The Junior League:
100 Years of Volunteer Service

The Association of Junior Leagues International Inc.

The Junior League: 100 Years of Volunteer Service

Copyright © 2001 by
The Association of Junior Leagues International Inc.
132 West 31st Street, 11th Floor, New York, New York 10001

Author: Nancy Beth Jackson, Ph.D.
Nancy Beth Jackson is a journalist and journalism educator in New York City. She has written for newspapers, magazines and websites in the U.S. and overseas and taught journalism at New York University, the University of Missouri, The American University of Paris, The American University in Cairo and Columbia University Graduate School of Journalism where she directs a college editors workshop. She graduated Phi Beta Kappa from the University of Missouri and received her graduate degrees from Columbia University and the University of Miami, Coral Gables.

Edited, designed and manufactured in the
United States of America by

FRP

2451 Atrium Way
Nashville, Tennessee 37214

Book Design: Steve Newman
Project Editor: Jane Hinshaw
Production Design: Sara Anglin

Library of Congress Number: 2001-132608
ISBN: 0-9710265-0-5
First Printing: 2001   7,500 copies

To order additional copies of
The Junior League: 100 Years of Volunteer Service,
call 1-800-243-1557 or contact the
Association of Junior Leagues International.

Mission

The Junior League is an organization of women committed to promoting voluntarism, developing the potential of women and improving communities through the effective action and leadership of trained volunteers. Its purpose is exclusively educational and charitable.

Vision

Through the power of our association, Junior Leagues strengthen communities by embracing diverse perspectives, building partnerships and inspiring shared solutions.

Reaching Out

The Junior League reaches out to women of all races, religions and national origins who demonstrate an interest in and commitment to voluntarism.

Front cover photographs, clockwise from the center:
Junior League of Houston volunteers work with Habitat for Humanity, photo: King Wong; Mrs. William Walling at the Junior League Baby Shelter, New York City, The Junior League of the City of New York Archives; The Junior League of London Volunteer Drive; Junior League members of the Women's Ferrying Squadron, World War II; Donna Smith, President of Junior League of Halifax, 1985, at the Halifax Child Development Center.

Back cover photographs, clockwise from the top center:
Volunteer caring for the elderly through Project Reach Out, The Junior League of Tulsa; Junior League Policy Institute delegates on Capitol Hill; Jack and the Beanstalk at the Junior League of Portland, Maine; Equal Suffrage League marches for "Votes for Women," The Junior League of St. Louis.

The Junior League: 100 Years of Volunteer Service

Service
Service
Service
Service
Service
Service
Service
Service
Service
Service
Service
Service

Introduction

This is a book about a simple but powerful idea—that women with energy and passion can lead their communities in change. That idea, advanced by Mary Harriman in 1901, became the founding vision of the Junior League. One hundred years later, Mary Harriman's powerful idea lives on in the mission of the Junior Leagues as organizations of women committed to promoting voluntarism, developing the potential of women and improving communities through the effective action and leadership of trained volunteers.

This book tells the story of the Junior League through the stories of individual Leagues and the women who shaped them. It is being published as part of the celebration of the Centennial of the founding of the Junior League by Mary Harriman in New York City in 1901. The Centennial is an occasion to share the rich history of the Junior League movement with all of our members and with the many people who admire the work of this important women's organization. The story told in this book is not only the story of the Junior Leagues but also of women's lives and how they have changed from the beginning of the century. Through it all, there is a strong common thread—that women as volunteers are powerful leaders for community change.

Mary Harriman's vision of women volunteers improving their communities is taken for granted today, but it surely was not a widely accepted one at the turn of the century when the Junior League was founded. The world was changing for women, and organizations like the Junior League were important forces in expanding leadership opportunities for women. In the 1890s and 1900s, women were making significant educational gains and small numbers were entering higher-status occupations such as education, law and medicine. Women came together in clubs and organizations to broaden their education and to learn more about the social issues around them. Both expanded opportunities and their discussions with one another about important social problems gave them increased self-confidence to address issues that were important to them. Organizations like the YWCA, the General Federation of Women's Clubs, the National Council of Jewish Women and many African American women's groups were founded during this period. These organizations gave women a vehicle through which their voices could be heard on those social issues that were traditionally considered their domain—issues of women, children and family. The experience that women gained in these organizations gave them confidence to express their views on matters of broader civic concern as urbanization and immigration brought to the fore significant social problems.

It is against this backdrop that Mary Harriman founded the Junior League in New York City in 1901. While the Junior League had similar origins to many other women's organizations founded during this period, it was different in one important respect—Mary Harriman understood that it was not enough to do good. In the 1904 report of the organization, Mary Harriman observed that the greater contact with the settlement houses and their clients also exposed the ignorance of the volunteers, and she and her colleagues set out to rectify this gap with courses not only on specific useful skills, such as a pedagogy, but also on economic, political and social issues. Thus began the concept of the Junior League as a training organization, a hallmark of the Junior League experience that remains so today. Indeed, throughout its one-hundred-year history, Junior League members have cited

➤

the training and the emphasis on personal development as core values that they took from the Junior League experience.

Mary Harriman and her early founding members also understood that women had an important leadership role to play in improving communities and that organizations like the Junior League could unlock their potential for service. She demonstrated this in her own life through public service, as did many other Junior League members chronicled in this book. She also understood that leadership is exercised in many ways and not just through positions of power. Junior League members exercised their leadership in large and small ways through their volunteer activities, by chairing a committee, organizing programs to improve the public schools or working in a soup kitchen to deliver hot meals to the homeless. To this day, this more expansive view of leadership and the way women exercise it is also a hallmark of the Junior League.

Throughout its one-hundred-year history, Junior Leagues have provided a venue for women to move beyond the limitations that society places on them. Junior Leagues were founded by women of privilege and still are largely made up of highly educated, upper-income women. But from the very beginning, League leaders have advanced a powerful message that with privilege comes an obligation to address the pressing needs of society. From the outset, League members defied convention, often with great pluck, and moved beyond the narrow confines that society would place on them because of gender and class. Instead, they rose to Mary Harriman's great challenge, which she put forth in her League's 1906 Annual Report: "It seems almost inhuman that we should live so close to suffering and poverty . . . within a few blocks of our own home and bear no part in this great life." This book chronicles their story and the story of the organization that nurtured them.

Junior League membership has expanded well beyond Mary Harriman's narrow social class. Today, it is more reflective of the communities in which Junior Leagues exist and is a mirror of the changes and expanded opportunities for women since the Junior League was first founded. Today, the majority of Junior League members work outside the home; women of color, women of various nationalities and a variety of religions make up the Junior League membership. Nor is the Junior League solely an American institution; Leagues exist in Canada, Mexico and England. What unites all of these Junior League members is a strong commitment to the Junior League mission.

In 1922, Dorothy Whitney Straight, the first President of the Association of Junior Leagues, addressed the Annual Conference with these words: "Given this conception of a continuous educational process, acquired through, and in relation to living itself, we see in clear perspective the place of the Junior League. It becomes our vocational, our continuation school . . . it directs our activities into channels of useful service . . . it trains us for special tasks and it enlightens us regarding the state of our society . . . It becomes something more than a school teacher, it becomes, in part, a life teacher."

Fifty-five years later, Sandra Day O'Connor, Supreme Court Justice and former President of the Junior League of Phoenix, also addressed the Association of Junior Leagues International Annual Conference and said: "I love the Junior League . . . Within the Junior League, I gained experience on how to organize and run a meeting, how to work with volunteers, how to get the most out of my time . . ." Throughout its one-hundred-year history, the Junior League has emphasized hands-on training, and first-hand volunteer and leadership experience. The story of the Junior Leagues is thus both the story of the Leagues' contributions to communities and also the story of the Leagues' contributions to the development of women.

Dorothy Straight and Sandra Day O'Connor are decades apart and had very different life experiences, but both moved beyond the restrictions that society might have placed on them and used the Junior League as a way to propel them into a different future than society had assigned. The development of women—the "life teacher"—was never an end in itself, however. As important as developing the self, was using the training and skills gained in the Junior League to address important social issues in the community and nationally. Throughout its history, Junior Leagues have been actively engaged in the issues of Mary Harriman's "great life." Leagues have been at the forefront of the suffrage movement, child welfare, tenement housing reform, childhood immunization, historic preservation, and education reform, to cite just some. Leagues individually and collectively have contributed to the volunteer community as leaders of the Civil Defense Volunteers Bureau during World War II and as early founders of Volunteer

Centers around the country. Throughout all of these endeavors, Leagues have collaborated in their communities and with national partners to improve communities through the action of trained volunteers. These stories, too, are told in this book.

The Junior League history is one of both tradition and change. Over the years, Leagues have looked forthrightly at both society and themselves. They have worked hard to change even as they have remained true to the fundamental values of developing women and serving the community. Many have addressed candidly their past exclusivity and worked hard to open their doors to all women who share their mission. They have addressed critics who say that volunteering devalues the role of women. Instead, Leagues have stood firmly for the principle that volunteering is an essential role for citizens in a democracy.

This book tells all of these stories and others to give a picture of how the Junior League has evolved through its first century. It is organized by decade. Each chapter describes the major developments and themes in Junior Leagues for the period and looks at these against the backdrop of women's social history at the time. The chapters feature

selected stories of individual Leagues and League members that are emblematic of the decade. Whenever possible, we have had Leagues and League members tell these stories in their own words or through their pictures.

This is a rich and thrilling story. Junior Leagues have made contributions in big and small ways throughout their history. They have set an example for others of the ability of an organization to adapt and change and the power of women to lead and contribute. The result is a story that all Junior League members should be proud of and one that can inspire others.

Jane Silverman
Executive Director
The Association of
Junior Leagues International Inc.

August 2001

Contents

1901

Junior League founded

1920

27 Junior Leagues, including the first League outside of the U.S.

In 1901, Mary Harriman, a 19-year-old New York City debutante with a social conscience, founded the first Junior League. Moved by the suffering she saw around her, Harriman mobilized a group of 80 other young women—hence the name "Junior" League—to work to improve the squalid conditions in which immigrants were living on the Lower East Side of Manhattan. Mary Harriman's vision for improving communities by using the energy and commitment of trained volunteers caught on. The second Junior League was started in Boston, Massachusetts, in 1907 and was soon followed by the founding of the Brooklyn, New York, Junior League in 1910. The rest is history.

During the 1910s, Junior Leagues shifted their focus from settlement house work to social, health and educational issues that affected the community at large. The Junior League of Brooklyn successfully petitioned the Board of Education to provide free lunches in city schools. During World War I, the San Francisco Junior League formed a motor delivery service that served as a model for the nationwide Red Cross Motor Corps.

In 1921, the Association was formed to provide professional support to the Leagues. During the 1920s, the Junior League of Chicago pioneered children's theatre, and the idea was taken up by more than 100 Leagues across the country.

Junior Leagues responded to the Depression during the 1930s by opening nutrition centers and milk stations. They operated baby clinics, day nurseries for working mothers, birth control clinics and training schools for nurses. Junior Leagues also established volunteer bureaus to recruit, train and place much-needed volunteers in the community.

During World War II, Junior League members played a major role in the war effort by chairing hundreds of war-related organizations in virtually every city where Junior Leagues operated. In 1939, the Mexico City League began development of a comprehensive, internationally recognized center for the blind.

In the 1950s, nearly 150 Junior Leagues were involved in remedial reading centers, diagnostic

1930

108

Junior Leagues

1939

144

Junior Leagues

1949

167

Junior Leagues

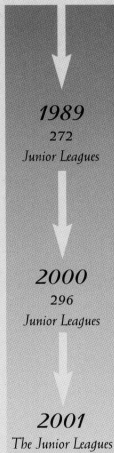

1959
189
Junior Leagues

1969
211
Junior Leagues

1979
235
Junior Leagues

1989
272
Junior Leagues

2000
296
Junior Leagues

2001
The Junior Leagues celebrate the 100th anniversary of the movement's founding.

testing programs and programs for gifted and challenged children. Leagues collaborated in the development of educational television and were among the first to promote quality programming for children. By the end of the decade, Junior Leagues were involved in more than 300 arts projects and multiple partnerships in many cities to establish children's museums.

During the 1960s, many Junior Leagues added environmental issues to their agendas. The Junior League of Toledo produced the educational film, *Fate of a River,* a report on the devastating effects of water pollution. Leagues also established programs addressing the education, housing, social services and employment needs of urban residents.

Throughout the 1970s, the Association expanded its participation in public affairs issues, especially in the areas of child health and juvenile justice. In 1973, almost 200 Leagues worked with the national Commission on Crime and Delinquency and the U.S. Justice Department on a four-year program that sought to improve the criminal justice system.

During the 1980s, Junior Leagues gained recognition for national advocacy efforts to improve the nation's child welfare system. Leagues helped gain passage of the first federal legislation to address domestic violence. Leagues also developed a campaign that actively and comprehensively tackles the impact of alcohol abuse on women. The campaign, called *Woman to Woman,* involved more that 100 League communities.

In 1989, the Association was presented with the prestigious U.S. President's Volunteer Action Award.

In the early 1990s, 230 Leagues participated in a public awareness campaign to encourage early childhood immunization called *Don't Wait to Vaccinate.* At the end of the decade, the Leagues prepared to launch a public awareness campaign on domestic violence.

In 2000, with nearly 200,000 members in Canada, Mexico, Great Britain and the U.S., the 296 Junior Leagues of the Association of Junior Leagues International planned for the Centennial celebration of the Junior League movement in 2001.

New Century, New Needs, New Women

Mary Harriman, before 1920.

1900–1910

*G*irls coming of age as the 20th century began *were already on their way to becoming modern women. Since 1860, when a brewer named Vassar established a college to offer women the same rigorous academic training received by men, more and more middle-class women attended new women's colleges or progressive co-educational institutions in the west. After Frederic A. P. Barnard, president of Columbia University, failed to win admission for young women, a women's college named after him opened across Broadway in 1889, joining what would be called The Seven Sisters, private educational institutions that took women seriously and challenged them intellectually. It was at Barnard just after the turn of the century that a young woman named Mary Harriman decided to form a "junior league" of affluent young women, volunteering their energies to help solve the social ills of their city. The Junior League Movement built upon and expanded a new awareness that women could make a difference in society beyond home and hearth.*

Our League, as I see it, was organized as a means of expressing the feeling of social responsibility for the conditions which surrounded us. We have the responsibility to act, and we have the opportunity to conscientiously act to affect the environment around us.

—Mary Harriman Rumsey, 1912

Women's magazines at the end of the century talked much of the "New Woman," who was making her convictions known outside the home. Charles Dana Gibson, a magazine illustrator, created his popular "Gibson Girl," freed of the Victorian's restrictive clothing and dressed in simple skirts and blouses, "shirtwaists" modeled after men's shirts. The Gibson Girl was often pictured playing golf or tennis, cycling or at the beach. Susan E. Meyer in *America's Great Illustrators* described her as "taller than the other women currently seen in the pages of magazines . . . more spirited and independent, yet altogether feminine."

Other independent young women, though far less privileged, came to America's cities in hopes of finding employment in the new industrialized society. These "working girls" earned one-half to one-third the wages of men and often worked up to 18 hours a day in sweatshops. Around the turn of the century, their numbers swelled by new immigrants from Central and Southern Europe, glovemakers, laundresses and shirtwaist workers staged dramatic strikes to call attention to their exploitation.

Women's organizations thrived at the end of the 19th century, the most famous—and feared—the Women's Christian Temperance Union, was founded in 1873 to campaign for prohibition and stricter moral codes. Carry Nation, one of the best-known members, was often pictured with a hatchet in one hand and a Bible in the other, but by the end of the

century—with membership of nearly 170,000—the WCTU was also a strong voice for women's suffrage.

The WCTU was the first truly national women's organization, but others soon followed, using the revolutionary words "women" and "club" instead of "ladies" and "society" as had been the custom. Many women's clubs began in the 1870s as lecture circles, but soon societal reform and suffrage were paramount. The prestigious Chicago Woman's Club, established in 1876, stressed philanthropy and education and required members to complete a course as intellectually challenging as a first-year college program. Its elite membership included African-American and Jewish women as well as white Christians. Women throughout the country organized, working collectively across class, color and religion for social good. Even without the vote, they found political voice.

Empowerment

Thomas Beer, a best-selling social historian in the 1920s, looked back on the 1890s in awe of "the Titaness," the powerful influence of "pure and enlightened womanhood." Much of that energy was concentrated in Chicago where in 1889 Jane Addams, "without parade or notice," according to Beer in *The Mauve Decade*, had established Hull House, a settlement house to serve the poor. Because of the impact the Settlement Movement would have on

A generation of girls reared in this shadow, the shadow of suffrage parades, mass meetings, women militant, could not but absorb a craving for action.

—Winthrop B. Palmer,
Junior League Bulletin, 1927

the lives of women and the nation, Beer called 1889 "a year of triumph for American womanhood."

In the 1890s, two rival suffrage groups joined together as the National American Suffrage Association and over 60 women's clubs formed the General Federation of Women's Clubs, a nondenominational voluntary service organization. Women united in the National Consumers League to fight for fair, safe and healthy working conditions that would foster quality products for consumers and a decent standard of living for workers. The NCL issued its own "white-label" to manufacturers who met the League's requirements.

At the World's Columbia Exposition in Chicago in 1893, the power of women seemed to explode. "The World's Fair definitely set afire the suffragists," Beer observed. Organized to celebrate the 400th anniversary of Columbus' arrival in the New World, the fair included a women's Board of Management and an International Congress of Women. "At receptions of the Woman's Club in Chicago there had been a parade of quietly effective professional women—Jane Addams, Florence Hunt, Jane Logan and the rest. Suffrage now woke with a roar," Beer wrote.

Frances Willard, WCTU president, reported on the exposition at the WCTU convention in October 1893. "The World's Fair in Chicago has been indeed the eighth wonder of the world, and no one has appreciated its splendour more than women have done, nor has any class probably reaped more of help and hope from the great show than we. Never before has such provision been made for women."

A congress of women "such as the world has never seen" was held in May 1893, attracting audiences of 20,000 to 30,000 "eager to learn what had been wrought, and to know what could be undertaken by the suppressed half of the human race," she observed. "It is the universal testimony that no single meeting ever held by women was so representative in the character of its attendance, so progressive in the tone of its utterances, or so phenomenal in the size of its audiences."

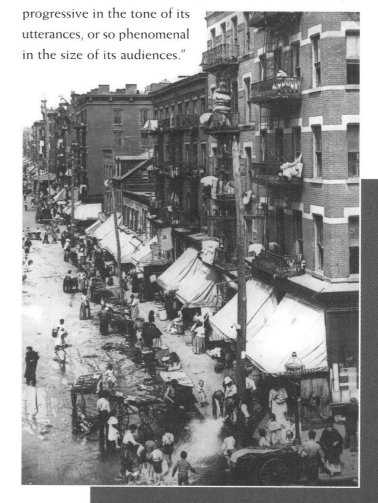

The Junior League for the Promotion of Settlement Movements started in neighborhoods like this one along Hester Street on New York City's Lower East Side.

Photo: Brown Brothers, 1890. The Museum of the City of New York Print Archives

15

organizations like these, 19th century women found they could influence public policy whether in improving local garbage collection or achieving major reforms like the Pure Food and Drug Act.

Founder Mary Harriman

Much of the social activism in the last decade of the 19th century involved older women of the middle classes, but after the new century opened, daughters of the upper classes began to address the inequities they saw in their cities.

"It was in New York that a youthful trumpet sounded the new call—Mary Harriman, daughter of the man who flung railroads in careless triumph across a continent called together a little group of friends," Mrs. Palmer recalled in the *Junior League Bulletin* in 1927. "A girl in the shadow of the Mauve Decade flinging across America a web as vibrant, taut, electric as her father's network of steel."

In the middle of the 20th century, Nathalie Henderson Swan recalled the exact moment when the Junior League had been conceived 50 years earlier. She and Mary Harriman, daughters of New York City's "400" elite, were traveling down Riverside Drive after preparing for their Barnard College entrance exams. Mary, a horsewoman from childhood, drove her light carriage behind a trotting horse named Gulnair, but her mind was on the lecture they had heard that morning. The young women, still in their teens, were among the first of their crowd to go to college. Most of their friends concentrated their energies on planning glittering debutante balls for the 1900–1901 season at posh establishments like Sherry's.

One of the most impressive speakers at the Congress was Fannie Barrier Williams, who within the year helped organize the National League of Colored Women, which advocated job training, wage equality and childcare. Hannah Greenebaum Solomon organized a Jewish Congress at the World's Parliament of Religions at the World's Fair to explore religious, social and philanthropic questions. Out of that congress grew the National Council of Jewish Women, "to improve the quality of life of women, children and families . . . and ensure individual rights and freedom for all."

The YWCA, the Daughters of the American Revolution, the Association of Collegiate Alumnae (later the Association of University Women), and the Congress of Mothers (later the National Parent-Teachers Association) all came into being in the late 19th century. Through

They would be making debuts, too, but Mary wanted more from the year than a series of parties. "What can we do to make it a particularly good year, and to show that we recognize an obligation to the community besides having a good time?" Mary had asked Nathalie several years earlier while playing golf. She began exploring possibilities, dismissing church, welfare and hospital work as much too limited. "She talked with several of us about her feeling that we debutantes when we came out had an opportunity and the responsibility of making an important contribution to the New York City community. That we, as a privileged group, besides having a good time, should consider what we could do to improve conditions, and that we should lead the way," Nathalie recalled when the New York League celebrated its 50th birthday.

An unusually large group of 85 debutantes to be introduced to society that season knew little of the social conditions of New York beyond their mansions on Fifth and Madison Avenues. They had no reason to venture into the slums of the Lower East Side, but that morning at Barnard Mary and Nathalie had learned about the Settlement Movement. Social reformers like Lillian Wald in New York and Jane Addams in Chicago had established "settlement houses," community centers in poverty-stricken neighborhoods swollen by immigration. Students and people of means worked in the centers, offering adult education, Americanization classes, public health services and after-school activities for children. America's first settlement house, still in existence as University Settlement in New York, began in 1886, Hull House following in Chicago in 1889. By 1890 over 100 settlement houses had opened around the country. Women operated most of them. Addams, who won a Nobel Prize in 1931 for her work, drew support mostly from middle-class women at Hull House. As Mary learned in the Barnard lecture, the settlement movement intended not only to help the poor but also "to assist young women of means in search of a moral purpose."

Mary was tremendously excited by what she had just learned. As she headed south from Morningside Heights, she suddenly shouted, "We will work for the College Settlement!" At the College Settlement on Rivington Street in Manhattan's Lower East Side, college students and graduates learned about neighborhood problems and needs by living and working among the immigrants.

"Her idea was an expression of the awakening social consciousness of the time," observed Nathalie a lifetime later. Mary invited friends over to her home to discuss how they could become a part of the movement. Dorothea Draper James, a founding member and an early League president, remembered at mid-century, "The thought was that we should organize to develop a wide conscientiousness and be useful, so that a general social betterment might ensue and a more democratic viewpoint be instilled in those of us so privileged." Mary, she said, was their "lamplighter."

Mary Harriman was among the most privileged of her generation. A hundred years ago, Carnegie, Morgan, Rockefeller and Harriman were names recognized by every American. What Carnegie was to steel, Morgan to money and Rockefeller to oil, Harriman was to railroads. Her father, E. H. Harriman, a Wall Street banker until he was 50, became one of the most powerful and combative men of the era as he made his way around a real-life Monopoly board collecting railroads. He created the Union Pacific-Southern Pacific system, extended rail service into Mexico and dreamed of building a global transportation system combining rail and water. At his death in 1909, the railroad baron was said to be worth between $70 million and $100 million.

Born in 1881, Mary was the oldest of six Harriman children, including a son who died in childhood. Another son, Averell, ten years Mary's junior, would grow up to become governor of New York and ambassador to Russia. E. H. Harriman doted on his children and took them with him even on trips to Alaska and the Far East. He and his eldest daughter shared both an emotional and intellectual bond and were alike in many ways. Her interest in the settlement houses of the Lower East Side may be traced directly to the Tompkins Square Boys' Club, founded by her father in 1875 to keep boys off the street. In addition to organizing and underwriting the club, he also spent many evenings on the Lower East Side working with the boys. As a young woman, her mother was active in charity work through the Episcopal Church in Ogdensburg, New York. When the couple wed in 1879, her clergyman reportedly said that the marriage had cost him "the services of a young lady who had become a leader in every good work, especially in helpful ministries, to the ignorant, the distressed and the poor."

Young Mary, while leading a sheltered life, was not cloistered. E. H. Harriman's biographer Maury Klein wrote,

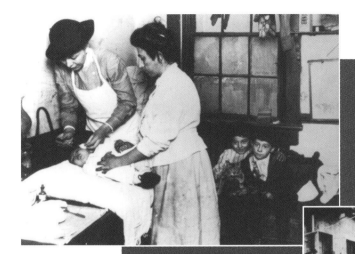

A League volunteer helps a mother care for her baby in a tenement, early 1900s.

View of a New York city tenement courtyard, c. 1900.

"Harriman expected no less of his daughters than of his sons. They too were educated in private schools and pushed to go as far as their abilities would take them. Mary blazed an impressive trail for the others to follow." Harriman had resisted Mary's plan to study biology and the new discipline of sociology at Barnard, but he couldn't say no to his eldest and favorite child, whose passion for eugenics, scientific breeding, led to her nickname "Eugenia." Independent, even headstrong, she drove her own carriage to campus, hitching her horse several blocks away so she could arrive on foot to avoid being identified as a member of the privileged class.

Klein describes Mary as "a dark, pleasant girl with an infectious laugh," and the child who was most like her father in wanting to take charge, although she strove for cooperation while he thrived on confrontation. As a young woman, she was "dynamic, magnetic and gay," according to her friend Nathalie. Whatever Mary did she did with total enthusiasm, enlisting others to join her.

She soon had enlisted the debutantes in "The Junior League for the Promotion of Settlement Movements," whose activities would continue beyond the coming-out year. They drew up a constitution, assessed five-dollar annual dues and began planning a musical evening as a benefit. In March 1902, the League issued its first annual report. In it, the board of managers with Mary Harriman as president and Nathalie Henderson as vice president explained why the young women had chosen the cause. All members could "lend their sympathies irrespective of church or creed" and it was "one of the broadest and most efficient movements of the times to aid in the solution of the social and industrial problems of a great city."

Social Activism

Initially, the young women set up a committee to send flowers from their parties and their summer homes to hospitals and the College Settlement, but soon these privileged "girls" were sending more than posies. They sent themselves into the neighborhood, which they knew about only through the writings of muckraking journalists who exposed the appalling social, economic and political plight of American cities, bloated by industrialization and immigration.

In the Lower East Side of Manhattan where the Junior League for the Promotion of Settlement Movements began its work, families from Ireland, Central Europe and Russia crowded into dark, airless quarters without indoor toilets, hot water or gas lighting. Fathers left for work in the mornings and were never seen again, with no one ever knowing if they had been murdered by robbers or had simply kept on walking west. In 1896, William Dean Howells, novelist and editor of *Harper's Magazine*, followed a friend down an alley barely as wide as a man's shoulders and found himself among buildings in a courtyard of despair. He wrote:

> One of them was a stable, which contributed its stench to the odors that rose from the reeking pavement and from the closets filling an end of the court, with a corner left beside them for the hydrant that supplied the water for the whole enclosure. It is from this court that the inmates of the tenements have their sole chance of sun and air. What the place must be in summer I had not the heart to think, and on the wintry day of my visit I could not feel the fury of the skies which my guide said would have been evident to me if I had seen it in August. I could better fancy this when I climbed the rickety stairs within one of the houses and found myself in a typical New York tenement. Then I almost choked at the thought of what a hot day, what a hot night, must be in such a place, with the two small windows inhaling the putrid breath of the court and transmitting it, twice fouled by the passage through the living-room, to the black hole in the rear, where the whole family lay on the heap of rags that passed for a bed.

Junior League House for Working Girls

If the early Junior League members had lived a century later, they would have been heading up Wall Street firms and launching their own dot.coms, but in the early days of the 20th century, Dorothy Whitney, president of the New York League from 1907 to 1909 was also the force behind one of the most visible League projects of the decade: the Junior League House for Working Girls, also known as the Junior League Hotel. For some years, the League had been concerned with how single working women fared in the city. They supported the Consumers' League campaign to make a free Saturday afternoon compulsory for all shop girls during the summer and discussed vacation camps for the young women. League members also began talking about how they could build a working women's residence, run as a business but with affordable rooms and social amenities. Nearly four dozen residences for working women existed, but they generally had restrictions about religious creed, hours, age or wages. None were self-supporting.

The Junior League project grew out of an urban experiment called the City and Suburban Homes Company, a forerunner of public housing. Founded by some of the most influential families in the city, the company sought to provide workers with an affordable and healthy alternative to the dismal tenements. The most ambitious and successful of the company's model housing was York Avenue Estates, a complex built on a block bounded by East 78th and 79th Streets between York Avenue and the East River, a great open space adjacent to John Jay Park and a school playground. Between 1901 and 1913, more than 1,200 apartments with radiators, cross-ventilation, hot water and privacy were designed by prize-winning architects. Part of the housing reform movement in America, the company contended that improving living conditions would also improve moral character.

Junior League members, many of whom were the daughters of company founders, believed the complex should also serve the young women who came from Europe and rural areas to work as domestics, dressmakers, milliners, office workers and teachers. In 1909, the Junior League bought $260,000 worth of stock in the company, sold $340,000 in capital stock subscriptions to finance construction and began erecting a six-story building with views across the East River to the green hills of Long Island. At the corner of 78th Street and East End Avenue, the building overlooked John Jay Park and had open piazzas facing the river. Residents, paying $4 to $7 a week, which included two meals a day and three on Sunday, enjoyed steam heat in winter, electric lights, telephone and elevator service, sewing room privileges, laundry facilities, a library, a gymnasium, a ballroom and roof garden. In her annual report, Dorothy Whitney called the project "perhaps the most important enterprise of the Junior League this year... it is hoped that the roof will prove a feature of great attraction."

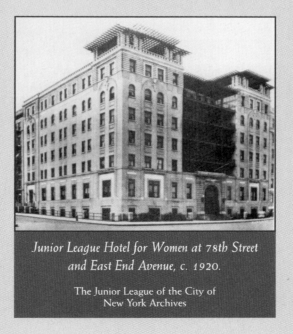

Junior League Hotel for Women at 78th Street and East End Avenue, c. 1920.

The Junior League of the City of New York Archives

Designed by Philip Ohm in 1910, the Junior League House matched the other buildings in the complex with its pale yellow brick trimmed in marble and could accommodate 350 women, 260 of them at one sitting, in the basement dining room. Each room had homey touches like a rocking chair and rug. Public areas included living rooms with fireplaces, small parlors to serve as "courting rooms," and tennis and basketball courts.

In 1912, the Bureau of Social Hygiene reported that "of the 58 organizations in Manhattan providing housing accommodations solely for women, the Junior League House is the largest and one of the few in which there is no discrimination against nationality or religion." Katharine Barnes, chairman of the League's Tenement House Committee, predicted, "If such a scale can be provided a financial success, and a demand found for a girls' hotel, The Junior League House may, we trust, become a model for many of the same kind." Indeed, as the Junior League spread across the continent, the Junior League House inspired Leagues in other cities to sponsor residential hotels, lunchrooms and other services for working women. The New York Junior League owned and operated the residential hotel through 1931.

The young women volunteered to spend Wednesday and Friday afternoons and Saturday mornings at the settlement house, handing out library books and singing for kindergartners. Three afternoons and two evenings a week, they taught art classes. Among them was Mary's good friend Eleanor Roosevelt, who joined the League two years after its founding.

After an introductory lecture on "Practical Sociology," the young woman threw herself into League activity. She served as League secretary in 1904 and taught after-school dance and calisthenics to girls at the Rivington Street Settlement House. Jean Reid, who played the piano for the classes, traveled to Lower East Side by carriage, but Eleanor took an elevated train or trolley even though it meant walking through the Bowery. "I often waited on a corner for a car, watching with a great deal of trepidation,

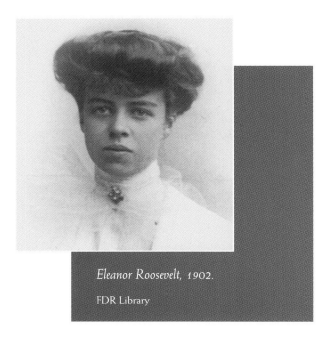

Eleanor Roosevelt, 1902.

FDR Library

21

men come out of the saloons or shabby hotels nearby, but the children interested me enormously," she recalled. The classes were "the nicest time" of her day, she wrote Franklin Delano Roosevelt, her husband to be. She later invited him to accompany her into the crowded neighborhoods of the Lower East Side, the first time he had seen such poverty.

Joseph Lash, in *Eleanor and Franklin*, noted that Eleanor quickly emerged as one of the leaders of the Junior League. "She was finding a vocation and a role, and she

New York Junior League volunteers working at the New York College Settlement on Rivington Street, c. 1911.

The Junior League of the City of New York Archives

applied herself with scrupulous diligence to the settlement tasks. Already her debutante friends were classing her with Mary Harriman and Nathalie Henderson, whom they regarded as 'superior beings.'"

Despite their energy and enthusiasm, the young women soon found that they knew little that they could share with others. "Although the Settlements were always asking for more of our volunteers my impression is that, while we gained through widened community contacts, most of the classes were not very successful," Nathalie Henderson Swan admitted years later. "Why? Because we did not know how to teach or to handle groups of children. We were untrained."

Mary Harriman pushed her friends to learn more and do more about the social problems of the city and extended their work beyond the Settlement programs. While going to college, she chaired League committees on tenement houses, parks and playgrounds, and neighborhoods. Her volunteer work led her to write her senior thesis on the needs of one public school district in the city. She then divided League membership into boards to survey neighborhood school districts. They investigated school conditions and provided recreation activities and tutoring for the students. Because they were who they were, their questions were more often answered than ignored, but for the same reason they also had to prove themselves. Pauline Robinson remembered being asked, "Are you here just for a fad or would you like to undertake some serious work?"

By 1904, "the tiny society" had become the Junior League for the Organization of City Districts, divided into eight boards of investigation between Washington Square and 86th Street. "You served the ward in the district in which you lived, you investigated: The Board of Education, Board of Health, the Board of Public Charities, the Tenement House Department, Settlements, Hospitals, Day Nurseries, Kindergartens, Factory Work, Churches, Parks, Playgrounds and Public Baths in your neighborhood," she explained. "Anxious, eager, girls investigating, asking questions. A little ridiculous perhaps (Public Baths) but very earnest," Winthrop B. Palmer wrote in her 1927 article looking back on the founding years.

Education

Through her Junior League investigations, Nathalie Henderson began to see education as a way to ameliorate many of the social ills of the city. In the *Junior League Bulletin* of January 1911, under the headline, "Education and Why It Should Interest Us," she wrote:

> It has been the experience of at least a few of us who have been doing social work through the Junior League, that we have found ourselves becoming slowly convinced that of all the socially constructive agencies at work in New York City, the most powerful potential instrument making for progress is the Public School. Like 'Alice in Wonderland,' trying all the paths in the garden for the way out and always finding herself bumping into the House, so we, setting out on different paths of social reform, seem invariably to bring us up in front of the School House.

Winthrop B. Palmer, c. 1927, Junior League of Brooklyn and Association of Junior Leagues President 1926–28.

The "few of us" included the committee headed by Eliza Morgan Bates (Swift) that looked at the research of the League's neighborhood committees and convinced the League to design a pilot project called "School and Home Visitors," the forerunner of the Visiting Teachers programs in public schools. Under League sponsorship, teachers for the first time would go into the homes of immigrants to help improve communication between schools and parents and help children succeed in the classroom. By 1909, the League was paying salaries of $1,000 a year to four Visiting Teachers and supplying volunteers to tutor children and hold special classes. The work of two Home and School visitors was supported by the proceeds of the League's first musical show "Girl o' Mine."

Eliza Morgan Bates (Swift), League president, was pleased to report that New York was taking responsibility for the Home and School Visitors. "In the City Budget for the fall of 1910 will be found a request by the Board of Education for $25,000 to establish 25 Home and School Visitors. No other commendation is needed of the work . . . for which the Junior League has been financially responsible, establishing and supporting four out of five visitors in the city." In addition, she had been appointed to the Local School Board of District 13, pointing to the League's growing reputation in educational affairs.

Junior League members remained involved in the visiting teaching project. In September 1911, Nathalie Henderson, chair of the Committee on Visiting Teachers of the Public Education Society, reported on the work to the Board of Education. Teachers had visited the homes of nearly 1,000 students, as many as ten times in some cases, as they looked into truancy, poor school work, troublesome conduct or home conditions that might be hampering academic performance.

Teachers found children burdened with taking care of smaller children or ill family members or doing "home work," which Nathalie described as "working on flowers or willow plumes or selling papers or working in a restaurant,

shop, bakery or stable." Often both parents were away working all day, neither parent spoke English or the mother was "overwhelmed by the conditions." Although results were difficult to measure scientifically, schools reported improvement in attendance, scholarship and conduct and the number of promotions were up.

The program led Nathalie Henderson Swan to become an activist in public education, chairing New York's Joint Committee for Education and serving as a trustee at Teachers College at Columbia University. When she died at age 83 in 1965, the *New York Herald Tribune* credited her with being a co-founder of the League but pointed out her "interests did not end with the Junior League."

Raising Money

In addition to volunteering, Mary Harriman also thought the young women should raise money to support their cause. She suggested they draw upon their musical and theatrical talents to stage an evening of entertainment for family and friends in the winter of 1901. "In those days our parents would have looked askance at 'Follies.'" Mildred Phelps Stokes Hooker said in 1951. "I don't think they had even been invented; and tableaus were considered the most fitting form of entertainment." She chaired the League's first art committee and convinced her mother, Mrs. Anson Phelps Stokes, to volunteer their Madison Avenue home for the fund-raiser.

"Edith Post and I were to have charge of the entertainment, which proved much more of an undertaking than we had realized," she said. "It never occurred to us to get any professional help and we spent hours painting

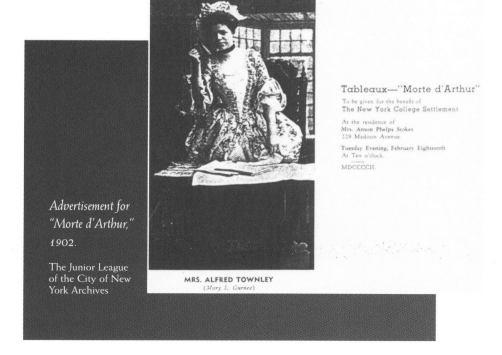

Advertisement for "Morte d'Arthur," 1902.

The Junior League of the City of New York Archives

Tableaux—"Morte d'Arthur"
To be given for the benefit of
The New York College Settlement

At the residence of
Mrs. Anson Phelps Stokes
229 Madison Avenue

Tuesday Evening, February Eighteenth
At Ten o'clock.

MDCCCCII.

MRS. ALFRED TOWNLEY
(Mary L. Gurnee)

24

gray castle walls for background and sticking gold paper leaves on tulle to give the necessary illusion for the angels behind the golden tree."

On a Tuesday evening, they dressed in elaborate costumes and played out the death of King Arthur in "Morte d'Arthur" and performed violin and piano solos and songs. They cleared $1,500 for the College Settlement.

As the decade progressed, their fund-raisers became more and more successful—and more and more professional, with League members showing off talents to rival Broadway showgirls. Ruth Draper, who made her debut in 1903, went on to an international career as actress, stage manager, scene designer and writer. One League benefit, directed by Miss Draper, featured an Egyptian dance costumed by a Metropolitan Museum designer. Their musical and dramatic performances became immensely popular, quickly moving out of members' salons into theaters.

Interviewed as the New York League's oldest member in the late 1980s, Margaret Trevor Pardee, who joined in 1912, remembered playing in the Junior League band at hospitals, settlement houses, Ellis Island and on stage at Sing Sing prison and also dancing in League productions. "I rode across the stage at The Plaza Hotel on a bicycle built for two accompanied by that old song. In another Junior League show, in which I danced a solo, I was asked by one of the audience, who happened to be Florenz Ziegfeld, to join his famous Ziegfeld Follies Girls. But father said 'No!'"

As the Leagues expanded beyond New York City, League Follies—often including husbands in the musical productions—became social and cultural events in communities far from Broadway as Leagues raised money to initiate and support projects in health, housing, education and culture.

In New York, the first League soon expanded its service beyond the settlement houses, making an impact throughout the city and setting models for programs in other communities. League members did everything from examining the teeth of 500 schoolchildren to being responsible for the creation of the Council of 100 of the Parks and Playgrounds Association, which used city funds to create parks to give children somewhere to play other than the streets.

Branching Out

By 1907, when Dorothy Whitney (Straight Elmhirst) was president, the organization had broadened into the Junior League for the Promotion of Neighborhood Work. She introduced the first formal training of new members, a "Social Problems" course, which was taught by a Barnard College professor and was the forerunner of League Provisional (first-year) training in community organization and problem-solving.

Dorothy Payne Whitney (Mrs. Willard Straight), President of the New York Junior League, 1907.

The League held special meetings on civic problems the young women had discovered in their investigations and invited experts to help them find the answers. The guest speakers included Prof. Gidding, Ph.D., on "Civic Responsibility of Women," Kate Glahorne, Ph.D., on "East Side Tenement Houses," William G. McAdoo on "Police Problems and the West Side" and the Rev. S. Gaynor White on "Immigration." McAdoo, later U.S. Secretary of Treasury, was then president of the Hudson and Manhattan Railroad completing construction.

The League grew quickly from "a training school for the modern debutante," as the *New York American* dubbed it initially, to an established community service organization. By 1909, the League was so busy that it rented an office at 42 East 39th Street and hired an executive secretary to work from nine to one o'clock five days a week. A good part of her job was answering letters and questions from women wanting to start Leagues in their cities in the United States, Canada and Europe.

As early as 1905 to 1906, inquiries had come from Baltimore and Budapest. Sister Leagues had formed in Boston, Brooklyn and Portland, Oregon, although without formal affiliation with New York.

In Boston, debutantes each year since the Civil War had joined sewing circles, first to sew for Union soldiers and later to lunch. In 1907, the eight newest circles decided to establish an organization resembling New York's Junior League. The Sewing Circle League of Boston began with a play committee to present entertainment in settlement houses and a lecture series, designed to train new members in philanthropic activity but open to other League members and outsiders. With speakers like Booker T. Washington, founder of the Tuskegee Institute, and Charles Eliot, president of Harvard, attendance soon averaged over 200.

In the spring of 1910, a League organized in Brooklyn, which only a few years before had been independent from New York City. Unlike the New York League, the Brooklyn members included young matrons as well as debutantes. One of their first projects was identifying the need for free lunches in the public schools and petitioning the Board of Education to provide them, creating a model for school lunches elsewhere. They also worked to turn vacant lots into playgrounds. "No matter whether we do just a little, we must put our whole heart into it," Mrs. George S. Frank explained at the first meeting of Junior Leagues in 1912.

On the West Coast, a young bride named Gretchen Hoyt Corbett, originally a New York League member, deeply missed her League activities after she moved to Portland, Oregon. "I wish we could do something like that here," she said to her mother-in-law, who replied, "Why

> *We all belong to a class which has leisure, education, wealth and power, and we owe a responsibility toward the community for the very opportunities these things give us.*
>
> —Elizabeth Gray
> Boston President, 1910–1913

don't you? Invite a group of the girls over and start a Portland Junior League." In 1910, she entertained 40 young women at an organizational tea. "It was the answer for young women who needed outside interests and did not want to be confined to society or children," she explained. "You had an obligation to contribute your services as a volunteer." They did casework for Associated Charities, delivered Christmas baskets to the poor and provided flowers to hospitals, but the young women also got the reputation of being somewhat radical when they initiated a study of community services. In committees of three, the members visited charitable organizations to find out just what welfare work was being done in the rapidly growing city. The committee visiting the Waverly Baby Home found deplorable conditions and asked the governor to appoint a committee to investigate, leading to a drastic reform of the Home and the child care system.

As the Junior League movement spread, the New York League restated its mission in an editorial in the *Junior League Bulletin*, the official magazine it had recently launched for its own members and to share with members of other Leagues as well.

> What the Junior League is is definite, clear, concise. An organization of the young society women of New York whose objectives are, first, to promote, among its members, an interest in all kinds of charitable and social effort. Second, to bring the members in touch with already organized philanthropies so that they may find the sphere of usefulness best fitted to their individual capacity. And third, to raise

Leagues Founded 1900–1910
New York City, New York
Boston, Massachusetts
Brooklyn, New York
Portland, Oregon

money for the assistance of those organizations in which the volunteer workers of the League are actively interested. What the Junior League does is manifold, often experimental, and changing from year to year.

League members could look forward to "an ever-broadening horizon and enlarged opportunities," but what they really stood to gain was "a broader knowledge of existing social conditions, through their own experiences, through our meetings and lectures and through personal contact with trained workers."

Through their training, these daughters of the Mauve Decade had found their calling. The *Bulletin* editorial noted: "If this knowledge helps us collectively and individually to take our place in the world of affairs with a broader viewpoint, larger sympathies, and more human understanding, then, and then only, can the Junior League be counted as an integral part of the great movement for civic and social betterment."

The Chicago Junior League provides dressmaking classes at the settlements.

*W*hatever was left of the Victorian Era disappeared in the second decade of the century as the role of women in the public arena continued to strengthen. Out of the Settlement House movement had come a new respect for social workers as professionals and women as volunteers. A band of well-trained women stood ready to assume even greater responsibility in the progressive era. Taking a lead from women's organizations, youth joined the Girl Scouts, Boy Scouts and Camp Fire Girls; men established the Rotary Club, Kiwanis and the American Legion. Women enjoyed greater personal freedom, the more daring of them dancing the Turkey Trot and Bunny Hug, championing free love and wearing lipstick and soft bras. Determined to be full and equal partners in society, women marched in suffrage parades and worked in war relief.

The thought was that we should organize to develop a wide conscientiousness and be useful, so that a general social betterment might ensue and a more democratic viewpoint be instilled in those of us so privileged.

—Dorothea Draper James, founding member

Early cover of the
Junior League Bulletin.

In this setting, the young women in many cities sought to form Junior Leagues in their own cities and looked to the New York League for inspiration and help. After the New York League launched its *Junior League Bulletin* in 1911 to improve communication among its own members, it offered editorial space to other Leagues wanting to share ideas and ideals, but no formal affiliation existed among the groups. In March 1912 the *Bulletin* announced that the Junior League of New York would sponsor a two-day conference in April for delegates from "all the Junior Leagues in the world." A sweeping statement, the author admitted, but justified because Philadelphia, Baltimore and Montreal already had Leagues and it was rumored that a Dutch woman had established a League in Holland after visiting New York.

"The conference is designed to bring them all together—to give advice to those just starting, find out how the others have done their work to the best advantage, and to gather inspiration and help from each other. There is nothing like comparison for showing the weak and strong points of an organization." The magazine urged members to put up some of the visitors, "thereby dispelling the idea that New York is the most unhospitable city in the world." In addition to inviting Charity Organization Society leaders to speak, the conference

committee also arranged an evening at the theater for 50 New York League members and delegates.

The session was held at the Harriman home at 1 East 69th Street. Montreal and Holland, which indeed had a service organization inspired by the Junior League but never affiliated, were not among the delegates, nor was Portland, where the League had formed in 1910, but Baltimore, Boston, Brooklyn, Chicago and Philadelphia all sent representatives. Mary Harriman Rumsey addressed the session, recounting the earliest days of the League as "the years when we felt our inexperience and realized how much we would have to know." To do that, she said, required organization.

"Our League, as I see it, was organized as a means of expressing the feeling of social responsibility for the conditions which surrounded us. We have the responsibility to act, and we have the opportunity to conscientiously act to affect the environment about us," she told the delegates as recorded in minutes of the meeting. "The Junior League, then, was started simply as an organized effort to express these feelings." She reminded them that even as they gathered to discuss greater unity, they must remember that improving individual communities was the goal.

. . . each city has its own conditions to cope with, and the organization should be founded on the conditions in each individual place.

—Mary Harriman Rumsey, 1912

By January 1911, the New York League had grown so large that it decided it needed a monthly newsletter to spread "a knowledge of our activities among the members, especially among the younger girls who still regard the League from the point of view of the debutante." Subscriptions started coming in even before the first issue of *Junior League Bulletin* appeared, delighting editors with the response.

"Very kind, indeed, are those who, having read their 'Sample Copy' of the Bulletin, have followed it up with a crisp dollar-bill. Truly we are grateful. But we are even more indebted to those who, having subscribed before reading our first endeavor, have not followed it up by withdrawing their subscriptions . . . Little Miss Bulletin is learning to lisp a 'Thank you,' as is only right for a well-bred child to do, to all her friends who are helping her first faltering steps."

The *Bulletin* began modestly, featuring in its first year reports of League activities such as the new residential hotel for "working girls" the League had built in the Upper East Side and outings for settlement house children. From the start,

the publication also set forth to stimulate the minds of members, few of whom had bothered with college. The initial issue invited readers to send in recommendations

"GOLDEN GATE NUMBER" JANUARY, 1917

for books useful to volunteers like John Dewey's *The School and Society.* Two issues later, the *Bulletin* floated the suggestion that it maintain a regular book review column.

"This sounds at first rather pretentious, but on examination proves itself an excellent and helpful suggestion. There are many books on social and civic questions which would be of benefit and assistance to our volunteer neighbourhood (sic) workers, and to the executive board of the League." Soon book reviews and a regular book column appeared, all written by members.

Initially, the readership was about 500 New York League members of various ages and members of other newly organized Junior Leagues. In the kind of chatty editorial note that would be favored throughout the publication's history, the editors confessed in the October 1913 issue that they felt the *Junior League Bulletin* should become "a uniting factor in the lives of the Junior League" as it spread to other cities.

"We have already requests for copies of the *Bulletin* from Boston and Cleveland," the editorial continued. "The biennial conference of the Junior

➤

League takes place this spring. Is it too much to hope that by that time the *Bulletin* will have become a flourishing organ, the mouthpiece of the Junior Leagues of America?" The response was immediate, with letters from Leagues in Brooklyn, Montreal and Boston, and the London Personal Service Association appearing in the November issue. News from Leagues in Chicago, Baltimore, San Francisco and Boston filled most of the four pages in December 1913. The Young Woman's Guild of Holland also sent news regularly although it, like the London Personal Service Association, did not develop into Leagues.

By June 1914, the *Bulletin* had established a network of "city editors" in the United States and Canada. "We are to double in size and circulation and we hope to teem with interest and news, and that no member of any League will feel she can afford not to be a subscriber."

The *Bulletin* would take on a far more professional air after January 1917, because rapid growth had forced the editors to think about practical concerns like card indexing and subscription renewals. In an item headlined, "We Learn Our Trade," editors reported on a visit to "the inner mysteries of the *Harper's Bazar* (sic) office." "Word cannot tell how helpful was this experience nor what countless ideas we gathered... ah, fatal words for our readers, for henceforth, we will try to run our *Bulletin* like other magazines." Readers were warned that they would be pestered for renewals instead of receiving "grace copies" and to expect the launch of "advertising propaganda on an unsuspecting bevy of League Members." That issue had a full-page advertisement from L.P. Hollander & Company, a Fifth Avenue clothing store, and quarter page ads from Brooks Brothers, a furniture store, a pantomime-and-dance specialist and Dutton's, which sold not only books but "correct social stationery." Brooks Brothers would become a loyal advertiser, anchoring the society news pages for decades.

The first issue had posted a notice for an "able" editor without specifying any qualifications besides availability; by 1918 the staff had grown to five and the following year the publication hired a business manager who also functioned as an advertising agent. Pages expanded to 44, and theater reviews became a regular feature. The *Bulletin* continued to diversify, adding general interest features like a book column, poetry contests and literary quizzes.

The same literary talents producing the magazine also ventured into film. In 1916, the New York League produced a "moving-picture melodrama" called "The City of Beautiful Nonsense," written by Grace R. Henry, the *Bulletin* editor. Although the action took place "in and around New York City," the plot revolved around a ruby called The Flame of India and a "Hindoo adventurer" named Ravan Varas, who posed as the Count di Ravano.

Grace R. Henry continued as *Bulletin* editor after the Association of Junior Leagues was created in 1921. The *Bulletin* steadily expanded, putting club news and Junior League engagements, weddings and births in the back of the book. Extensive coverage of the arts and discussions of social and political issues began attracting a broader readership. With each issue, the publication resembled less a club newsletter and more a general interest magazine, and soon began advertising itself as "the journal of youthful opinion."

In November 1923, the *Junior League Bulletin* introduced a new trademark, shaped like a magazine rolled ready to mail, but instead of an address label, the cylinder bore the words *Juvenus Potestas*, which the editors explained was Latin for Youth is Opportunity. The editorial copy was markedly different from earlier issues, this issue given over to politics, a topic previously avoided by the League. "We are not necessarily advocating a change of tactics at the moment but merely suggesting that the time may come when we will be forced into the position where we might have to take a definite stand one way or the other in order to render the most intelligence service to our community," Mrs. Charles A. Lindley, the editor wrote. In the following pages, League members Eleanor Roosevelt and Ruth Pratt, a prominent Republican from New York, explained their political affiliations.

Advertisements for costume rentals for Junior League follies, luxury hotels, photographic portraits and clothing for men and women were growing, but by January 1921, the editors were calling upon readers to send in post cards indicating that they read the *Bulletin* "...for our satisfaction and to prove we have interested readers to sundry skeptics in the advertising field who, when asked for ads, refused on the ground that, like a Mission Monthly, we are never read."

The Junior League Magazine *attracts major advertisers, 1911.*

By 1929, the *Bulletin* was a highly professional publication, rich with editorial content and fat with national advertising including full-color pages. The *Junior League Magazine* as "the voice of youthful opinion" was sold by subscription and also on newsstands next to *Vogue*. In 1929, a reader from Milwaukee wrote to congratulate the magazine on the October issue. "Compliments have come from all sides, but I should like to speak especially of the article from Honolulu on the sugar tariff. It bristles with facts, intelligence and information." A reader from New Haven added, "I do not belong to The Junior League and cannot as I am in my 75th year, but I have read your paper on Prohibition in the November number and want to congratulate you on its tone and spirits."

Even as the Depression deepened, the magazine continued to be an editorial force full of advertisements for fashion, cigarettes, automobiles and design. Wartime shortages forced a cutback and redesign from which the magazine never really recovered. In the post-war period, *Better Homes & Gardens* became the favorite read of League members, who were predominantly young matrons rather than debutantes. The magazine took on the more modest role of being a publication focusing less on what youth was thinking and more what the Junior League was doing. It later transformed into the *Junior League Review*, whose publication was suspended in the 1990s for economic reasons.

"This question of organization is all-important, if we are to direct our knowledge and sympathies effectively. Probably all of you are having the same troubles and the same facts to deal with; but there is one point I would like to make, and it is, that the sociological conditions in each city are different," Mary told them.

Then, in a roll count beginning with the youngest League, they told their individual stories. Baltimore, represented by Miss Margaret Carey, confessed to being in "an embryonic state of development," having organized only on April 1. Miss Carey explained although her city had other volunteer organizations, none offered young women "the opportunity to gain knowledge of social conditions or knowledge of the field of work open to them or knowledge of the means which can be used." Miss Katherine Hutchison of the Junior League of Philadelphia, which had grown out of the Agnes Irwin Alumnae group, asked for help from "older sister Leagues" in establishing a training system. Chicago, organized the previous year with the encouragement of Jane Addams, had placed most of its members in the settlements. One did such a fine job managing Saturday morning sewing classes, settlement officials asked her to take the job of head matron. She accepted the offer, carrying on the work "very creditably." Brooklyn reported on Lenten Bible study and the joys of laboring alongside professional social workers. The Boston Sewing Circle detailed how it had "already done something toward creating a

general sentiment that a girl can, and should, do something outside her own particular set."

At the end of the meeting, according to the minutes the New York League found a cause that united them all— a disaster "uppermost in all our hearts." The night of April 14–15, the Titanic had sunk after colliding with an iceberg. The Junior League House would be taking in 50 immigrant women from the ship. Asking delegates for donations, Caroline McCormick Slade collected $313 to be contributed to the Relief Fund in the name of the Associated Junior Leagues.

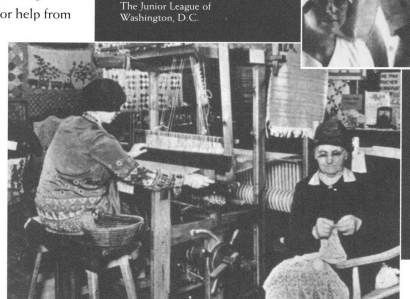

Child Welfare Group volunteers.

The Junior League of
Washington, D.C.

*The Junior League of
Montreal's Canadian
Handcraft Guild,*
c. 1910.

Junior League Bulletin filled the May 1912 issue with reports from "the first annual Junior League Conference." "We say 'first annual' advisedly, because no one could have attended the meeting without feeling sure that they will take place annually as long as there is work to do and methods to compare." At first, however, the conferences were biennial. In 1914, Chicago hosted 13 Leagues, who voted to form the International Junior League Committee made up of League presidents. At Philadelphia in 1916, committees were appointed to draw up a national constitution and to consider copyrighting the name Junior League of America. Delegates at the Cleveland conference in 1918 debated if war work should be counted as Junior League volunteer work and established a formal process for groups to become Leagues. After the Baltimore meeting in 1919, the Conferences became an annual event.

The idea of young Society girls volunteering to better conditions in their cities intrigued the press from the start. New York City newspapers regularly covered League social events like balls, amateur theatrics and changes in headquarters and recognized the contributions the young women were making to their city. The *New York American Sunday* on March 16, 1913, wrote: "The Junior League is the training school for the modern debutante. Through its theatrical entertainment, which it gives every Winter, the League has become known as a social-philanthropic organization, to which the fashionable debutantes belong. It is generally regarded as an exclusive club for the girl just out . . . Of the true work of the League, of its aims and purposes, the general public knows nothing. It knows nothing of its splendid work among the migrants, of its labors for the children and for the working girl."

The Movement Spreads

The Junior League movement rapidly spread across the continent as the decade progressed. West of the Mississippi, San Francisco, St. Louis, Kansas City, Denver and Omaha established Leagues. A League formed in the capital but also in smaller towns like Racine, Buffalo, Poughkeepsie and Utica. In 1916, Atlanta became the first Southern League with its 45 members sponsoring a "Butterfly Ball" to benefit the Churches' Home for Girls and enrolling young women in household arts and Red Cross courses essential to war relief. Chattanooga followed in 1917, organizing a canteen for servicemen at the train station.

Though versatile and ambitious, the women of St. Louis were sheltered from slums, poverty and suffering. In 1940, Virginia Elliot Fischel, an early St. Louis League president, shared her memories of how the League was born "in the shadow of the Great War." "It should be easy to be amusing about that so quaint yesterday when none of us could so much as lunch with a man unchaperoned; when most of us did not smoke, and if we did, it was daringly or behind closed doors beside opened windows; when a coordinated city-wide plan for social work had yet to be thought through, and when the young volunteer was the exception rather than the rule."

Twenty members signed on almost immediately. By the first of the year, membership had doubled. Three members were guests at the National Junior League Conference in Chicago where they met Jane Addams at Hull House. At the next conference when the Leagues met in Baltimore, St. Louis was represented by a full-fledged delegation that had much to report.

St. Louis and the Suffrage Battle

After Lincoln Steffens criticized St. Louis in his mucking-racking article, "The Shame of the Cities," the city had embraced the Progressive Movement, committed to reform. With a new city charter, Mayor Henry W. Kiel was determined to make St. Louis more than "first in booze, first in shoes and last in both (baseball) leagues." In March 1910, the Equal Suffrage League of St. Louis had formed, stirring much interest, but the issue grew in popularity even more after a statewide referendum on suffrage failed to pass in 1914.

On one fall afternoon in 1914, a small group of debutantes and suffragists, often one and the same in St. Louis, met at the home of Miss Margaret McKittrick on Pershing Place. But tea was not all that was on the table. The young women wanted to be part of the reform movement. They gathered to "clarify their ideas of what could be done to make themselves and other like-minded young women, informed and useful citizens," wrote Mrs. Harry January, a former Baltimore resident whose encouragement gained her the title "Grandmother of the St. Louis League."

From that first meeting, the St. Louis Junior League combined advocacy with service. The young women wanted to serve—but they also wanted the vote. They became the only League to organize to support the suffrage issue.

"They knew they believed in suffrage for women, they knew that industrial conditions were not as they should be for a great many women and child workers. And they wanted to find out how they could best take some intelligent action in these and various other phases of life about them," Mrs. January recalled later.

Sarah Chambers Polk, another early League president, remembered her involvement in women's suffrage more than anything else when looking back nearly 60 years in 1974.

"My husband was a proper Southern gentleman who believed that a wife should be dressed in dignified black silk with a white lace collar, sitting at home with needlework. She definitely should not be in the streets marching for woman's rights or at the polls where some men drank and used vulgar language. When the time came for me and many of my League friends to decide on this issue, we felt that for the nation's good women should be permitted to vote. To win our point, we threatened to march in the streets until our husbands promised to vote for suffrage."

After a suffrage referendum failed to pass in New York in 1915, St. Louis became a focal point in the campaign when the city hosted the Democratic National Convention in 1916. The local suffragists decided to demonstrate, but instead of the hunger strikes and sit-downs used elsewhere, the St. Louis women staged a "walkless, talkless parade." Wearing yellow sashes and carrying yellow parasols, which protesters purchased from a local department store for 50 cents, more than 7,000 women lined the route delegates had to pass to reach the hall. They made their point. The Democrats voted to include a plank for women's suffrage, the first time a national party had declared support for suffrage.

The St. Louis League participated when the National American Suffrage Association held its golden jubilee convention in St. Louis in March 1919 less than three months before Congress passed the 19th Amendment. Carrie Chapman Catt, president of the suffrage association, declared, "Arise women voters! In this your first union together, let the nation hear you pledge all that you have and all that you are to the new crusade." Members voted to dissolve the organization and replace it with a new group: The League of Women Voters.

On July 3, 1919, a month after Congress passed the Amendment, Missouri became the 11th state to ratify it, almost a year before it became the law of the land.

In 1920, when the Junior League held its annual conference in St. Louis, all thoughts were on women's suffrage and what the amendment's ratification would mean to women. Discussion turned to forming Legislative committees "for the study of all contemplated city or state laws, especially those affecting the social welfare of women and children." The St. Louis League established its Legislative Committee in 1920 with the goal "to develop into a vital factor for better city and state government." In less than a year, the League helped to pass the Missouri Children's Code Commissions Bills and to elect a nonpartisan school board. Members had sent letters and telegrams to legislators, signed petitions, rode in parades and displayed banners, but most of all they had carried on "the not-to-be-underrated verbal propaganda for the ends we desired," learning their skills in a public speaking class sponsored by the Legislative Committee.

The Junior League of St. Louis—Equal Suffrage League marches for "Votes For Women," c. 1919.

The Junior League of Portland, Oregon, begins work at the Flower Mission Day Nursery, 1919.

patients could learn marketable handicrafts. With war's end, the workshop overflowed with severely disabled veterans relearning basic skills and mastering new skills to support themselves. Out of the program grew the Washington University School of Medicine's Program in Occupational Therapy.

The League staged the Great Rummage Sale in 1918 for "the benefit of rehabilitation schools for battle worn soldiers after the war." The League convinced Mary Pickford to send an initialed handkerchief, the City of Richmond Heights to donate its old oil-burning lamps and Mayor Kiel to contribute his gold watch. The event netted over $9,000.

Issues affecting the well-being of women and children proved the common denominator for all Leagues. Like New York, the Chicago and Cleveland Leagues also created residential hotels for working women; other Leagues established lunchrooms or lunch programs. The New York League in 1917 began the first system of volunteers in an outpatient department in the city in the Children's Clinic at Bellevue Hospital. Many Leagues supported a national pure milk movement and established milk stations to deliver untainted milk to needy families. In Oregon, the Portland League organized a Fresh Air program for working mothers and their children. The roots of later League involvement in foster care and adoptions can be found in projects like San Francisco's home for underprivileged children.

The war soon overshadowed such local projects, but Caroline McCormick Slade of the New York League reminded members in 1917 that "in trying to help the misery and suffering abroad we do not forget our duties

Without any training, St. Louis League members went to work immediately, reading to the blind and taking "yesterday's party flowers" to the "sick poor." They volunteered to teach housekeeping, sewing and embroidery to working girls at Miss Gregg's Settlement House and maintained a children's lending library. Following the lead of other Leagues, they staged a play to raise money for a lunchroom where "wholesome lunches may be provided for working girls." After war was declared, they rolled bandages, took nurse's aide courses and helped care for wounded soldiers.

In their first year, the St. Louis League began a most ambitious project. In a tunnel at Children's Hospital, they established an occupational therapy workshop where and obligations at home." Leagues continued to follow Mary Harriman's advice to build their programs on "the conditions of each individual place."

Over There, Over There . . .
The Junior League Goes to War

The Montreal League "plunged into patriotic work" first as nearly every member had a brother or a friend among the 32,000 Canadian troops sent to Europe when war began in 1914. Although the U.S. would remain neutral until April 1917, almost all Leagues were doing something to help by 1916, mostly collecting money for war refugees or setting up "preparedness" projects, often in partnership with the Red Cross.

As the conflict spread, so did the Leagues' service on the home front. Kansas City League members wrapped bandages and sent Christmas boxes to soldiers. The Oranges League in New Jersey worked with the Red Cross to organize home nursing classes that drew over 100 participants. "The pupils are most enthusiastic and persistent . . . We are all better 'prepared for any fate.'" Philadelphia established a special Emergency Committee for War Relief. "Every girl is trying to do some little extra work besides her regular Junior League service with which it is not allowed to interfere in anyway . . . As our hearts and thoughts are with that valiant little country and her people—Belgium— we are making a special effort to do two things at once!"

In San Francisco, League members sold sugarless gum to benefit the Red Cross and set up a delivery service so successful that it became the model for the Red Cross Motor Corps. Responding to an urgent call from Herbert C. Hoover, then head of the Belgian Relief Commission, they donated food that was shipped to Europe in a vessel chartered by the Chamber of Commerce and established a Belgian Relief Committee to provide warm clothing. They also collected individual monthly subscriptions "notwithstanding the fact that it is not the policy of the Junior League of San Francisco, as a body, to contribute money for any purpose whatsoever."

New York Junior League hospital volunteers, c. 1915.

The Junior League of the City of New York Archives

Detroit, inspired by New York's work at Camp Upton, visited Fort Wayne where the *Bulletin* reported they found a "hospital of forlorn colored soldiers, tended by men nurses." Ignoring the segregation of the times, the Detroit League organized visits three times a week, bringing the soldiers "flowers, fruit, cigarettes, magazines and cheer," and set up a tent outside the ward to teach toy-making for those patients strong enough for occupational therapy. Reporting to the *Bulletin*, the League promised to send news of plans to see the "fascinating Noah's Arks, wooden animals, dolls' furniture, locomotives and airplanes."

In New York, the League addressed the problem of wartime shortages by working with Wanamaker's Department Store to create seven simple dresses in serge, Georgette and foulard, which "make possible a maximum of effect at an extremely moderate expenditure," according to one newspaper report. Mrs. Edith Morgan of the League was quoted as saying, "It is not our desire to standardize fashion or to persuade all women to dress alike. But we do want to make available in the ready-made trade simple, well-designed models for the street and the afternoon, which will make

"War Time Dress," designed and promoted by League members and offered by Wanamaker, to "conserve materials and labor and to eliminate waste."

Junior League Bulletin, 1917

dress less of a problem for the woman who is busy with all kinds of war work and who wishes to spend more of her money on war relief and less on clothes."

The demands on the volunteer's time were immense as Leagues not only joined the war effort but also maintained community projects like the Visiting Teachers. "The war with its disorganizing conditions has put bigger problems before the school inasmuch as it has put bigger problems in the lives of the children," Jane F. Culbert of New York reported in the fall of 1918.

League members also began serving overseas with a number of organizations. Volunteers included the president of the St. Paul League, the founder of the Philadelphia League and the editor of the *Bulletin*. Alison Elder of the Montreal League, serving as secretary of a Canadian general hospital, was stationed "somewhere in France."

Caroline McCormick Slade, then New York League president and chairman of the YMCA's Women's Division of the War Personnel Board, organized a League unit of 125 members, uniformed in designer shirts with special JL patches, to serve with the YMCA in France. The unit was such a success, the head of

League volunteers serve in France during World War I.
The Junior League of the City of New York Archives

Over 100 volunteers responded, with four Detroit girls doing "splendid work" at Aix-les-Bains in France. The number might have been larger if the YMCA hadn't stopped recruiting when its overall quota was more than full. Leagues members at home couldn't help but be jealous as well as proud.

"As it has been the biggest opportunity in the life of our men, so has it been for our girls, and the stories that come back to us of their achievements are often unbelievable," reported the *Bulletin*.

Under "News From the Front Lines," a Junior League volunteer near the front shared this dispatch written from Paris, July 23, 1918:

the YMCA cabled Mrs. Slade, "Would like 200 Junior League types for areas. Unit enthusiastically commended." Mrs. Slade went to work after scribbling on the cable, "Isn't this wonderful? Will you, through the Junior League, get us 200 as soon as you can?"

The *Bulletin* asked readers if Leagues could possibly contribute one or two members for the unit, saying that the YMCA would pay all expenses if volunteers could not do so themselves. Candidates were required to be over 25 years old, in good health and "having no father or husband in service."

The last week in Chalons-Sur-Marne has been as near hell, I guess, as anything on this earth can get. On July 14th we were wakened on the stroke of midnight by a great detonation close to the house. Simultaneously, pandemonium broke loose to the north and west. The continuous quivering vibration, which was rattling all the windows, was interrupted at five-minute intervals by the explosion of the shells, which were landing all over the town. At the hospital the next morning, we found that all the patients had been taken down to the cellar for the time. By this time the French wounded were pouring in, and we volunteered our services to help. . . . The field hospital which the

Americans had installed as a casualty clearing station, about 10 to 15 kilometers ahead of us, had been shelled to pieces the night before, and their nearest hospital to the line was 10 kilometers in our rear at least. They therefore wanted an emergency station at which to drop intransportables, who would not probably survive the stress of the additional trip. From that time on life has been a nightmare. . . .

After the war, Junior League members still volunteered to serve overseas during the Russian Civil War. The American Expeditionary Force, made up of the 27th and 31st Regiments, fought with the Whites in the Russian Civil War between 1918 and 1920. Carol Camp of the Milwaukee League, serving with the YMCA in Vladisvostok, Siberia, in February 1920 as the Red Army advanced eastward, found herself being evacuated to Japan. She reported back to the *Bulletin*, under the headline: "In the Grip of the Reds."

> *As it has been the biggest opportunity in the life of our men, so has it been for our girls, and the stories that come back to us of their achievements are often unbelievable.*
>
> —*Junior League Bulletin*, 1918

The last two weeks have been very chaotic ones. For some days we had heard that the Bolsheviki were coming . . . The opposing Russian Army sent out word that the city was under siege and that all civilians must obey certain military regulations. General Graves [expedition commander] immediately ordered all American women to go either to the Red Cross barracks or to the Evacuation Hospital, which places would be protected by American troops. We YMCA girls were sent to the Evacuation Hospital, which is four miles outside the city. It was a dark night and we jolted along over rough roads for an hour.

On arriving we were taken to the officers' ward, a cold barren building that had not been heated or used in weeks . . . That night we thought we heard the roar of guns trained on the besieged city. It was a flight of our excited imaginations, however, for the next day we heard the news of how quietly the Bolsheviki had taken over the town . . . There are many rumors about Japan. Her merchantships have ceased coming and some think that within a few days she may send her battleships to blow up the town. The situation is a serious one and we cannot but feel that General Graves is wise in sending American women to safer regions.

Part of a Nationwide Movement

The mission of the *Junior League Bulletin* throughout its history and name changes was to encourage League members to greater service no matter how great the challenge. In 1915, Harriet Alexander (Aldrich), the magazine's editor, wrote the following editorial, spurring Leagues onward. The *Bulletin* reprinted it as just as relevant 15 years later when Mrs. Aldrich chaired the 1930 Conference in New York City.

Very often during the past winter letters have come to us from officers and members of various Junior Leagues expressing real discouragement, even despair, at the seeming unfruitfulness of their efforts, or at the waning interest in League work. To some of these the answer must need be the cruel one, 'Work out your own salvation.' All of us must go through the 'storm and stress' period, beset by the indifference of others, and fear and doubt within ourselves. The example of other Leagues who have gone through the same experiences is a great help. New York as the pioneer League feels a great responsibility in helping young and growing Leagues to steer a straight course and emerge triumphant from the many dangers which surround them. Some of these dangers come from over-enthusiasm, others, on the contrary, from over-organization, and the latter are the worst. Whatever you do, don't let the spirit of service in your League die an unnatural death, bound and gagged by red tape! Do away with any unnecessary officers and committees, keep only those who have work to do, and as the work expands, add more committees, but not before. Don't hire an office and buy a typewriter till you really need it. Be satisfied to grow slowly, rather than to be inflated like a balloon, only to burst with a loud report!

Leagues all over this country. 'Failure' is a word which has not yet been written in the history of any League, and need never be, if only the right girls are entrusted with the work. You can have the best organization in the world on paper, and yet if the chairmen of the committees are vague or indifferent the machine doesn't work.

I sometimes dream at night of an ideal Junior League in which every girl possesses that great attribute of genius 'the infinite capacity for taking pains.' For that is what is needed.

Leagues Founded 1911–1919

Baltimore, Maryland	Oranges & Short Hills, New Jersey	Atlanta, Georgia	Greater Utica, New York
Chicago, Illinois	Washington, D.C.	Milwaukee, Wisconsin	Wilmington, Delaware
Cleveland, Ohio	Detroit, Michigan	Racine, Wisconsin	Denver, Colorado
Montreal, Quebec	Kansas City, Missouri	Albany, New York	Buffalo, New York
Philadelphia, Pennsylvania	St. Louis, Missouri	Chattanooga, Tennessee	Omaha, Nebraska
San Francisco, California		St. Paul, Minnesota	Poughkeepsie, New York

New Freedoms and Responsibilities

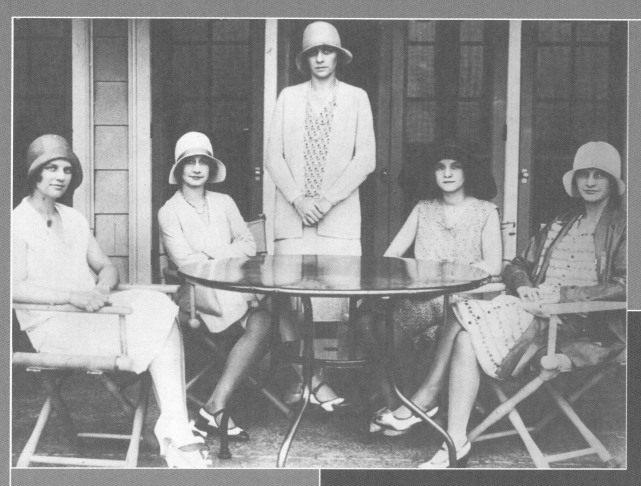

The Executive Committee of the Junior League of Kansas City, Missouri, 1929–1930.

1920–1929

*N*o image better symbolizes the Roaring Twenties *than the flapper, recognized by her bobbed hair, scarlet lips and fringed skirt barely covering rouged knees. Equipped with a ready-to-party attitude, she smoked, she drank, she necked with handsome young men driving roadsters, not a care in the world as she frolicked through F. Scott Fitzgerald's Jazz Age. She created a language and style all her own and changed forever how women acted, thought and dressed.*

If the flapper appeared giddy, so did the times. Fitzgerald estimated that "the whole upper tenth of a nation (was) living with the insouciance of a grand duc and the casualness of chorus girls." A growing middle class enjoyed the materialistic rewards of Model Ts, refrigerators and radios. The Great War and its incredibly bloody battles were over and a revolution was underway in the United States as well as in the Soviet Union. "The war tore away our spiritual foundations and challenged our faith. We are struggling to regain our equilibrium," a self-confessed flapper wrote in OUTLOOK *magazine in 1922.*

In accepting membership in the Junior League a woman steps forthwith into the wider citizenship of her city. . . It is only as we add our contributions of service that we can be rightly said to have won our final citizenship papers.

—Dorothy Whitney Straight

Dorothy Whitney Straight, first president of AJLA, 1921–1922.

other walks of life." In the Roaring 20s, the Junior League would experience immense growth in individual memberships and number of Leagues.

For nearly two decades, the Junior Leagues had multiplied across the continent, a loosely organized confederation of earnest young women. By 1920, the 39 Leagues shared a name, a newsletter and an annual conference but little more. It was apparent that the Leagues "could not run on enthusiasm alone," as Winthrop B. Palmer, an early Association president, recalled in the *Junior League Bulletin* in 1927. "It was the genius and creative imagination of Dorothy Whitney Straight that consolidated the little group of local societies into a National Organization that doubled its size, power and potentiality in ten years."

Dorothy Whitney Straight

In the spring of 1921, Dorothy Whitney Straight was a 34-year-old war widow with three children under age nine. Since her husband's death in France, she had dedicated her immense energies into creating a memorial for him at Cornell University and organizing the growing collection of individual Leagues into a unified association.

This was the same Dorothy Whitney who had headed the New York League so brilliantly in 1909 and supervised the ambitious construction of the Junior League House for working women. Not long after the residential hotel was completed, she married Willard Straight, a foreign correspondent and diplomat who had also courted Mary Harriman. Maury Klein, E. H. Harriman's biographer, describes Straight as "tall, charming, possessed of boyish good looks and brimming with talent." Son of

Young women, empowered by the vote, searched for new roles. "To understand the young girl of today, we must grasp the fact that first, last and all of the time, she is an experimentalist," Dorothy G. Noyes of the St. Paul League wrote in the *Bulletin* in November 1923. "Now, as a natural result of the Women (sic) Movement, she has thrown over all authority and has decided to find out for herself by actual experiment what she wants to be and what she will think about the world and all its works." It was through the Junior League work, she said, that "many girls get their first glimpse of the problems of people in schoolteachers, Straight trained as an architect but headed to the Far East after graduation. He was serving as vice consul in Seoul when he met Mary, traveling with her father, in 1904. Although Harriman opposed the romance, he used Straight as his contact in exploring business ventures in China and Manchuria.

The Whitney-Straight wedding took place in Switzerland in 1912 with the couple living briefly in what was then Peking. Back in New York, they became leaders in shaping American intellectual life, and Dorothy Straight returned to Junior League work. In 1913 the *New York American* noted that she was as one of "the well-known young matrons" active in the League.

As the war approached, the Straights launched *The New Republic,* "a journal of opinion to meet the challenge of the new time," with Walter Lippman among the first editors. When her husband joined the army in 1917, serving in France as a major, Dorothy worked for women's rights and the war effort. Drawing upon her Junior League experience, she raised money for the Women's Liberty Loan Committee, the Young Men's Christian Association, and the Red Cross. She chaired the Women's Emergency Committee of the European Relief Council, which helped feed over three million children in Europe. On December 1, 1918, her 38-year-old husband died in Paris after pneumonia developed from a case of influenza.

It was the genius and creative imagination of Dorothy Whitney Straight that consolidated the little group of local societies into a National Organization that doubled its size, power and potentiality in ten years.

—Winthrop B. Palmer, 1927

The question of a national organization came up in the spring of 1921 when the annual Conference, meeting in Montreal, resolved "that a council be called for consideration of a national name, constitution and policy to be submitted to the membership at large at the next conference." They wasted no time. A special meeting was held in New York in May, delegates agreed to form an association dedicated to giving service to the community and training and educating its members. Dorothy Whitney Straight was elected president of the national board.

Article 2 of the new Constitution laid out the organization's purpose. "The object of this Association shall be to unite in one body all the Junior Leagues and to promote their individual purposes, i.e., to foster interest among their members in the social, economic, educational and civic conditions of their own communities and to make efficient their volunteer service." The Association was charged with admitting new Leagues, publishing the *Bulletin,* supporting the Conference and acting as an information bureau.

Under Dorothy Straight's leadership, the Association of Junior Leagues of America, Incorporated, resolved to harness the strengths of the individual Leagues for greater community service and "to train and educate" League members for a lifetime of volunteer work.

Education—A Continuous Process

At the Atlanta Conference in 1922, Dorothy Whitney Straight, first president of the Association of Junior Leagues, set the standard for volunteer training with these remarks:

In order to form any fair estimate of the Junior League we must see it in relation to education as a whole. In the thought of previous generations, education was something which ran a definite course, commencing in a girl's life at the age of six or seven and continuing for a period of ten or twelve years. The acquisition of knowledge—so called—was crowded into these years and upon graduating from school a girl was pronounced educated with a triumphant note of finality. Thereafter nothing more was required of her except her plunge into society and matrimony and a complete baptismal immersion in both.

Today our concept of education is quite different, as well as our conception of a woman's place in the world. We see education now as a continuous process, commencing the day we are born and lasting as long as life itself, provided we have the will to learn and the spirit of inquiry motivating us. We see our school life as merely one stage in our great voyage of discovery. And we recognize that our subsequent years offer us untold opportunities for learning—both from experience and from books

as well as from contacts with people. We desire to see ourselves grow in social power and insight, in effective self-direction, and in the 'willing ability to identify both insight and capacity with the interests of the world and man.'

Given this conception of a continuous educational process, acquired through, and in relation to, living itself, we see in clear perspective the place of the Junior League. It becomes our vocational, our continuation school. It picks us up at the point where the preparatory school dropped us and it carries us through our second stage of education. It enables us to make our first contacts with the conditions of the big world in relation to which we are going to play out our lives—it directs our activities into channels of useful service—it trains us for special tasks, and it enlightens us regarding the state of our society. It becomes something more than school teacher; it becomes, in part, a life teacher. It becomes the means of revealing to us certain scenes in the great drama of humanity which is being enacted all around us.

In accepting membership, therefore, in the Junior League, a girl becomes at the same time a member of her own community. She steps forthwith into the wider citizenship of her city. And the first training course she takes or the first bit of social work she does is equivalent to taking out her citizenship papers. Thereafter she will endeavor to

qualify for full membership in that society, which implies, in the first instance, knowledge of the community, of its people, its needs, its activities, problems—and in the second instance, a realization and understanding of the technique of dealing with social situations. It is only as we show readiness to bear the burdens, to identify ourselves with that common life—and to add to it our contributions of beauty or of service, that we can be rightly said to have won our final citizenship papers.

In emphasizing so dominantly the educational aspects of the Junior League it may appear that I have overlooked the various services that it renders the social agencies of our cities. This, however, is not the case. The Atlanta Conference has in fact brought home to all of us I believe a realization of the useful and valuable work that the Junior Leagues are performing all over the country. But this work, it seems to me, can almost be taken for granted, for the very reason that once knowledge is vouchsafed to us once we have seen poverty and disease, of waste and of maladjustment—it will follow as "the night the day" that we will want to do something about it. The first and the great one is the awakening—the initiation—the raising of the curtain, as it were, on the drama—the introduction to the pain and sorrow and suffering of the world. Once we develop eyes that see and ears that hear, and hearts that understand, we will almost automatically constitute ourselves workers in a great human body whose aim is creation of the perfect community wherever we happen to be.

One defect in our Junior League education seems to arise from the fact that we do not meet the people or the problems of our cities until they come up to us through the social agencies—in other words, it is only at the point where people have gone under, only at the point where problems have become acute, that we learn something about them. Our whole attention is then directed to remedies. If I should criticize the Junior League for any weakness it would be this one. As an organization it is too much concerned with the effect and not enough with the cause. It is concentrating too much on remedy in relation to prevention. It is not going back far enough in trying to understand the forces that precipitate conditions. For this reason the training courses seem to fill a special need, or they, at least, attempt to indicate and interpret some of the forces that are at work in the world, some of the factors of human nature, and some of the elements that underlie our modern industrial life, causing the conditions that we see before us. It is only as we can diagnose our trouble—only as we can throw light on the cause of social as well as physical ills, that we can hope to effect any remedy and cure.

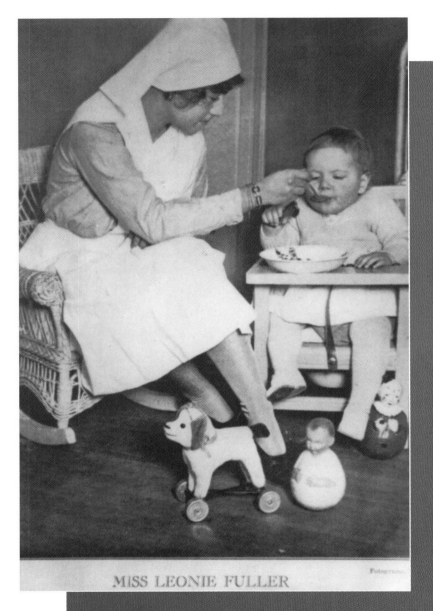

MISS LEONIE FULLER

The Junior League Baby Shelter provides for those in need, 1926.

The Junior League of the City of New York Archives

49

"In accepting membership in the Junior League a woman steps forthwith into the wider citizenship of her city . . . It is only as we add our contributions of service that we can be rightly said to have won our final citizenship papers," Dorothy Whitney Straight told a new generation of Junior Leaguers.

Expanding Roles

Throughout the decade, Junior League women stepped forward to serve. Chicago pioneered children's theater. Augusta opened a milk kitchen providing 35 quarts of clean milk a day to needy children, Cincinnati established a health clinic, known as the Junior League Welfare Station, to treat infants and children of indigent families. Tucson started and staffed the city's first day nursery. Tulsa founded a convalescent home for crippled children from all over Oklahoma. In Chattanooga, the League established the city's only women's exchange shop. "There were myriads who scoffed at the idea of a lot of inexperienced girls and women succeeding with a business," Emily Miller Smith reported to the *Bulletin* in 1923. " We thought that if we could just make a little over expenses the first year, we would do well. But it has prospered and prospered beyond the fondest hope of the most sanguine."

The Association set up new bureaus to serve Leagues' expanding responsibilities: Civic Welfare, Art and Lecture Exchange, the Players Bureau, the Arts and Crafts Exchange and a Shop Bureau to help the Leagues run the thrift shops, tearooms, libraries, handicapped crafts shops and even a beauty shop, which helped raise funds for their various projects.

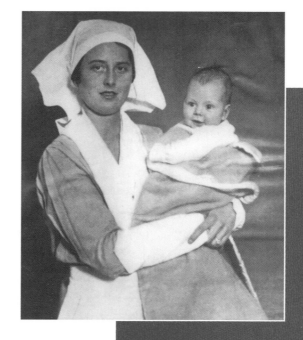

Mrs. William H. Walling, chairman of the Volunteer Workers, at the Junior League Baby Shelter, New York City, 1927.

The Junior League of the City of New York Archives

As the number of Leagues rapidly expanded, the Annual Conference quickly became an institution. Delegates traveled often for days to share League experiences, learn more about volunteering and develop friendships. Atlanta hosted in 1922 "in the midst of the famous Southern hospitality." Detroit the following year put on "a most efficient conference with fast motorcars and Ford factories." The Denver League sent cowboys on horseback to meet the train and a special Junior League train carried delegates westward across the country to Portland. Nashville featured Bobby Jones, the famous golfer and a Junior League husband. New Orleans greeted delegates with "a carpet of hyacinths." Delegates were houseguests of local League members and were royally entertained with theatrical skits, sing-a-longs, teas and dances when not hearing talks on welfare and children's theater. In 1979, Mary Ellis Peltz, a former New York League president and early *Junior League Magazine* Theater Editor, looked back on conferences of the 1920s.

She had been invited to join the League in 1915 but, busy as a journalist, she didn't "take a chance" on a Conference until 1925 when she traveled by bus to Concord and Lexington to an "Open Forum" of 500 Junior League leaders. The " burning subjects of the hour" were how to run a uniform fiscal year and what to do about transfer members, but in the evenings, they played bridge or mah jong. In May 1926 she went to Nashville. "What I remember most clearly was the three-course breakfast served in my bedroom by Mrs. John M. Gray of Nashville and the ingenuity of another hostess, Mrs. Foskett Brown. When a power failure extinguished every light in her home, Mrs. Brown, undaunted, merely instructed visitors to focus their automobile headlights through her windows so that the delegates could see to finish their meeting . . ." In 1928, Mrs. Brown would become the first member outside of the New York area to head the national association.

Pregnant in 1927, Mrs. Peltz missed a long train ride across the continent to the Portland Conference, but the following year she went to Buffalo where "The Place of Non-Partisan Politics in the Junior League" and "Children's Theater" were the major items on the agenda.

But it was New Orleans in 1929 that she remembered the most fondly. "The Conference was the best for hospitality and ease of management yet encountered. With me on the hot, dusty train sat the national officers and delegates from Boston, Philadelphia and Washington, D.C., who joined us as we made our way down the line. We arrived at New Orleans station at daybreak where hardy conference hostesses turned out to meet us, despite the hour, and then led us to wonderful morning coffee and doughnuts at the French Market."

By the time of the New Orleans Conference, when Mexico City was accepted as the 109th League, over 100 women's service organizations a year were asking for League affiliation. The Association was fielding an average of 150 letters a day asking for information on all kinds of things from how to run a clinic to how to stage a play outdoors.

The *Bulletin,* which had started so modestly, was filled with national advertising and running over 100 pages an issue. At the request of the Baltimore League in 1931, H. L. Mencken, editor of the *American Mercury* and a revered press critic, agreed to write an appraisal of the magazine but decided to submit an article instead. "When I went through the copies of the *Junior League Magazine* I found so many merits and so few defects I hesitated to make a critical report upon it, so it occurred to me that an article such as the enclosed (on the sad state of American literature) might be better.

By the time of the New Orleans Conference, when Mexico City was accepted as the 109th League, over 100 women's service organizations a year were asking for League affiliation.

51

Thrift Shops

*I*f walls could talk, Junior League thrift shops could tell the story of how people dressed, furnished their homes and saved a dime during much of the 20th century. Many of them were the first projects Leagues launched and remain their longest running fund-raisers.

"Money was not the only thing gained from fund-raisers; members came away from these events with both an *esprit de corps* and improved skills in organizing, motivation, planning, budgeting, marketing and public relations," Ellen Kingman Fisher, historian and former League president, observed in her history of the Junior League of Denver.

In 1923, the Denver League opened its Junior League Exchange and Shop as "The Little Shop with a Big Purpose." The shop grew and expanded to include a tearoom and circulating library and branches were even opened in Estes Park and Evergreen. Until 1939, the League thought it had created a great success. Then the League president asked the professional manager to see the shop's books, only to discover the manager hadn't kept any. The League was forced to liquidate the business to pay its debts and turned to other ways to raise money. In the 1970s, the Denver League became

shopkeepers again, this time building its thrift shop on a solid financial basis only to have it destroyed by fire in 1981. Through "heroic effort," the League reopened the shop in a new location. By 1993, when Dr. Fisher wrote her history, the shop at its various locations had generated a net income of nearly $1,500,000.

At the end of the century, 71 Leagues in the U.S., Canada and Mexico had thrift shops run and staffed by members, and another 74 sponsored rummage or thrift sales. Their histories tell the story of broader League service. Just listen to the tale the Salvage Shop, the League's first thrift shop, told to Mary Johnson, a Junior League of Buffalo Sustainer:

Some of my first memories are of people coming to shop in their horse-drawn carriages. The automobile was just beginning to be seen around town when the Junior League, then only two years old, purchased me in 1921 for one dollar from the Red Cross that had used me as a fund-raiser during World War I with great success. Soon the luncheon café opened and our existence was solidified. Throughout the years of the Great Depression, good hot meals were available to neighbors at reasonable prices. I still remember the looks of despair in the

Eye-catching bags advertise the Chicago Junior League's secondhand clothes sale.

The Junior League of Chicago

eyes of our customers. We tried to help as many as we could, but it never seemed to be enough.

The post-depression era was a happier time. I was finally full of the laughter that had been missing for so long. Ironically, as prosperity grew, the profits diminished. In 1939, the Board voted to close my doors. The chairman and a few new members of the committee worked to reverse the decision— and it worked! The League's minutes noted that too many dances would have to be held to make up for my annual profits. Later that year, my profits were used to buy Bundles for Britain pins. We were all concerned about the war and what was happening in Europe.

Then, all too soon, we were involved in the "War to End All Wars." This was the most vital time in my life. We filled the physical needs of our customers by selling clothing and the emotional needs by sharing good news and bad. I was proud that my profits were used to buy defense bonds. We all felt that in some small way we were making a difference.

The end of the war brought new worries: tuberculosis and later polio. Our community faced more tragic times, but we made it through.

In 1961, I turned 40—time to begin my mid-life crisis. I wondered how I'd find the energy to keep on going, but those women in the League didn't know the meaning of the word quit. Their time and enthusiasm brought me back stronger than ever. The year I turned 70, sales were up $3,000 over the previous year and we showed a profit of $20,000. The last

40 years have been a whirl as I began to advertise, target audiences and added donations from area retailers to keep my shelves stocked with quality merchandise. I have often heard that history repeats itself, and I, your grand lady of the fundraisers am living proof. Yes, I've had my ups and down, but over the years I have returned over $1 million to the community through grants and Junior League projects.

The original Junior League of Buffalo Thrift Shop, purchased in 1920 from the Red Cross for $1.00.

Photo: Elizabeth Kahle

The Junior League of Portland, Oregon, thrift shop.

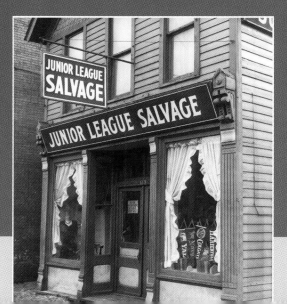

The Junior League of Atlanta is one of many Leagues with a thrift shop, but theirs is on wheels, 1968!

Junior League Fiction

The *Junior League Bulletin* encouraged members to submit poetry, plays, book reviews, artwork, photography and short stories, often announcing special literary contests months in advance. One children's plays competition drew so many entries, the editors had to put off announcing the winner to give judges enough time to read them all. Helen Cassin Carusi, a Washington League member, wrote this for the January 1925 issue:

THE MASTER MIND IN FOUR PARTS

Part 1
Scene:
A Peaceful Little Rural Town.

Bang! Bang! Bang! Three shots rang out in the midnight air. Detective Willie Ketchum arrived at top speed upon the scene.

"Which way did he go?" he asked one of the numerous bystanders attracted by the night life of the village.

"To the right," was the reply.

"Thanks," threw Willie, the astute, loping madly in the opposite direction.

"To the right, I said," bawled one young blade, a newcomer in the town and ignorant of the genius of the lynx-eyed detective.

"The approved modern psychological method of apprehending criminals is to proceed always in the opposite direction of the point in view thus bringing the pursuer face to face with the pursued," explained Willie as he ran.

"Read 'How to Grow Roses'," the detective added as an illuminating afterthought.

After five miles of careful consideration, the detective decides that the murderer can wait and hurries back to the scene of the crime.

The house was ablaze with light!

The Fiend flaunted this crime!

In a room on the second floor the body lay in a pool of blood. From the mouth of the victim trailed four black hairs!!!!

"The killer was a blond woman," said Willie to his assistant. "Find the knife!"

"But the hairs are black," pointed out the canny young fellow.

The Master Mind paused. No trace of annoyance marred the perfect tranquillity of his features.

"What would any woman do before she committed a murder? Why dye her hair, of course."

The young man looked crestfallen.

"Never mind, my lad, you'll get on," said Willie, kindly patting his head.

The detective seized his microscope.

"It remains to find a woman with dyed hair," he mused.

Just then a blood-curling shriek arose from the room below. Willie, the ever-resourceful, poked a hole through the floor, looked down,————and even the valiant detective turned gray as he saw——???

(to be continued in the February *Bulletin*)

Junior League of Savannah Provisionals completed classes in Parliamentary Law as part of their training, 1928.

Photo: Foltz Studios

after the Association was formed, a well-organized training course for Provisionals, first-year members, became the cornerstone of the League experience. Within this framework, each League would prepare its Provisional members to recognize and meet local needs.

An example of the rigor of the training can be seen in the assignments for New York League Provisionals in December 1929. The young women attended a series of lectures and wrote a paper on each in preparation for a comprehensive examination. The lectures included a Seth Low Junior College instructor on "The Homeless Man," the executive director of the Welfare Council of New York on "Our Social Agencies go in for Team Work" and Gertrude Ely of the League of Women Voters on "Why Not Take an Interest in Our Government?" Other talks explored "The volunteer of 1930 vs. 1890" and "Opportunities for the Volunteer in New York." The group also had a field trip to City Hall, leaving the Barbizon "at 10:00 o'clock promptly."

Suggested readings, 14 in all, included *The Art of Helping People Out of Trouble* by Karl de Schweinitz, *The Problem Child in School* by Sayles, *Schools of Tomorrow* by John Dewey, *The House on Henry Street* by Lillian D. Wald and *Spirit of Youth and City Streets* by Jane Addams.

Full of energy and excitement, Winthrop Palmer, writing in 1927, saw Junior League women marching forth as leaders unlike any known before:

> The future of America we are seeing for ourselves is the beginning of a new culture, a new meaning to life, a new philosophy. The girl of today unlike the mauve girl of 1900 is not standing in the shadow.

If it doesn't fit into your plans, please don't hesitate to throw it away." Circulation by subscription and newsstand sales was 24,000.

The Junior League had grown into an organization that set agendas, influenced opinions and provided volunteers for the community. From its earliest days, the League educated its members through lectures and readings, but

The Modern Girl's Reaction to Life

Borrowing a questionnaire from the Seattle League's "Puget Soundings," the *Junior League Magazine* asked the same 35 questions of the whole organization in November 1929 and reported the results in the first issue of the new decade.

Question	Percentage of Responses
What type literature do you prefer?	
Fiction	47½
Historical	17½
Biography	20
Biography and Fiction	10½
History and Biography	2
Miscellaneous	2
Whom do you consider the greatest woman in politics?	
Lady Astor	30
Ruth McCormick	10½
Ruth Pratt	5½
Alice Longworth	5
Do you vote?	
Yes	79
No	17
Sometimes	4
What three magazines do you prefer?	
Time	11½
New Yorker	11
Junior League Magazine	8½
Vogue	8½
Atlantic Monthly	7
Harpers	6½

Question	Percentage of Responses
Have you read *Ulysses*?	
Yes	67½
No	30½
Partly	1
Cannot get it	1
Is constant association with the mother beneficial to the children?	
No	61
Yes	22
Bad for mother	1
Do you believe in the principles of Margaret Sanger?	
Yes	78
No	12
Partly	10
Do you go to church as much as once a month?	
No	55
Yes	45
To What Church?	
Episcopal	40
Presbyterian	9
Catholic	8
Do you ever go without stockings?	
No	51
Yes	49
If not, why not?	
Unsuitable legs	19
Dislike looks	16
Comfort	5
Father or Husband	2

Question	Percentage of Responses
Do you believe in going Dutch?	
Man pay	52
Dutch	25
Depends on the circumstances	17
Do you believe in the double standard?	
No	60
Yes	25
Could you be happy with a man who was not a success in business?	
Yes	51
No	27½
Doubtful	16
Do you think necking is wrong?	
Yes	36
No	33½
Not wrong but foolish and in bad taste	13
Do you think that the abolition of the chaperone was a dangerous thing?	
No	84½
Yes	10½
Do you think that a brainy woman has any advantage in modern life?	
Yes	67
No	24
If she conceals them, yes	3½
And, after all, do you think that men really prefer the old-fashioned girl?	
No	48
Yes	26
Compromise	13
No, but they like to think so	2½

Crucible for Children's Theatre

Children's theatre, for all practical purposes, began in 1920 with an investment of $22,000 by the Junior League of Chicago. "The Chicago Junior League has done a bigger thing than it has any idea of," a Chicago newspaperman wrote in 1922. At first, the children's plays were used to raise funds for other League projects, but by 1929, children's theatre had become an art form and a national movement under Junior League leadership.

In less than a decade, The Children's Theatre of Chicago was producing Broadway-quality shows, nearly 90 other Leagues had established theatre programs in their communities and the Association added a manuscript library and a Bureau of Information for Children's Theater to provide professional guidance. The *Junior League Magazine* ran a regular column called "The Play Box" and encouraged League members to write children's plays. The November 1929 issue notes three new plays, one by Ellenor Cook of Hartford and two by Brownie Brace of Grand Rapids.

In previewing what was called "America's first conference on children's theatre" to be hosted by the Chicago League the following month, Eleanor Brush Cochran of the Chicago League reminded readers that only eight years before, Chicago had produced its first children's play, with troupers going from hospital to hospital. The first production in a regular theater was *Alice in Wonderland* by Alice Gerstenberg.

The Chicago Junior League presents Alice Gerstenberg's Broadway adaptation of Alice in Wonderland in 1921.

Out of the conference came a national Junior League production of Maeterlinck's *The Blue Bird*, which was seen by 35,000 children in a 15-city tour. The costumes and scenery, created by the Chicago League, traveled from city to city, but in each city local casts performed under local directors. When the play opened in Louisville in February 1931, the local newspaper reported, "The purpose of the Junior League in bringing this production to Louisville is not a monetary one, but an attempt to put Louisville in a chain with other cities so that a little theater movement may be worked up here." The Utica, New York, newspaper noted that "the business end of the tour is handled from the League's own theatrical bureau in New York City."

Children's theatre had become a community service—introducing theatre to children who otherwise would have never seen live performance—and also a creative outlet for League members. At first, professionals

57

Children's Theatre Expands

Throughout the Depression, World War II and the post-war era, children's theatre continued to thrive, expanding into puppetry, radio and television. On the West Coast in 1925, Portland staged marionette shows; three years later the Chattanooga and Roanoke Leagues began using hand puppets. The Birmingham, Alabama, League staged *Sleeping Beauty* as its first production in 1929, added a half-hour radio program in 1940 and introduced puppets, made by League members, in 1944.

By 1931, plays were staged by 80 Leagues, 42 presented marionette or puppet shows, 20 showed films and one gave "shadow picture" shows. At the Chicago World's Fair, the League presented three plays a weeks over four months. By 1938–1939, Leagues counted 900 performances of 200 players, reaching 350,000 children in person and even more in radio broadcasts, and almost all the 148 Leagues were involved in children's dramatic productions of one kind or another.

Grand Rapids and Cincinnati were among the first Leagues to take theatre into the public schools. In 1933 the Chicago League was staging performances in every elementary school in the city. By the end of the 1950s, nearly 80 Leagues took theatre into the schools.

"From its inception, the purpose of the Children's Theatre project has been to bring live theatre to children who would otherwise never be exposed to the art form," noted the Junior League of Houston when it celebrated 70 years of children's theatre productions in 2000. "Children's Theatre has always been reflective of the times. Children's Theatre productions, pioneered by the Junior League of Chicago and taken up by more than 100 Leagues across the country, began with the idea that early exposure to this form of the arts would be an educational and beneficial experience for school children."

From the start, Leagues incorporated education as well as entertainment into the theatre. In 1941, the Children's Theatre Department of the Seattle League began the

Kukla, Burr Tillstrom and Ollie; Tillstrom began his career with the Junior League of Chicago children's theatre productions years earlier.

The Junior League of Chicago

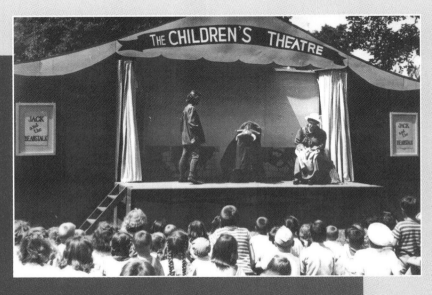

Children's Recreation Project, a story-telling hour, in low-income housing projects where children were facing "grave problems of adjustment" because of wartime anxieties. From story telling, the children moved into dramatizations and finally simple creative dramatics with plays written, produced and acted by the children. The program was continued after the war and was used as a model by UNESCO in helping children overseas adjust to post-war traumas.

Many children's theatre groups in Leagues moved into radio and television as the mediums developed. In the late 1940s in Chicago, Burr Tillstrom staged puppet shows with the Junior League that grew into Kukla, Fran and Ollie, a wildly popular show for both children and adults in the early days of television. The show premiered in Chicago on pioneer TV station WBKB on Oct. 13, 1947, two months and two weeks before Howdy Doody went on the air in New York.

Two years later, it was one of the first shows to be shown over a new network in the East and Midwest. In Pittsburgh in the 1950s, Fred Rogers helped organize WQED, the nation's first community-supported public TV station. With League help, he developed a daily, one-hour program called The Children's Corner, a forerunner of Mister Rogers' Neighborhood.

By the end of the Junior League's first century, many Leagues had turned over their children's theatre projects to independent boards or other organizations in the community. The Nashville Children's Theatre, begun by the Nashville League in 1931, no longer has direct League involvement but remains the oldest established continuing children's theatre in the United States. Nearly 60 Leagues remain active in children's theatre or puppetry projects used either for entertainment or in substance abuse or sex education programs. The Chicago League's longest running project is the Mad Hatters, a traveling theatre group that uses fun hats to tell a story and encourages children to read. In many cities, the Junior League roots of the local children's theatre have long been forgotten, but the curtain continues to go up.

Margaret Hamilton, later famous for her role as the Wicked Witch of the West in The Wizard of Oz, *got her start acting in the Junior League of Cleveland's children's plays, such as* Chatterbox, *shown here.*

The Junior League of Kansas City opened their children's theatre with an enchanting production of Aladdin, *c. 1927.*

were hired to play the roles, but Junior League volunteers soon replaced them. Margaret Hamilton of the Cleveland League, who played the Wicked Witch of the West in *The Wizard of Oz,* began her professional career in children's theatre as a Junior League member.

Not everyone, however, thought that producing plays for children fit into the larger League mission of social work.

"Some of the Leagues had scruples about beginning a play program because it might interfere with their welfare work," Helenka Adamowkska conceded in the November 1929 "Play Box," but she quickly pointed out that productions often provided the income "to support the very charities" critics had feared would suffer. "More than that, so far as the charity end of it is concerned, children's plays are not only a means to this end—they are the end in itself. Giving free performances for poor children, presenting them at Cripple Homes and asylums— can it be called anything but charity?"

In Chicago, where the League's children's theatre became nationally known, the troupers had gone from hospital to hospital with the first play and then finally into a regular theater with *Alice in Wonderland,* which Alice Gerstenberg, who headed the Chicago League's new drama department, had written for Broadway. Many of the early productions were based on fairy tales, because the children could more easily identify with the plot, but soon Junior Leagues were creating so many scripts that the Samuel French Company began publishing them. Sarah Spencer, who began writing and directing plays for the Charleston, West Virginia, League, founded Anchorage Press, specializing in children's plays.

Leagues Founded 1920–1929

Eastern Fairfield County, Connecticut
Cincinnati, Ohio
Dayton, Ohio
Duluth, Minnesota
Hartford, Connecticut
Knoxville, Tennessee
Lincoln, Nebraska
Louisville, Kentucky
Montclair-Newark, New Jersey
Rhode Island
St. Joseph, Missouri
Sioux City, Iowa
Syracuse, New York
Tacoma, Washington
Greater Princeton, New Jersey
Birmingham, Alabama
Dallas, Texas
Indianapolis, Indiana
Kingston, New York
Little Rock, Arkansas
Memphis, Tennessee
Nashville, Tennessee
Orange County, New York
Pittsburgh, Pennsylvania
Portland, Maine
Springfield, Massachusetts
Charleston, South Carolina
Charleston, West Virginia

Columbus, Ohio
Fall River, Massachusetts*
Honolulu, Hawaii
Greater New Haven, Connecticut
Elizabeth-Plainfield, New Jersey
Stamford-Norwalk, Connecticut
Tulsa, Oklahoma
Greater Waterbury, Connecticut
Winston-Salem, North Carolina
Colorado Springs, Colorado
Evanston-North Shore, Illinois
Jacksonville, Florida
Lancaster, Pennsylvania
Lexington, Kentucky
Minneapolis, Minnesota
New Orleans, Louisiana
Reading, Pennsylvania
San Antonio, Texas
Seattle, Washington
Columbia, South Carolina
Erie, Pennsylvania
Grand Rapids, Michigan
Norfolk-Virginia Beach, Virginia
Parkersburg, West Virginia
Santa Barbara, California
Spokane, Washington
Wichita, Kansas
Worcester, Massachusetts

Akron, Ohio
Charlotte, North Carolina
Houston, Texas
Los Angeles, California
Montgomery, Alabama
Pasadena, California
Savannah, Georgia
Toronto, Ontario
Asheville, North Carolina
Fairmont, West Virginia
Miami, Florida
Richmond, Virginia
Boise, Idaho
Flint, Michigan
Greensboro, North Carolina
Oklahoma City, Oklahoma
Roanoke Valley, Virginia
Tampa, Florida
Winnipeg, Manitoba
Augusta, Georgia
Harrisburg, Pennsylvania
Lynchburg, Virginia
San Diego, California
Troy, New York
Williamsport, Pennsylvania

(*League that disbanded in the 1990s)

The Depression: Voluntarism's Finest Hour

The Junior League of Eastern Fairfield County keeps kids busy at the Occupational Therapy Shop at Bridgeport Hospital.

The Junior League of Eastern Fairfield County, Connecticut

W omen responded with energy and dignity to the economic hardships of the Depression, but it was the election of Franklin Delano Roosevelt in 1932 that gave them greater political participation. Social welfare, which had been the heart of the Junior League and other women's organizations for decades, became the focus of New Deal policies. "An exceptional group of women with a common perspective built on shared history and long-term friendships had attained high positions. They were the last generation of women educated in the Victorian world of female social reform networks that had shaped the Progressive movement," wrote Sara M. Evans in BORN FOR LIBERTY, a history of women in the United States. "Eleanor Roosevelt was the emotional center of the network." As the President's wife and a woman with a strong social conscience, she spoke for people in need and supported her fellow Junior League members in doing the same.

In the present emergency special emphasis shall be put upon the League's welfare activities . . . it shall endeavor insofar as possible to offer increased volunteer service and raise additional funds to be used in actual relief work.

—League policy, 1932–1934

The Junior League movement, growing from 30 Leagues in 1920 to 112 only a decade later, had become well known across the continent by the 1930s. League members seemed to be offering their volunteer services everywhere. *Esquire* magazine poked a little fun at the League in April 1934 in a cartoon that showed a matron in a fur-collared coat offering her card to a police officer at the scene of a four-alarm fire and saying, "I'm president of the Junior League—perhaps there's something I can do!" But the message was clear: the Junior League always came to the rescue.

Tenth Annual Conference of the Association of the Junior Leagues of America at the Plaza Hotel, New York City, April 1930.

Photo: Price Studios, Inc.

The League members had become known as women who got things done in the community, whatever the challenge. But in its fourth decade, the League concentrated on its welfare roots as the world spiraled, rather than crashed, into an economic depression. The Association created a Welfare Bureau in 1931 and the following year formulated a five-point emergency welfare policy in response to "unprecedented economic and social problems." Social service agencies everywhere received a flow of destitute families. One agency reported an increase of 300 percent, with clients including white-collar families who had never asked for aid before, according to the *Junior League Magazine* in 1932. Families whose needs would have been considered "extremely desperate" only the year before were turning up daily. Evictions were frequent and threats of eviction more so.

The League found itself thrust into "a new era of maturity and sacrifice," Eleanor Pratt recalled in 1980. As Association President in 1932–1934, she encouraged Leagues to set up bureaus to recruit, train and place much-needed volunteers in their communities and to pool their resources. Drawing upon 30 years of experience in putting trained volunteers to work solving community problems, the Association charged its member Leagues to attack the problems in their local communities. "The A.J.L.A. believes that a community's greatest need at this time is a well-rounded social work program," the policy stated. "In the present emergency special emphasis shall be put upon the League's welfare activities. In addition to the work already carried on by the League, it shall endeavor insofar as possible to offer increased volunteer service and raise additional funds to be used in actual relief work." Cleveland, Providence and Montreal were among the Leagues matching local volunteers to agency needs.

Many Junior Leagues operated milk stations, nutrition centers, nurseries for children of working mothers and soup kitchens. League thrift or salvage shops thrived and multiplied. Washington, Newark and St. Joseph, Missouri, Leagues opened unemployment bureaus. Dallas worked through the local YWCA to help people find jobs. Volunteers at the Pittsburgh thrift shop helped people find jobs.

The number of Leagues grew steadily throughout the Depression, with 1934 the peak year when seven Leagues joined the Association. The Monroe, Louisiana, League, founded in 1930, was one of those "Depression" Leagues. Those early days are recalled in the Monroe League's official history: "The desperate welfare situation at that time was the inspiration for a small group of concerned friends to organize and help the needy children during the crisis. The years were a struggle because of the times, but with the unforgettable luncheon benefits in the homes of Monroe, charity balls at the country club, and style shows, enough money was made to establish and operate the first large project, a baby clinic for underprivileged babies and very young children."

Tampa, which became a League in 1928, started off its community service by giving partial support to the Pine Health Preventorium, a tuberculosis clinic and treatment center. By 1931, as the Depression deepened, the League assumed total support, including building an addition. In 1933–1934, members logged over 8,000 service hours at the center, helping to care for nearly 150 children. All the proceeds from League fund-raisers went toward supporting the Preventorium. The League continued to support the Preventorium until it closed in 1938.

Knoxville, the Girls Relief Corps until it became a League in 1921, built a preventorium, or children's cottage, at the county tuberculosis sanitarium as its first permanent project in 1922. Proceeds from the second annual charity ball, which netted $641.50, and the first Follies, which netted $3,000, helped pay for construction. In 1930, Nashville opened a home for crippled children. Tuscaloosa's preventorium made headlines in 1940 with the announcement that in the 1940 summer season two dozen children would receive "three months of excellent care and good food."

The Junior League of Monroe begins a baby clinic in the basement of St. Francis Hospital in 1930 in response to the Depression.

The Junior League of Monroe, Louisiana

Children's Welfare

RIGHT: *The Junior League of Minneapolis teaches constructive play to handicapped children at its Curative Workshop, 1936.*

Minneapolis Public Library, Minneapolis Collection

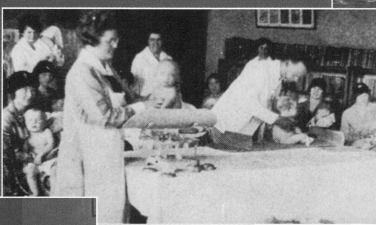

RIGHT: *In 1933–34, the Junior League of Lincoln's Well-Baby Clinic treated 3,280 babies.*

The Junior League of Lincoln, Nebraska

BELOW: *The Junior League of Honolulu's Kindergarten Nutrition Work program, c. 1930.*

The Junior League of Honolulu

LEFT: *The Junior League of Washington, D.C., contributed funds to the Children's Hospital for more than 60 years.*

The Junior League of Washington, D.C.

Junior League Advocates

The urgencies of the 1930s encouraged greater involvement in the political system than the League members had ever had before. Until the mid-1920s, the Junior League studiously avoided any discussion of politics, because many Leagues feared politics could cause division within the membership. "Politics and religion, as far as we know, are almost the only two fields into which the Junior League (as an organization) has not penetrated," Mrs. Charles A. Lindley, editor of the *Junior League Bulletin*, wrote in November 1923. "There are some Leagues who feel strongly that politics are absolutely 'taboo.'" Then she broke the taboo by devoting the entire issue to politics.

Mrs. Lindley carefully avoided any charges of partisanship by inviting two prominent New York League members, Eleanor Roosevelt and Ruth Pratt, to write about why they chose their political affiliations. Eleanor, wife of the recently defeated Democratic candidate for vice president, had recently begun her own political career by joining the League of Women Voters. Ruth Pratt had been appointed vice chair of the Republican National Ways and Means Committee in 1918—even before she could vote. Both encouraged League members to become involved in the political process.

"The general consensus of opinion seems to be that while the Junior League cannot enter the field of politics with the power to try and swing a candidate or an issue, nevertheless it should try and educate its members by means of legislative work committees, who would look into the whole question thoroughly and impartially," Mrs. Lindley wrote. "We are not necessarily advocating a change of tactics, at the moment, but merely suggesting that the time may come when we will be forced into the position where we might have to take a definite stand one way or the other in order to render the most intelligence service to our communities.

In the years that followed, Eleanor Roosevelt and Ruth Pratt as well as Mary Harriman Rumsey and Isabella Greenway would become major figures in the nation's politics. All of them could trace their social consciousness to their League work in the Settlements in New York. Ruth Pratt was the first to establish her own political presence.

"It was great satisfaction for me to fight, fight, fight for abolishing tenements unfit for human beings," Ruth Pratt said of her League work. Like many League members, she assumed highly responsible volunteer posts during World War I when she chaired the Women's Victory Loan Committee, overseeing 35,000 workers in 72 countries and raising more than $600 million for the war effort. She didn't seek a political career when she was elected the only woman among 64 Aldermen. "I might as well act instead of asking others to," she explained.

Ruth Baker Sears Pratt, the first Junior League member to serve as a U.S. Congressperson.

Wellesley College Archives and *Wellesley Alumnae Magazine,* March 1966

Mary Harriman's husband, Charles Cary Rumsey, a sculptor and polo player, died in a car accident in 1922, leaving Mary a widow with three young children. She spent more and more time at her country home in Virginia, throwing her energies into scientific cattle breeding and holding office in agricultural societies. As the Depression deepened, she organized an Emergency Exchange Association to barter skilled labor for merchandise and also established the Eastern Livestock Cooperative Marketing Association as a model for farm cooperatives across the nation.

Because of her work with cooperatives, President Roosevelt appointed her in 1933 as chair of the Consumer Advisory Board (CAB), making Mary Harriman Rumsey the first government voice for consumer rights. She encouraged her younger brother Averell, a New York banker, to join the administration, too. Although all the Harrimans had always been Republicans, they had supported their old friend Franklin in his presidential campaign. Averell was already serving as a business consultant to the NRA, but Mary thought he should do much, much more.

"You ought to take a job down there, that's your responsibility," the big sister told the little

Mary Harriman Rumsey, c. 1920.

Courtesy of Rotofotos, Inc.

brother, Averell Harriman recalled much later. He resisted; she insisted. He finally gave in and became the administrator of the National Recovery Administration, cornerstone of the New Deal.

"I don't think I would ever have done so if it hadn't been for her influence. That started off my career in government, so Mary is really responsible for it," he said in 1983. "I was affected by all Mary's interests and certainly politics. She had an influence in preventing me from remaining a Republican."

During World War II, Averell Harriman was President Roosevelt's representative in Lend-Lease negotiations with Churchill and Stalin and served as ambassador to both Great Britain and the Soviet Union during crucial years in the mid-40s. He became prominent in the Democratic Party. Appointed Secretary of Commerce in the Truman Administration, he later was elected governor of New York and represented the United States in the Paris peace talks with North Vietnam.

His sister provided him with the model for government service in her work with the Consumer Advisory Board. "Labor wanted higher wages and business wanted higher prices. She had to fight both of them," he said. "They had a great respect for her because,

fundamentally, she was socially conscious and she knew, to make the system work, both wages and prices had to stay in line."

She also knew how to bring people together, whether around a conference table or in the rented house in Georgetown she shared with Frances Perkins, a friend from the Settlement Movement and, as Secretary of Labor, the first woman appointed to the Cabinet.

Mary simply knew everyone in Washington. Her octagon house on O Street soon was the center of the city's social, artistic and political life. Guests included Margaret Bourke White, George Russell, Bernard Baruch, Will Rogers and, of course, Mary's old friends Eleanor Roosevelt and Isabella Greenway, the Arizona Congresswoman. Mary, Eleanor and Isabella lunched together regularly "to air" their minds.

Mary had long seen newspapers as a way of influencing public opinion. In 1932, she explored the possibilities of acquiring the *Washington Post* in order to turn it into a "new voice for liberal principles in the capital." She enlisted her friend Raymond Moley, part of Roosevelt's Brain Trust, and with Averell and Vincent Astor made a bid for the failing newspaper in 1933. They lost out to

Eugene Meyer, former chairman of the Federal Reserve Board.

They decided next to publish "a liberally oriented national public affairs magazine" with Moley as the editor. In explaining why they had decided to establish *Today*, Mary told *The Literary Digest*, "A weekly paper is something that I've been keenly interested in for 10 years, and now is a magnificent opportunity to start one. This paper will be completely independent, backing up all the movements and keeping the New Deal going. Of course we will back the President." But they didn't plan to be the mouthpiece of the administration, even though the president contributed an article to the first issue and was the first subscriber. Moley told *Time* magazine, "We want this to be a popular journal written in plain, square-toed English for the man in the street and the man on the farm."

Moley gave Mary all the credit for the genesis of the magazine. "The idea of the magazine originated in the fertile mind of Mary Harriman Rumsey," he said. But Mary died before she saw how successful her brainchild would be. In 1937, *Today* acquired a publication called *News Week* and created *Newsweek*, which later would become part of the *Washington Post* publishing empire.

➤

On Saturday, November 17, 1934, Mary's 53rd birthday, she fell from a horse during the first steeplechase of the season near her Middleburg estate where she relaxed on the weekends. The accident made the front page of the *New York Times* the following day. Riding sidesaddle and clamped to her mount, the expert horsewoman suffered a compound fracture of the right thigh and four broken ribs when her horse stumbled at a stone wall toward the end of the hunt.

She was rushed to Emergency Hospital in Washington where she received a blood transfusion, but Mary herself didn't seem to think the injuries were serious. She continued working from her hospital bed. She sent regrets that she would be missing a CAB staff meeting, dictated notes to her social secretary each morning, advised her son Charles and his new wife on decorating their home and planned a speaking tour for her friend, George Russell, the Irish poet and economist.

But complications slowed her recovery, and a month later, Mary Harriman Rumsey died, her three children, Frances Perkins and her brother at her side. Pneumonia was given

Averell Harriman, brother of Mary Harriman Rumsey, presents a photo of Mary on her horse to Association of Junior Leagues President Anne Hoover, 1981.

Photo: Robert L. Knudsen

as the official cause of death, but her brother demanded an autopsy, which found she had suffered a transfusion reaction. Doctors found her death "a tragic, mystifying affair."

Her friends were devastated. Isabella Greenway said, "The color seems to be wiped from the face of life with the going of Mary. I miss her a thousand ways over the hours." Eleanor Roosevelt canceled all her appointments for two days. She attended the funeral services at St. Thomas' Church with all the cabinet members, and left that night with Frances Perkins to attend gravesite rites at the family estate at Arden, New York. At a

memorial service, Eleanor mourned the loss of her girlhood friend who had been responsible for her first social activism and who, like herself, believed that "the sole reason for the existence of any government is to improve the condition of its citizens."

The press loved her, calling her "the lovely Mrs. Pratt" as she used her experience in finance—gained as a volunteer—to point out that the city could save $50 million a year simply by cutting the fat from the budget. Often at odds with Mayor James J. Walker, she introduced legislation calling for a referendum to revise the city charter. She also proposed measures that led to the construction of the Triborough Bridge and tunnels under the East River. She made reforms from inside the system, inspiring a *New Yorker* cartoon showing her in an arena, whip in hand, taming the Tammany tiger. She didn't like being singled out as "the first woman" and said so in 1928 when she became the first New York woman sent to Congress:

> A man enters public life and not the slightest attention is paid to the fact that he is a man. A woman runs for office and there is more interest in the fact that she is a woman than her qualifications for the job she seeks. It is then she learns how tenacious the tag woman is—how palpably she is a woman, how completely shackled by her sex. At every turn she is confronted with the fact that the activities of the world are cut from a pattern, that it has always been a man's universe and that while she isn't exactly an interloper she's different. The woman label follows her around like a faithful dog.

In her first House speech, she criticized a tariff bill that raised the duty on sugar without improving the wages and conditions of sugar workers. She also sponsored a bill to acquire and publish books for the blind, reflecting a traditional concern of the Junior League.

It was a great satisfaction for me to fight, fight, fight for abolishing tenements unfit for human beings.

—Ruth Pratt

She won a second term, defeating controversial journalist and socialist Heywood Broun, but the Roosevelt landslide ended her political career even as it brought Eleanor Roosevelt, Mary Harriman and Isabella Greenway into positions of prominence in Franklin Delano Roosevelt's New Deal.

Eleanor Roosevelt, whose story has been chronicled in many biographies, transformed the role of president's wife from hostess to activist. Later first ladies, including Nancy Reagan and Barbara Bush, also Junior League members, championed causes, but Eleanor Roosevelt changed the nation. Some scholars credit her with the New Deal, pointing out it was she who introduced her husband-to-be to the realities of poverty, taking him along when she volunteered in the Lower Eastside settlements.

When she moved into the White House, Eleanor continued to lunch and dine regularly with her old friends Mary Harriman and Isabella Greenway, who had been one of Eleanor's bridesmaids when she was Isabella Selmes. Isabella had been appointed to fill a Congressional seat after the elected representative from Arizona died.

The First Lady Addresses the Junior League

Eleanor Roosevelt was among the earliest Junior League members in New York and credited her work in the settlement houses to expanding her social consciousness. Throughout her life, she remained close to the League. Even when she was the wife of the President of the United States, she found time to drop by the Junior League office in Manhattan for tea. In 1938 she wrote an article for *Reader's Digest* praising the League. Toward the end of the Depression, she shared her thoughts in the *Junior League Magazine*.

"Women at work," the First Lady paused thoughtfully. "The first thing that comes to me on that subject," she said "is the question I've had asked of me several times—one time in particular when I was talking to a Junior League group. Do you think we ought to take paying jobs? they asked. I realized that the majority hoped for and expected a negative reply, but they did not get it. For I believe that today about the only gauge of merit we have is a monetary one. We don't ask young men to work for the glory of it and, however wrong it is, we do rate success in dollars and cents. I also believe that young women take paying jobs generally for two reasons: one, to supplement of necessity their family incomes, or, two, to exercise a talent they possess. The first reason is

obviously valid—the second is equally important with a reservation. If the girl who is paid for her ability does not need her earnings, she should use that money to create work for others. That is her obligation. Her pride in her own work should be enriched by her desire and willingness to help someone else to work.

"The Junior League was founded on a sound idea—the efficacy of group work, even an inspired individual cannot accomplish much these days in the face of the interdependent pattern of life. That same idea applies to a group itself. The Junior League must, and I know in many instances does, work with other groups. If it remains isolated it suffers from the same frustration and ineffectiveness that affects the individual working alone. I am aware of the policy that prevents the Leagues from backing legislation and taking, as an association, any stand on controversial matters, but this policy does not prevent the Leagues in their communities from allying themselves with other groups, exchanging ideas and working toward a clearer understanding of all the forces for progress and stability existing in their cities.

"I believe strongly that the Junior Leagues should interest themselves positively in the problems being faced by other young people in their communities—young men and women of the same ages as themselves whose hopes and fears, whose problems and difficulties differ not in kind but only in the possibility of fulfillment from those possessed by the

Eleanor Roosevelt continued the work she began as a Junior League volunteer when she moved into the White House, speaking out on social injustice at a national level.

Photo: George Hurrell

members of the Junior League. Young wage earners want to enjoy themselves, they want companionship, romance, homes, babies, good schools for their children, and the respect of their communities. They want, too, the privilege of helping others. In the last few years the age group of unemployment has made a significant and disturbing switch. There are now more young people out of jobs than ever. This is a constant problem that the young laboring people are primarily concerned with, and it is one that should be shared with them by the young women in the Junior League from the point of understanding it in all of its phases.

"The will to helpfulness which brings a young woman into the Junior League must be supplemented by a desire to think straight, to understand—and this understanding must have that concreteness only achieved by actual co-operation and contact with as many viewpoints as possible. The Junior League is, as I see it, an entering wedge into the vital pattern of any community. The members, through the League, learn first about a baby clinic, let us say, one already established or one badly needed in a certain district. From that point of awareness the League should continue as a group to study and observe what lies back of this necessity. In almost all cases they will find that the path leads to the basic trouble, the economic insecurity of the people for whom the clinic has been established. I believe that the Junior League members are not too young or too inexperienced to analyze this basic trouble. They have the security, the background, and the education which should enable them to push their inquiries into the fundamental causes of poverty and disease without being labeled

Eleanor Roosevelt and Shirley Temple, past and future Junior League members.

FDR Library

radicals. They may be called busybodies, but if they are sincere in their desire to understand and see their communities' problems in a clear light, they will live down that label.

"I am delighted, for example, to know that a president of one of the large Leagues plans to be here in Washington to attend the Citizenship Institute of the Youth Congress. She will meet and hear some of the most idealistic young people in the country. She will also hear people of her own age discuss the great—the almost overwhelming—problems that the majority of young people in our country must wrestle with day after day. It would have been a wonderful thing if every League in the country had

sent delegates. You are a youthful organization with a youthful board, and you share with young wage earners the right to better a world that other generations have failed to make peaceful. You have a right to break away from a pattern of life in which matters that should be relegated to a few hours of pleasant leisure have become paramount. The Junior League program today, wisely balanced with study and participation, can give you an ever-increasing understanding of problems that are universal—problems that must be solved before the ideal of peace among men can be realized."

—Junior League Magazine
October 1933

Eleanor also invited Dorothy Whitney Straight Elmhirst and her family to breakfast when they came to town and often saw her cousin Corrine Robinson Alsop, another League member. Biographies of Eleanor go into detail about how important these friendships were to her. Joseph Lash wrote in *Eleanor: Eleanor Roosevelt and Her Friends,* "Their friendships went back a long way. They too were women who were making it in a man's world, and that added to the spice of such occasions. It was one of the ways that all of them kept in touch with what was going on in Washington." In 1934, when the Washington League sponsored a "Wear Something New" ball to boost the local economy, Eleanor, Mary and Isabella attended, dressed in their debutante gowns, with adjustments for mature figures.

State Public Affairs Committees

But it wasn't just in Washington that Junior League members were making a difference. The dramatic need for social services during the Depression pushed Junior Leagues toward advocacy as well as service. State Public Affairs Committees (SPACS) began to influence public welfare policy.

In Virginia, Leagues in Norfolk, Richmond, Roanoke and Lynchburg decided something had to be done to improve child welfare programs as the general suffering caused by the widespread economic depression put more children in need than their state could aid. They united to influence government policy.

A White House Conference on Child Health and Protection in the early 1930s had established that states most adequately handling the problem cared for only about 36 children for every 10,000 inhabitants, but public and private agencies in Virginia together served half that number. Private agencies cared for about 3,800 children; the State Department of Welfare cared for about 150. The conference formula suggested that another 4,000 dependent, neglected and delinquent children should be receiving help.

Constant pleas for help from all over the state backed up the numerical projection. It was obvious many more children needed to be cared for outside their own homes.

"Realization that the private agencies of the state not only could never possibly care for these 4,000 additional children but that they were at the present unable even to carry their assumed responsibilities forced the

Junior Leagues into taking action," Frances Leigh Williams of the Richmond League wrote in 1934. "The evidence was too overwhelming to be ignored by the Virginia Junior Leagues."

Annual reports from private agencies in 1932 showed an approximate income of $700,000 and an expenditure of $735,000. Not only were the agencies unable to take on any new charges, but they were going broke taking care of children already in their care. Since 1922, the state had the legislation in place to act. What it didn't have was appropriations.

"Our path was mapped out. The Leagues would have to gather together sufficient data to prove this need to our lawmakers and arouse public opinion so that the citizens would insist that this money be made available now to prevent delinquency and crime later on," Mrs. Williams explained.

The Leagues embarked upon an ambitious survey to help formulate a child welfare program for Virginia, but they drew upon professional sources, including the Children's Homes Society of Virginia and the Child Welfare League of America. The Child Welfare League sent a trained worker to each of the Leagues to teach members how to make a cross-section survey within a 50-mile radius of each of the Leagues, which covered most of the state and

Realization that the private agencies of the state not only could never possibly care for these...children but that they were at the present unable even to carry their assumed responsibilities forced the Junior Leagues into taking action.

—Frances Leigh Williams, 1934

prepare a comprehensive needs assessment. The goal: "a sane and workable program," which would be "a basis for demands for sufficient appropriations" from the Virginia State Legislature in 1936.

The Association's Welfare Department at the time called the Child Welfare Study "one of the most vital and far-reaching League projects today" even though Association policies prevented the Leagues from lobbying for the legislative changes their research supported.

After the 1937 Conference, the prohibition was even greater. After a "week of bitter debate," delegates decided: "Junior Leagues shall not lobby any legislative body; they shall not allow the Junior League name to be used in support of any bill except where a council of social agencies or another established federated group of which they were a member, lists its member agencies in so doing; they shall not use the Junior League name to encourage any candidate for public office; they shall not in any way use the Junior League as a political threat to influence government decisions."

In 1940, delegates modified the prohibition by outlining criteria allowing individual Leagues to act on local public issues.

Our Times—Are They Your Times?

There's goin' to be a change in
    The weather,
Goin' to be a change in the sea,
From now on there'll be a change
    In me.
My walk will be different,
My talk and my name,
There's nothin' about me goin' to
    Be the same.

The words of the old ballad might be well a theme song for the New Deal. "There'll be some changes made," the song goes on, and, whether we like it or not, we must face the fact that these changes are being made right now. Although our names may remain unchanged, we already talk in a language new to most of us and walk in strange paths indeed. Just how much about us is "goin' to be the same," it seems to me, depends on our personal adjustments to the new order of things.

Home Economics has taken on a new meaning and budgets are necessarily elastic. "Keeping up with the Joneses" is no longer the problem; it's keeping up with Uncle Sam. Even those very conservative people who consider that any change, except small change, is for the worse, should be glad of this change of pace.

Ours has been a breathless generation. Most of us can remember a little of the days before the war.

There were labor troubles and panics and the fervor of the Progressive movement, but the times yet had a placidity that we have not known since. The war, then the reaction and "Normalcy," the "New Era" of the late 'twenties,' the depression; and now the "New Deal"—these are the periods of sharply contrasting tendencies that have trod closely on each other's heels in less than twenty years. We should be used to change by this time.

We have adapted ourselves quickly enough to the physical changes of the two decades. The automobile in America spread like the English sparrow. The moving picture became our chief recreation. Even the more timorous of us took to the air occasionally. Home was where the radio was, and, in many cases, where the chromium-plated furniture was. We kept abreast of the times in all these things, and in the changing lengths of our hair and skirts, and the changing lines of our silhouettes . . . A few, only a few, I am afraid, of the more discerning of us may have protested against some characteristics of these hectic years; but most of us were quite in accord with the spirit of the age. We changed with the times, we changed constantly, but the changes presented no real difficulties to moderns such as we are.

Now, however, we are faced with conditions vitally different from anything our generation has ever known before. The past three years should have been as educational as a postgraduate course in any

university. I know I spent them unlearning a lot of "facts" that had been taught me as gospel truth. When I think of the time I spent in classrooms being filled with knowledge with which to face the world, it makes me regret that I didn't play hooky more often. At any rate, most of us have now learned enough to avoid some of the worst pitfalls into which we plunged so blithely a little while ago.

But this hard earned knowledge is only negative at best. We know some of the paths to avoid in the future, but probably have only the vaguest ideas as to which paths to follow. . . .

. . . Mere compliance with the different aspects of the New Deal will not be difficult for most of us. We have always been good compliers. We made small sacrifices during the war for patriotism and during the depression through necessity; and we can make them again. . . . We can change, if need be, our way of living, as we have done before. All this is necessary, of course, vitally necessary. But what is still more important for us, I think, both as individuals and as citizens, is a more fundamental change. We must change our ways of thinking, our philosophies. . . .

. . . I don't pretend to understand all the ramifications of the various projects now being undertaken throughout the nation; but what I do understand is that behind all these plans and proposals lies a new social idea—an ideal that in American has never before been given practical application. It runs counter to many of the dogmas we have always accepted, and some of it manifestations must prove shocking to the more conservative of us. But it is an ideal that we must understand if we are to be truly modern, to be anything more than uncritical spectators of this great drama now unfolding.

The technique for being "modern," in the best sense, for keeping pace with events, is rooted, I think, in curiosity. One need not always be interesting, but one must be eternally interested . . . It's the everlasting wanting to know what it's all about, that makes one really a part of one's own times. Mr. Einstein says that time stands still, but in this whirling new world of the 'thirties, I can't believe it.

Excerpts from a prize-winning essay written by League member Catherine Allison Patten, who described herself thus:

When I was nine, an iron sewer pipe rolled over me and flattened my head. At sixteen, I went to Sweet Briar for two years and flunked English. Then I married a red-headed newspaper man, had three red-headed children, became infected with the writing bug. Am an associate member of the Chattanooga League.

Movie hero, Tom Mix, visits the Nashville Junior League's Crippled Children's home, 1923.

Leagues Founded 1930–1939

Fort Worth, Texas	Halifax, Nova Scotia	Phoenix, Arizona
Mexico City, Mexico	Huntington, West Virginia	Columbus, Georgia
Raleigh, North Carolina	Berkshire County, Massachusetts	Morristown, New Jersey
Rockford, Illinois	Rochester, New York	Peoria, Illinois
Des Moines, Iowa	Shreveport, Louisiana	Canton, Ohio
Greater Elmira-Corning, New York	Toledo, Ohio	Macon, Georgia
Mobile, Alabama	Tucson, Arizona	Topeka, Kansas
St. Petersburg, Florida	Austin, Texas	Butte, Montana*
Greater Vancouver, British Columbia	Cedar Rapids, Iowa	Durham & Orange Counties,
Binghamton, New York	Hamilton-Burlington, Ontario	North Carolina
Schenectady, New York	Saginaw Valley, Michigan	Great Falls, Montana
Youngstown, Ohio	Salt Lake City, Utah	
El Paso, Texas	Wilkes-Barre, Pennsylvania	
Bergen County, New Jersey	Oakland-East Bay, California	(*League that disbanded in the 1990s)

The Junior League Goes to War

Junior League members of the Women's Ferrying Squadron who moved military aircraft between U.S. airfields during World War II. Third from left is Cornelia Fort, member of the Junior League of Nashville, who died in an accident during ferrying maneuvers in Texas in 1943.

Women had rallied to the patriotic call in the first world war, and they threw their energies and organizations into war relief efforts at home. Some young women even volunteered to support troops overseas, but few women actually entered the workforce during the nineteen months the United States was at war. When war came again in the 1940s, it was a different story. Women planted Victory Gardens and recycled tin cans, but they also joined production lines, the federal government and the new women's branches of the armed forces. More than six million women, including married women, went to work for the first time between 1941 and 1945, mostly in war-related industries. In a world turned upside down, the conflict demanded a massive mobilization of resources. Who better than women, seasoned in volunteer activities, knew how to mobilize themselves and their communities?

If we and those who come after us have courage and wisdom, we will be singularly privileged to be able to use our physical stamina and youth to look ahead to the time when war shall end and we can help build a lasting peace on earth.

—Nancy Martin, 1943
Association President

Nancy Martin, of Winston-Salem, spoke for all Junior League members when, as Association president, she pledged to serve the Allies' cause at the Association of Junior Leagues Conference in New York in May 1943. The world was at war and so was the Junior League.

"We are an organization of youth sharing the realities of this conflict. If we and those who come after us have courage and wisdom, we will be singularly privileged to be able to use our physical stamina and youth to look ahead to the time when war shall end and we can help build a lasting peace on earth," she declared.

Long before that December Sunday when the Japanese attacked Pearl Harbor, Junior Leagues individually and as an international association had prepared for the global conflict, creating a civil defense model built on community volunteers. Community volunteers have always been at the heart of League activity, but the Leagues were particularly well positioned to join the arsenal of defense because of their efforts to match volunteers with agencies during the Depression. A number of Leagues including Cleveland, Louisville, Montreal and New Orleans had organized citywide bureaus to match volunteers with agencies in need of help.

For the first time in League history, however, they acted in concert against a community threat they all shared. As a Junior League report noted at the end of the war, the Association "passed on the imperative MUST of pooling all man power and jobs and placing the right volunteer in the right job. It was outlined and based on the fiat: Community work as usual and war work as UNUSUAL, though essential."

Canada Goes to War

Canada declared war on Germany on September 10, 1939, and armed for attacks on either coast. Two days later the Association headquarters in the Waldorf-Astoria Hotel sent the six Canadian Leagues a memo outlining how central volunteer bureaus could be organized in each city and offering to send help.

The Canadian Leagues mobilized immediately. Halifax, looking eastward over the Atlantic Ocean, worried about saboteurs and German spies as the League volunteers went to work in hospitals, bid farewells to the soldiers "sent aboard the great gray ships" and to its own League members who went overseas as ambulance drivers, nurses and air ferry pilots. The 2,900 volunteers enlisted through the Toronto League found themselves feeding and entertaining over four million young men headed off to the battlefields, working in three shifts a day, 60 to 80 volunteers a shift. In Vancouver, always on the alert for attack, the League balanced air raid drills with ongoing community needs. Hamilton, though a relatively small League, provided 428 young women for volunteer duties. In 1944 alone, nine League

We could not have completed those arrangements in coordinating both war and civilian volunteer work without the aid of a volunteer bureau.

—Canadian Deputy Minister of Health

members serving in the Hamilton motor corps covered 29,532 miles and ran 2,302 errands.

The Winnipeg League, organized in 1927, staged a salvage drive that collected shoes by the thousands and an astonishing 30 tons of scrap metal in just one day. "Grimy and toil worn," the women raised $10,000 by collecting rubbish. By 1941 the Winnipeg League had sent two mobile kitchens to Britain, with a third in the works. But an even more important contribution was its prototype volunteer clearinghouse, a "specimen copy," which would become the model for civilian volunteer bureaus supported by the Canadian and U.S. governments.

Accepting the Association's offer of help, Winnipeg based its prototype on a volunteer clearinghouse the Montreal League had created in the 1930s and outlined how each block or home could be marshaled into action immediately. The Deputy Minister of Health in the Provincial Government said, "We could not have completed those arrangements in coordinating both war and civilian volunteer work without the aid of a volunteer bureau." In 1941 the Canadian government took over the volunteer bureaus as a division of the Women's Voluntary Services under the Department of National War Services.

Canadian Leagues sheltered English children during World War II.

Junior Leagues Mobilize

Realizing that war was coming to the United States as well, the AJLA executive committee held a special meeting in July 1940 to commend the Canadians on their success and to urge all the U.S. Leagues to establish central volunteer bureaus as part of the defense program. In August 1941, all Leagues received "A Central Volunteer Bureau in Defense," a plan for coordinating community volunteer efforts. Shortly after that, the newly organized U.S. Office of Civilian Defense invited Junior League executives to Washington to help write a booklet called "Civilian Defense Volunteer Office," which explained how volunteer services and the war effort could work together.

Civil Defense and the Junior League

The cultural icon of Rosie the Riveter and the image of G.I. Jane donning her military uniform are easily recognizable salutes to the contributions women made to the war effort. Their stories have become part of the greater narrative of American history, but the role of the women who worked within their traditional voluntary associations remains an unheralded contribution to the war effort. The AJLA's involvement in World War II grew out of the tradition of activist women. In wartime, as in times of cultural upheaval, activist women accepted public leadership roles in their communities.

On June 25, 1940, President Franklin D. Roosevelt broached the subject of home front defense for the United States. His original image for a nationwide civil defense network was based on the Association of Junior Leagues of America's concept of locally driven activism to access locally defined community needs. And no wonder. His wife Eleanor, a member of the Junior League of New York, was assistant director of the Office of Civil Defense, although her tenure was turbulent. Her appointment created violent controversy as criticism focused on whether or not the First Lady should assume such a politically driven position.

The Junior League's volunteer program so influenced the Office of Civil Defense that the OCD's implementation manual is almost identical to the

Members of the San Antonio Junior League in wartime uniform.

AJLA pamphlet, A Central Volunteer Bureau, which had been distributed nine months earlier. The AJLA plan, which was praised by Harper's Magazine and professional journals, was modeled on the Depression-era Central Volunteer Bureaus established by local Junior League chapters. The CVBs drew local volunteer and fraternal organizations, welfare agencies, and religious groups into partnership. Local Junior League chapters developed, implemented and directed community welfare efforts by forming coalitions among agencies,

channeling resources efficiently and imposing order on chaos with a centralized distribution system. These bureaus attempted to coordinate services, utilize volunteers efficiently and avoid unnecessary duplication of limited resources. The OCD's Fall 1941 plan described in the official manual called for a national network of Civil Defense Volunteer Bureaus, a network beginning with the AJLA's seventy pre-war Central Volunteer Bureaus. The OCD and AJLA leadership encouraged the bureaus to "allow themselves to be nuclei in their communities for the development of civilian defense volunteer offices." Each of the original bureaus complied.

The local Junior League chapters, where they existed, always provided the primary contact in each new city. Within one year the initial network had grown to 235 Civil Defense Volunteer Organizations and the number continued to climb rapidly. By the end of 1943, 4,300 active CDVOs were registered.

As part of the national network, the CDVOs worked to recruit volunteers. They were charged to maintain community welfare; coordinate day care centers; provide housing lists for migrant war workers; work to ease the strain on community services such as schools, transportation and utilities; assist in setting up social activities for soldiers and teenagers; place volunteers in hospitals; provide school lunches; run classes on first aide and quality nutrition during rationing; help develop Victory Gardens, and organize salvage drives.

Defense industry boomtowns, displaced families in search of work and those following soldiers introduced new migration patterns and a new set of challenges into the local communities. Each CDVO identified a wide variety of volunteer opportunities to meet the needs of their own community and then shaped their program accordingly. They worked to fill the gaps and create a stronger community in spite of the war.

—Julia M. Siebel, PhD.
Junior League of Orange
County, California
Silent Partner/Active Leaders
PhD. Dissertation, University of
Southern California

Junior League war work extended beyond the borders of the United States; the Motor Transport Corps of the Red Cross delivering parcels to Camp Hill Hospital in Halifax.

Oveta Culp Hobby, Houston Junior League member, organizer and commander of the Women's Army Corps, and Chief of the Women's Interest Section of the War Department, 1941.

Photo: Paul Peters

as well." Canada established The Royal Canadian Air Force—Women's Division (RCAF-WD) in July 1941 and the Canadian Women's Army Corps (CWAC) the following month. Needs were so great that women soon were serving as air and ground crews for the Air Force and as drivers, cooks, clerks, messengers and canteen helpers in the CWACs.

Flight Officer Kathleen Walsh Walker of the Montreal League assumed leadership of the RCAF-WD. Margaret Eaton of Toronto was one of the two highest-ranking officers in CWAC with Frances S. Aitkins (Riley) of the Winnipeg League taking the first contingent of CWACs overseas. By the end of the war, over 45,000 Canadian women had signed up for duty, and 3,000 CWACs were serving in war zones.

In the United States, Oveta Culp Hobby volunteered as the $1-a-year Director of the Women's Interest Section of the War Department, where she drew upon organizational skills gained as the first professional member of the Houston Junior League and parliamentarian of the Texas legislature. Through her efforts, the Women's Auxiliary Army Corps (WAAC) was created in May 1941 "for the purpose of making available to the national defense the knowledge, skill, and special training of the women of the nation." The day after President Roosevelt signed the bill, she became Major Hobby, director of the new corps. Her job was not only to organize and train but also to convince the public that women could be soldiers and ladies, too.

Major Hobby explained that "the gaps our women will fill are in those noncombatant jobs where women's

They also assumed a disproportionate role in organizing and administrating volunteer corps of women who would see service on all fronts as the governments of Canada and the United States established units in which women other than nurses held military rank.

The Canadian Military Headquarters in London initially suggested that perhaps women might be useful overseas filling a great need for laundresses, one senior official noting that he saw no reason to "tie up 150 men on the washing of clothes, when women could do the job just hands and women's hearts fit naturally. WAACs will do the same type of work which women do in civilian life. They will bear the same relation to men of the Army that they bear to the men of the civilian organizations in which they work." She responded with grace to frivolous press questions about WAAC dating habits and the color of WAAC underwear (khaki) and launched the new military branch with a strong philosophy of women as helpmates.

The president announced a recruitment goal of 25,000 in the first year, but it was easily surpassed by November and the Congress' original ceiling of 150,000 put in place. Initially WAACs worked as aircraft warning observers, motor pool drivers, clerks, typists and secretaries, but they took on an increasingly broad range of responsibilities as the war continued.

By 1943, WAAC was such an unqualified success that the Army struck the word "auxiliary" from the title and converted the corps into Regular Army with pay, privileges and protection equal to what male soldiers received. Major Hobby became Colonel Hobby and her officers given the ranks of captains and lieutenants. WACs were assigned everywhere in the world, handling mostly clerical and communication responsibilities overseas.

Lieutenant Jean Tilford Palmer of the WAVES.

U.S. Navy photograph

In 1945, a month after the victory in Europe, she retired from service, exhausted. Her husband carried her by stretcher to a train for New York, where she would spend a month recuperating.

For her wartime efforts, she received the Distinguished Service Medal, whose citation noted that "without guidance or precedents in the United States military history to assist her, Colonel Hobby established sound policies and planned and supervised the selection and training of officers and regulations. Her contributions to the war effort of the nation has been of important significance."

Other League members played prominent roles in the new women's military, including Jean Tilford Palmer of the Omaha League. A graduate of Byrn Mawr, she worked in banking before joining the Association staff in New York in 1930, creating her own job of business manager. In 1942, she became one of many League members who joined the Navy's newly created WAVES (Women Accepted for Volunteer Emergency Service). Before the war ended, she was Captain Palmer and WAVES director. Returning to New York after the war, she became director of admissions and general secretary of Barnard College.

The Home Front

Not all Junior League members went marching off to war, but they were at work everywhere. They volunteered in daycare centers, ran blood drives and entertained servicemen at recreational centers like the U.S.O. Over 7,000 Junior League members volunteered to sell U.S. Treasury War Bonds and Stamps. Partial accountings from 40 Junior Leagues showed sales of over $43 million. Working for the Red Cross was so much part of the Junior League experience that nobody bothered to count the hours members worked, but over 1,000 Canadian League members volunteered for Red Cross projects.

What's more, the war effort did not replace the Junior League's ongoing community service commitments. Junior League members found ways to do both. Nearly a year before Pearl Harbor, delegates attending a conference in St. Louis looked ahead to the coming conflict and carefully worded a message to President Roosevelt: "We believe the maintenance of community services is the very foundation of any program of total defense." No one ever calculated just how many hours Leagues contributed to the war effort, but one staff member at the time remarked that "everything that makes an individual, a family or a community stronger . . . healthier . . . improves morale, is part of the defense effort."

Surveys by the *Junior League Magazine* in the mid-'40s hinted at the contributions the Junior League had made. One finding indicated that 158 wartime Leagues had completed 320 "indispensable" projects. The efforts included health, community arts, civic education and action, radio broadcast and councils, recreation for civilians and military,

central volunteer offices and other civilian organizations including teen centers and children's libraries. The grand total of volunteer jobs assumed by League members was nearly 75,000, which suggested that many members did more than one assignment. In 1946, with the number of Leagues increased to 160 in the U.S., Canada, Mexico and Hawaii, which had yet to become a state, membership numbered only 44,000.

Junior League members were also among the women who went to work in the war effort. "Women who know . . . say there is nothing like a motor mechanic's course for testing the strength and sincerity of one's belief in the single standard," the *Junior League Magazine* observed in March 1942.

Realizing the importance of providing comfort and continuity to children, whose lives had been disrupted by

The Junior League of Charlotte, North Carolina, at work on an Army Air Force bomber.

war, Leagues made children's activities a priority. In May 1941, when a fire destroyed the Halifax children's library, which had been staffed and financed by the Junior League for seven years, the League not only rebuilt but doubled the space, serving 1,315 children a year even during the war. Leagues staged 783 theater performances for 368,449 children in the 1944–45 season alone. In the last year of the war, Leagues reported presenting 36 live radio programs for children. Although radio personnel were in short supply, the Winston-Salem League managed to find professional leadership to direct its community radio plan. Attendance at art classes at children's museums doubled during the last year of the war as League volunteers replaced professional staff.

Tightening the Belt

The Association continued to function during the war and a much-altered *Junior League Magazine* continued to publish. Printed on cheap newsprint, without advertising and only a few over-sized pages, it struggled to keep Leagues in touch. Editors apologized for condensing reportage of the 1942 Conference in Kansas City "so sturdy and bold in structure and design." In October 1942, Helen Hickham Martin of the Washington, DC, League reported on the changes war had brought to the capital—and to the League. In only one year, the League had received 175 transfer and inter-League members. They included wives of young officers posted to the capital and women "training for highly important and confidential jobs with the Army, Navy and Civilian Defense." The 32 members of other Leagues, who requested transfer status in one summer

During World War II, Junior League members supported many different kinds of war efforts, including salvage collection in Kansas City.

month, begged, despite the Washington heat, for immediate volunteer placements, according to Mrs. Martin. Even members whose wartime jobs allowed little time for volunteering wanted to help. One night a month, they met to make surgical dressings and do knitting and sewing for the Red Cross.

Mobile, Alabama,
Junior League
Red Cross
Motor Corps.

After completing
the Russian Relief
Drive the year
before, volunteers
from the Columbia
Junior League
pose with clothing
gathered from
wholesale and retail
merchants for the
Victory Clothing
Drive, 1946.

The Junior League
of Columbia,
South Carolina

"No other League has ever absorbed so many new members in so short a time. Yet the Washington League, undaunted, keeps its welcome sign out, and reports the greatest satisfaction with the impressive industry and skills of its adopted members. New arrivals, on the other hand, find interesting jobs, friends, information and a sense of belonging—all calculated to take the sting out of moving to a strange city," she noted.

The 1942 Conference was held in Kansas City with delegates, as was the tradition, staying in the homes of members of the host League, but by the following year, times were grave. Heating oil, gasoline, staples such as meat and sugar, and even shoes were rationed.

For the first time in League history, the Conference was held in a hotel. Meeting at the Waldorf-Astoria in New York, the Junior League invited the heads of all women's national organizations to lunch to discuss how all organizations could work for the good of the whole and not individual credit. Margaret Meade was the speaker.

During 1943, as the war grew worse, Margaret Hickey, chair of the Woman Power Commission in Washington, appealed to the Junior League to spread the word that more women were needed to work in industry and on the farms to free more men for the Armed Forces. "It was felt that a great amount of women power in the Junior League was untapped, and that our Placement Chairmen should point out the need for paid jobs as well as unpaid," Nancy Martin, Association President 1942–1943, recalled in the 1980s. "The response was remarkable. The way volunteers all over the country rose to the occasion was absolutely thrilling. They had been trained to take responsibility in their communities."

The Junior League canceled its 1944 Conference because the war was at such a frightening stage, but even in the darkest days of the war, the Junior League looked ahead to its role in peacetime. Nancy Martin recognized that six million women putting on slacks and going to work would alter forever the role of women and women's organizations. Junior League members would no longer be "the sheltered young women of pre-war years," she warned in 1943.

"This was the time to take inventory of our organization," Mrs. Martin remembered. "It was felt that to accomplish our purpose in the post-war world, we must have a membership who had an interest in the total community and were responsible, intelligent and thinking citizens."

At the 1943 Conference, she said, "America is undergoing terrific changes and if the Junior League is to survive, it will have to change, too. We are going through such a social revolution today that in the days to come an organization such as ours will surely and most certainly fall by the wayside unless our members prepare and equip themselves for the challenges ahead."

Even when victory was still in doubt, the Junior League began looking ahead to those challenges, assessing what communities would need and how the Leagues could help.

"When the flags and ticker tape had settled, a new life ahead was the goal," Eleanor Oakes Skinner of Philadelphia, Association President in 1950–1952, remembered thirty years later. And when peace came, the Junior League was ready.

Returning U.S. vets greeted by members of the Boston Junior League.

Killed in the Service of Her Country

On December 7, 1941, Cornelia Fort, a member of the Nashville League, was teaching a young man to fly over Honolulu when she looked around casually and spied a bomber with two red balls painted on the wings. She immediately recognized the Rising Sun insignia of Japan.

"I looked quickly at Pearl Harbor and my spine tingled when I saw billowing black smoke," she wrote. She watched as a bomb exploded in the harbor but did not panic. *"Most people wonder how they would react in crisis: if the danger comes as suddenly as this did you don't have time to be frightened. I'm not brave, but I knew the air was not the place for our little baby airplane and I set about landing as quickly as ever I could. It was as if the attack was happening in a different time track with no relation to me."*

A burst of machine gun fire erupted from the Japanese aircraft, but Cornelia said nothing to her student. As they landed, he asked, "When do I solo?" "Not today, brother," she replied. They jumped from the plane and raced towards the hangar as the plane strafed the airfield. Another instructor landing at the same time was killed. Several other small planes that had been up in the air that morning never returned.

Cornelia Fort (second from left), at Long Beach Army Airfield posing with a B-13, two weeks prior to her death in the line of duty.

Photo courtesy of the Fort family

"It crossed some of our minds that possibly we were the first Americans to run from invaders on American soil," she observed.

Not long after Pearl Harbor, Cornelia received a telegram from the War Department, announcing the organization of the Women's Auxiliary Ferrying Squadron (WAFS) and inviting her to report for duty within 24 hours if she was interested. She eagerly accepted, becoming one of the original 28 members of the squadron who ferried some of the largest and fastest military aircraft of the war between U.S. airfields.

In January 1942, she wrote to her mother about the experience. "For all the girls in the WAFS, I think the most concrete moment of happiness came at our first review. Suddenly and for the first time we felt part of something larger. Because of our uniforms which we had earned, we were marching with the men, marching with all the freedom loving people of the world."

Cornelia knew she was going to join the WAFS even before the organization was a reality, "before it was anything but a radical idea in the minds of a few men who believed that women could fly airplanes," she wrote in a 1943 issue of Woman's Home Companion.

"Because there were and are so many disbelievers in women pilots, especially in their place in the army, officials wanted the best possible qualifications to go with the first experimental group. All of us realized what a spot we were on. We had to deliver the goods or else. Or else there wouldn't ever be another chance for women pilots in any part of the service . . . We have no hopes of replacing men pilots. But we can each release a man to combat, to faster ships, to overseas work. Delivering a trainer to Texas may be as important as delivering a bomber to Africa if you take the long view."

By the time the article appeared, 24-year-old Cornelia Fort was dead, the first American woman in the war to die on active duty. She was ferrying a BT-13, a basic trainer, to Texas when her plane plummeted to earth after a mid-air collision with another plane in the convoy. The pilot of that plane, who survived, was a man.

An airport in Nashville has been named in her memory. Her relatives continue to serve in the Nashville League.

Leagues Founded 1940–1949

Scranton, Pennsylvania
Wheeling, West Virginia
Ft. Wayne, Indiana
Jackson, Mississippi
Pelham, New York
Sacramento, California
Lehigh Valley, Pennsylvania
Corpus Christi, Texas
South Bend, Indiana

Holyoke, Massachusetts*
Amarillo, Texas
Beaumont, Texas
Waco, Texas
Greenville, South Carolina
Greater Orlando, Florida
Central Westchester, New York
Texarkana, Arkansas-Texas
Albuquerque, New Mexico

Battle Creek, Michigan
Bronxville, New York
Lansing, Michigan
Long Beach, California
Galveston County, Texas
Wyandotte and
Johnson Counties, Kansas

(*League that disbanded in the 1990s)

Junior League of Portland, Oregon, runs a physical therapy program for polio patients.

Courtesy of Photo Art

When the men came home from the war, the women were sent home from their jobs. Their patriotic duty done, women were to surrender their jobs and retreat to the home and hearth, settling into a peacetime life of ranch houses, all-electric kitchens and swirling Christian Dior–style skirts. Instead of chauffeuring in military car pools, they ferried their children around the suburbs in station-wagon brigades.

"The female task was to oversee the quality of this private life, to purchase wisely and to serve as an emotional center of the family and home. The principal obstacle to this vision, however, was the possibility that women might now choose to play their publicly condoned role," observed Sara M. Evans in BORN FOR LIBERTY. Yet contrary to the domesticity portrayed in the media of the day, women did not flee the workplace and become full-time wives and mothers. After a brief drop immediately after the war, employment of women started rising again. Nearly a third of all women were still on the job in 1951, and more middle-class women began entering the job market to supplement the family income.

Once considered only a giddy band of footloose playgirls, Junior Leaguers are now obsessed by such dedication to duty that their benefactions make the philanthropy of the average heiress look like a miser's gestures.

—Coronet magazine, June, 1954

The demographics and democratization also began to transform the Junior League. No longer were teenaged daughters of industrial titans in major metropolitan areas the backbone of the League. Membership had become decidedly middle-class and matronly. In the 1950s, women in smaller cities and suburbs aspired to join the Junior League movement, now led by the wives of businessmen and professionals. The young matrons often saw the meetings as the social event of the month, the time to wear "your best dress, white gloves and the prettiest hat and plan to spend all day," Mrs. Wiley Perry Ballard of Atlanta remembered. But the growing number of working women who were members was re-setting the clock. By the end of the decade, Jean Vaughan Smith of Los Angeles, Association president in 1958–1960, saw a much different League developing. "We saw glimmerings of change in membership composition—more professional members, somewhat of an ethnic mix, a greater use of volunteers in more sophisticated jobs."

Leagues began scheduling meetings and other activities after 5 p.m. to accommodate working women. So many members were employed in 1950 that the New York League enrolled 115 members in its new evening program.

Cicely Kershaw Rosenberry, New York League president from 1948 to 1950, later described how the average post-war League member differed from earlier generations. "She was usually a college graduate, who was professionally employed. When she married, she was often servantless (and) probably at least 30 before she had time to participate in the daytime activities of the League ... This meant a decreasing number of volunteers

Actor and future President Ronald Reagan makes a special appearance at the 1953 Annual Conference, thanks to his wife Nancy, member of the Junior League of Los Angeles.

to carry out programs and fill the many community requests for volunteers. It explained the increased support of evening events and points to the need for further activities for this group." The New York League determined that the community needed volunteers in the evening as well as during the day. Projects included Library-by-Mail, which served homebound children and adults with books and friendly letters; teaching conversational English to foreign-born professionals; and an indoor garden program at homes for the aged.

A Mobile Society

Another sociological development that affected the League was the Corporate Wife, who followed her husband from community to community as he climbed up the company ladder. The League, established to train young women for a lifetime career of volunteering in their communities, was faced with two big questions:

■ Should Leagues invite young women to join if they were likely to move on to another community?

■ What should be done about "Transfer" members?

Some members felt that the organization—and community service—would be weakened by so much mobility. Mrs. Kenneth B. Page of Springfield, Massachusetts, disagreed. She wrote a letter to the editor of the *Junior League Magazine* in June 1954, expressing her concern about hearing Admissions Committees stressing the point, "Will she be in town next year?" She supported a Transfer policy, which would recognize the reality that women were on the move.

"Even new members to carry on the home League activities should be asked to join each year, but why not give their moving-away sisters an equal chance at League work in another city? If this policy were adopted by all Leagues, then each could count on transfers from other communities . . . It seems to me that Leagues are being shortsighted when they deny a chance of membership to excellent girls because they are leaving home. Sponsoring such a girl does put an added responsibility on the sponsor. Will this girl be acceptable not only to those at home who, of course, know her so well but to any League to which she may transfer? Will her League have reason to be proud that they recommended her for transfer?"

Comparing the Association to a big company with each League "a sort of branch office, a part of the whole," she said the answer to her question should be affirmative if the League, like a big company, picked the right person for the job.

Adele Hall, who received the Mary Harriman Award in 1996, was one of those transfers in 1953. Daughter of an early member of the Lincoln League, she began Provisional training in her hometown but before the year was out, she had transferred to Kansas City where her new husband's older sisters were League members. Provisional training there taught her things about the city she would not have learned as a businessman's wife, she believes. Not long after, she became Transfer Chairman herself. One of the young women transferring to Kansas City that year was Vereen Huguenin Coen, who had joined the League in Charleston, South Carolina, where she had met and married a Navy officer. Shortly after their wedding, they moved to his hometown. She found herself embraced by two new families—her husband's and the Junior League of Kansas City. When they returned to South Carolina not long after, she, like her mother before her, became president of the Charleston League.

The League provided incredible support and instant entrée for a generation of young women who moved from city to city because of their husbands' careers. Stephen Birmingham, the writer, observed that during those post-war years the League was "a national security blanket for transient businessmen's wives." In *The Status Seekers*, Vance Packard cited a Cornell study in which admission to the League, admission to private clubs and admission to exclusive residential areas were used as measures of social acceptability. The status extended beyond the United States. In Canada, *Maclean's* magazine in 1956 called the League "the most exclusive women's service club in the Americas."

A New Profile

Sociologists and journalists regularly examined the League and what it meant to society as well as Society. *Look* chose Mrs. Lauren Dwight "Sissie" Dreisbach as its glamorous yet all-American cover girl in February 1948 when it profiled the League. Mrs. Dreisbach, a 26-year-old war widow with two children, was "like 46,500 other well-bred young women," according to *Look.* Daughter of a League member, she had joined the Phoenix League right after finishing school and found support there in rebuilding her life after the war. Her League, the magazine noted, had recently been cited for its work in legislation, radio and children's theatre.

Rebuilding their communities after the war, Leagues often tackled needs unnoticed or ignored by others, going "where angels had feared to tread," observed *Coronet* magazine, reporting on an epilepsy consultation clinic that the Chicago League established shortly after the war. The Louisville League launched a Cancer Clinic on Wheels, perhaps the first of its kind, taking cancer care and cancer prevention to farm families far from medical centers. In both projects, the women did more than donate money. They became trained assistants in the work itself.

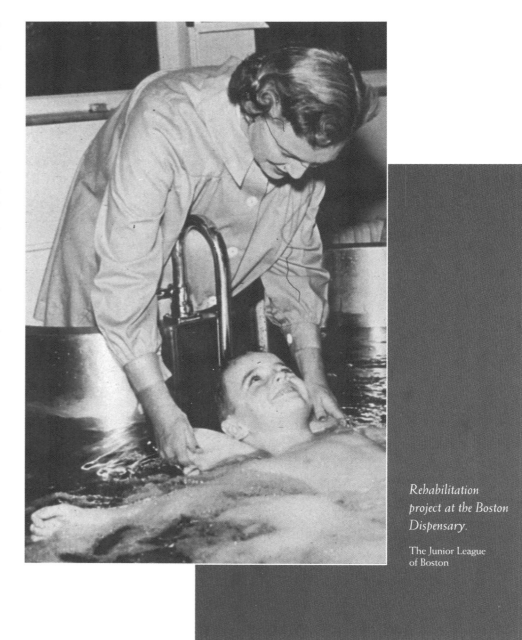

Rehabilitation project at the Boston Dispensary.

The Junior League of Boston

TV dinners, fast foods, microwave ovens and working mothers should have spelled the end of home-cooked food. So how to explain the phenomenal success of Junior League cookbooks, which have sold more than 18 million copies and raised tens of millions of dollars for good works?

"Each of these regional cookbooks has a flavor all its own. As our country becomes increasingly more homogenous, these recipe collections continue to reflect the individualistic best of unique communities," a writer for *Traditional Home* wrote in 2000, a half-century after the Charleston League published *Charleston Receipts,* now in its 30th printing.

Charleston was not the first League to issue its favorite recipes as a fund-raiser. Minneapolis in 1943–1944 published a cookbook of handwritten recipes and cleared over $3,000. But Charleston was the first to market its cookbook aggressively, with members doing everything from researching the recipes to sending out press releases. League cookbooks allowed members to develop and polish their business as well as culinary skills.

The Charleston project began modestly and at a time when perhaps less than 40 percent of the women in America even owned a cookbook. Mary Vereen Huguenin and Anne Montague Stoney asked 21 Sustainers to collect local recipes to raise funds for the

The Junior League of Baton Rouge celebrates thirty years of River Road Recipes *in 1989.*

League's school of speech correction, which was established in 1947 as the first such school in the state. After only three years, the school desperately needed more space.

Mary Vereen's daughter, Vereen Huguenin Coen, like her mother a president of the Charleston League, laughed when she remembered how it all began. "They all had cooks!" she said. The women launched their project "with spontaneous enthusiasm and commitment," spending a month collecting the best recipes in town, two months testing and four months spicing their cookbook with phrases of Gullah, the only Atlantic Creole language spoken on the U.S. mainland. More than just recipes, the book recorded cultural history. "Cooking and food told the lifestyle of the area. There's no better way to tell the way people live," Vereen Coen said.

The first print order at a cost of $150 was for 2,000 copies. Priced at $2.50 each, they all sold within two days of publication. Vereen remembers going up and down the highway with her mother to sell the book in dining rooms of motels, which were just becoming part of the American landscape. Her mother also took the book to New York to sell, using any contact she could find and her own charm to market it to B. Altmann's on Fifth Avenue. The book's reputation soon extended beyond the state as the League marketed the book by sending food editors around the ➤

country press releases featuring seasonal specialties. Craig Claiborne added his praise to the book. Sales steadily climbed and the book went into one new printing after another, reaching 100,000 copies by 1960.

Over the years, more than 750,000 copies have been printed and *Charleston Receipts Repeats* and *Party Receipts* added to the bookshelf. Both the original *Receipts* and its sequel have been inducted into the Walter S. McIlhenny Hall of Fame for Community Cookbooks, honoring books that have sold over 100,000 copies and benefit charity. Branching out in 1986, the League also sells gift baskets and bags of local food products.

From that initial investment of $150 has come nearly $1 million to support community needs, including the school of speech correction, which grew into the Charleston Speech and Hearing Center, a United Way Agency.

Other Leagues soon began to publish cookbooks to build their Community Trust Funds. In 1969, when the Tampa League, home of the *Gasparilla Cookbook*, hosted a cookbook workshop, more than 22 Leagues had published cookbooks celebrating—and, in many cases, saving—recipes unique to their communities. Other civic groups and commercial publishers followed their lead. The *American Home* food editor at the time

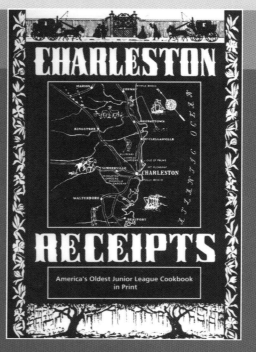 

The evolution of Junior League cookbooks through the years.

The Junior League of Charleston, South Carolina

explained the popularity: "In an era characterized by constant change, people want to assume roots. One of the ways they have found to do this is through regional cooking."

With names like *True Grits* (Atlanta), *I'll Cook When Pigs Fly* (Cincinnati), *Crème de Colorado* (Denver), *Heart and Soul* (Memphis), League cookbooks captured the imagination—and market share. *River Road Recipes*, Baton Rouge's collection of Cajun and Creole dishes, has sold more than

1.7 million copies since it appeared in November 1959, making it the best selling of all community cookbooks. Many Leagues have published more than one, with some years seeing as many as 200 different League cookbooks in print. The Boca Raton League entered the market in 1999, becoming the first League to include a CD-ROM. The women hired to produce the CD-ROM became so involved in the project that they joined the League.

Almost from the beginning, League cookbooks have attracted attention beyond their city limits. The Mobile League's *Recipe Jubilee* was featured in *House and Garden, House Beautiful* and *Southern Living* before the end of the '60s. The Tampa League's *Gasparilla Cookbook* was photographed at the 1964–65 World's Fair under the arm of Jacqueline Kennedy. When *Good Housekeeping* looked at hundreds of community cookbooks in 1994 to pick its regional favorites, four out of five of the recipes featured in the report were from Junior Leagues in Kansas City, Jackson County (Medford, Oregon), Houston, Rochester, New York, and Galveston County, Texas.

League cookbooks dominate the prize lists of cookbook competitions such as the TABASCO® Community Cookbook Awards, whose Walter S. McIlhenny's Hall of Fame includes League cookbooks from Atlanta, Charleston, DeKalb County (Decatur, Georgia), Eugene (Oregon), Hampton Roads, Houston, Morgan County (Decatur, Alabama), New Orleans, Norfolk (Virginia), Pasadena, Savannah and Huntsville, Alabama. Cookbooks by Leagues in Albuquerque, Houston, Little Rock and Mobile were added in 1999. After winning a Tabasco first place award in 1996, Houston's *Stop and Smell the Rosemary* went on to win a slew of other best cookbook and best design awards.

"The competition in cookbooks right now is incredible—especially nationally. There's just not enough room on the bookshelves at bookstores," said Cathy Hollis, co-editor for the Denver League, which has published cookbooks in 1978, 1987 and 1995 with total sales of nearly two million books raising more than $5 million.

Production schedules now take several years, with books often featuring original artwork by prominent artists. Food editors all over the country review new League books, including the Association's *Junior League Centennial Cookbook*, a compilation of over 750 recipes from 200 Leagues, and *The Junior League: Celebration Cookbook* featuring the 400 most requested recipes from Junior League cookbooks.

Is the market saturated? Doubtful. Cookbooks have become collectibles with out-of-print editions now being sold over the Internet. Earlier editions are being updated to replace canned mushroom soup and processed cheese with natural ingredients and to make the recipes more health conscious. And Leagues have only begun to tap specialty areas like Rockford, Illinois' *Brunch Basket* or Augusta, Georgia's *Tea Time at the Masters* and its sequel, *Second Round*.

The Junior League of Boca Raton moves cookbooks into the digital age. Savor the Moment *received a 2001 James Beard Foundation/Kitchenaid Book Award for the best cookbook in the "Entertaining and Special Occasions" category.*

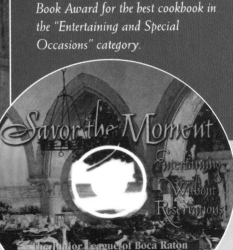

The Junior League of Boca Raton

Out of the Great Depression and World War II came not only a new life but also a New World. Few suspected just how revolutionary that world would be. According to Eleanor Oakes Skinner of Philadelphia, Association President in 1950–1952, League members were encouraged "to grow and serve beyond their own four walls...We were out to have grass-roots power with our energies released from the war efforts." Many post-war League members had little patience with the 1937 policy statement prohibiting any "action on any public question." "In the brave new world, this seemed to be stultifying and untenable," Linn Hamilton Jones of Washington, DC, Association President immediately after the war, said in the mid-1980s. "Many Leagues felt that efficacy demanded changing the causes of evil by venturing into sponsorship and legislative action. There were members who were timid but...in retrospect, the concept of legislative activism does not seem so drastic, and at the time, it appeared to be fundamentally necessary...or better, necessarily fundamental."

Except for the suffrage issue, Leagues had largely avoided involvement in politics, fearful of limiting their effectiveness if they appeared partisan. As the 1937 policy statement mandated, "The Association shall not endorse or sponsor any organization, movement or program or take action on any public question." But the Depression and the war had taught Leagues that sometimes they had to take a stand. In the years to come, they would battle to improve education, improve the environment, enrich cultural life in their communities and help those who couldn't fight for themselves.

The number of League public affairs and legislative programs grew steadily. By the end of the 1950s, 11 states had Junior League legislative committees. League activities began to appear on the front page as often as on the society page. "Dayton Housewives Impress Legislators" was the headline on a story describing the testimony of two League members before the Ohio Legislature in opposition to a bill that would have required the names of all persons receiving public aid to be posted. A little tentative at first, they rallied as they presented their carefully researched recommendations.

Junior League members assumed high-profile public service posts in the post-war years. Eleanor Roosevelt, appointed a delegate to the United Nations, helped draft the Universal Declaration of Human Rights and was an international figure in her own right.

In 1955, Oveta Culp Hobby was named to head the new Department of Health, Education and Welfare. She managed one of the world's largest medical research centers and hosted the First White House

> *The League initiated me into volunteer work in Minneapolis. This training as a volunteer case worker, as well as the further work I did in New York for the League in helping to develop their welfare program and other projects closely associated with humanitarian problems, gave me an excellent foundation for future responsibilities.*
>
> — Mary Pillsbury Lord
> *Junior League Magazine, 1953*

Conference on Education, but her biggest achievement was standing firm when faced with the panic of the 1952 polio epidemic. She held off announcing Dr. Jonas Salk's discovery of a polio vaccine until it had been properly tested. The Junior League, which had long been active in helping crippled children, was instrumental in promoting the vaccine once it had been approved. It received the March of Dimes Service Award in 1957 for education efforts, encouraging the use of the new vaccine and rehabilitation of polio patients.

President Eisenhower named Mary Pillsbury Lord as U.S. spokesperson on the United Nations Commission for Human Rights. She had also chaired the U.S. Committee for the United Nations International Children's Emergency Fund and was an ex-officio member of UNICEF. She joined the Minneapolis League in 1927 after graduating from Smith College and later served as president of the New York League.

Those responsibilities took her in April 1953 to a semicircular table at the United Nations headquarters in Geneva where, as the voice of the United States in humanitarian affairs, she helped craft a two-part covenant on human rights.

Sponsoring the Arts

Even in the darkest days of the war, the Junior League knew that it would return to sponsoring cultural activities in communities as soon as conditions allowed.

From the earliest Junior League days, the arts had been a major concern. In the 1920s and 1930s, Leagues volunteers served as museum guides or docents and many

Mary Pillsbury Lord, center, and Eleanor Roosevelt, incoming and outgoing U.S. representatives on United Nations Human Rights Commission, with Edith Evans Asbury, right, President of New York Newspaper Women's Club, 1953.

Leagues had mounted art exhibits in their headquarters or tearooms. In 1924 the New York League garnered a positive review from the *New York World* for its daring exhibit of young artists, including Georgia O'Keeffe. In 1933, delegates from 16 of the 20 Leagues nearest New York City attended an "experimental institute" to develop Junior League–Museum affiliations. The president of the Metropolitan Museum of Art encouraged the Leagues: "What are people going to do with their leisure time? They now have too little culture for leisure rather than too little leisure for culture. We must help educate the public to make the best use of its free hours,

The Junior League of Portland, Oregon, was one of many Leagues that used the arts to educate and entertain children.

Courtesy of Photo Art

to express their character in an abundant life which is largely defined by "the things we do that we do not have to do."

Leagues continued to produce Children's Theatre productions and taught art classes, but the immense needs of the Depression and then the urgencies of war required the Leagues to concentrate on what Nancy Martin, a wartime Association president, called "social planning."

During the war years, the Junior League began cultural resource surveys that grew into action projects enriching the arts throughout North America. As part of the self-study the Association initiated under Mrs. Martin, Virginia Lee Comer, an arts consultant, prepared an outline for surveying community arts resources in 1944.

Published in a brochure called "Arts in Our Town," the plan was sent to all Leagues before the war ended. The study spurred great interest among the Leagues in establishing arts councils in their community. The Vancouver League invited Virginia Comer to help in establishing art classes in the public schools, but that was only the beginning in Vancouver. Working with the arts consultant, the League surveyed resources in the city and presented the findings to a public meeting attended by over 400 persons in 1946. Out of this effort was born the Community Arts Council of Vancouver, the first arts council in North America. Other Leagues soon followed, including Winston-Salem, Baton Rouge and Corpus Christi.

Immediately after the war, only 33 Leagues reported community arts projects, but, inspired by Virginia Comer's plan, many Leagues initiated surveys of arts resources and followed up with programs meeting local needs. By the end of the 1950s, Leagues reported over 300 community arts projects. Just as they had in children's theatre, Leagues became prime movers in children's museums to introduce youngsters to the worlds of art, nature, and science and technology. Denver, Kansas City, Charlotte, Miami, Milwaukee, Knoxville, Nashville, San Francisco and Jacksonville, Florida, were among the Leagues creating museums for children in their communities.

The Denver Junior League wanted to interest children in art in 1945 when it co-sponsored a new children's museum with the Denver Art Museum. Ellen Harris, who organized the project, shared her memories with Ellen Kingman Fisher in *Junior League of Denver: Leaders in Community Service, 1918–1993.* "When we opened we expected about

200 to 250 people; we had a cake and some lemonade. As it happened, 10,000 people came. These were counted by the police," she said. A police officer arrived to help handle the crowd and said to Ellen, "Next time you give a party, I wish you would call the police first." By 1948, the Children's Museum had its own full-time curator. Phillip Gilliam, a juvenile court judge at the time, called the museum one of the community's most important developments. "It gets kids started off on the right track and helps them find new and lasting interests." The museum served as a pilot project for the nation and UNESCO.

The Junior League of Miami opened the Junior Museum of Miami in 1950 in a small frame house downtown. In its first three months, the museum attracted more than 2,000 children and matched that figure in the fourth month alone. Out of that tiny museum grew the Miami Museum of Science. The San Francisco League joined with the National Foundation for Junior Museums and civic groups in 1953 to establish the San Mateo County Junior Museum, which became the Coyote Point Museum for Environmental Education, a living museum informing people of all ages about their environment. In Charlotte, the League opened a children's museum in an abandoned day nursery in 1946. Five years later, the museum had moved into a $68,000 building paid for by the League through Follies, fashion shows and a citywide barbershop quartet contest.

The Junior Museum of Miami, forerunner of the Museum of Science.

Photo: Walter Marks.
The Archives, Miami Museum of Science

The Museum of Science, financed by the Junior League of Miami.

The Archives, Miami Museum of Science

Leagues also found ways to introduce children-friendly sections at existing museums. In New York, League volunteers staffed a new "Please Touch" Gallery financed by the League at The Museum of the City of New York. The New Orleans League was responsible for the addition of a junior gallery at the Delgado Museum.

Expanded Social Projects

In child health, Leagues continued and expanded projects begun before the war. In San Antonio a Children's Free Clinic grew into a children's hospital and foundation with the League organizing and staffing the first auxiliary of the Santa Rosa Children's Hospital. In Tulsa the League's Convalescent Home, set up in 1926, became the Children's Medical Center in 1952 with 55 agencies aiding in the transition. Leagues also pioneered new services. Louisville took cancer care on the road in 1948 with a mobile clinic going to isolated rural areas. The Evanston, Illinois, League opened the first aphasic clinic for children and trained members to be technicians when none could be found. Toronto established the first cerebral palsy nursery school in Canada.

The Baby Boom following the war put incredible pressure on schools, playgrounds and other resources for children. Teachers were in short supply everywhere. Leagues stepped in—often literally—to help. League volunteers could be found in the classroom and working with special programs that might not have been possible without League support. Nearly 150 Leagues served through remedial reading centers, diagnostic teaching programs, and programs for gifted and challenged children. As in the

earliest days of the League when Mary Harriman championed city playgrounds, over 100 Leagues by the mid-1950s had created public areas where children could play safely.

Leagues all over the nation made it a priority to increase the number of qualified

A Junior League of Little Rock volunteer assists a child with grammar activities at The Speech School, 1950.

Photo: Tom Harding

teachers. In Dallas, the League helped school administrators recruit more teachers in a project called, "Teachers for Texas—the Dallas Plan." The League also produced a film, "Why a Teacher," shown on television and at community meetings in Texas and employed by Leagues all over the country in teacher-recruitment projects.

In Atlanta, the League used film to illustrate how deaf children were taught at the League's School for Speech Correction, started in 1938 with one teacher and 50 children. By 1959, when Callie Huger, a League volunteer at the school, initiated, wrote and produced "A Sound Life," the professional staff numbered 25 and League volunteers were contributing 12,000 hours a year. In February 1959, *Variety* reviewed the film, calling it "a dramatic insight into the world of the deaf, a realistic documentary presentation that is at once heartwarming and eye-opening to the uninitiated who could not possibly conceive of what goes on behind the doors of a school for speech correction."

The Leagues increased their activities in radio, winning eight national awards in just two years. All the New York Leagues sponsored a series on New York State history produced by the Albany League. In Pittsburgh, where Mr. Rogers honed his talents with League support, the League produced a program encouraging reading. The Leagues also expanded quickly into television. As early as 1944, Virginia Lee Comer had forewarned League members that the new technology would be found in every home after the war "come what may." When the Federal Communications Commission set aside channels for education in 1952, Leagues were among the first to promote quality children's programming, and League women soon were found behind and in front of the cameras. Several Leagues produced weekly live TV shows, featuring teenage panel discussions. San Francisco spurred community interest in the new medium by hosting a one-day institute for several hundred delegates from area organizations and agencies.

By June 1954, when membership had grown to 63,000, the League was featured on the cover of *Coronet*. The magazine pictured the average Junior League member as a woman dressed for housecleaning. "Once considered only a giddy band of foot-loose playgirls, Junior Leaguers are now obsessed by such dedication to duty that their benefactions make the philanthropy of the average heiress look like a miser's gestures." Forget the old image of League members as social butterflies. They were really worker bees. A Charlotte, North Carolina, truck driver, praising a League-run school, told the magazine, "Don't worry about those girls and their amateur Follies. When their pictures are in the paper, you can bet it's for a mighty good cause."

> We are simply trying to live up to our duties as Americans. We must do more than vote and pay our taxes. The giving of ourselves is a sort of rent that we pay for living in today's kind of world.
>
> —Mrs. DeLeslie Allen
> Association President, 1954

Three Generations of Follies

Junior League Follies had their roots in the first musical evenings Mary Harriman and her friends staged in the early years of the 20th century to raise funds for the Settlement Movement and other League projects as they developed. Over the years, the musical evenings moved from members' homes to Broadway theaters. As the number of Junior Leagues multiplied, League Follies became a staple in the cultural life of many communities. The productions raised funds to meet local needs and also provided League members with creative outlets when few were available to young women.

Leagues occasionally produce Follies today, but since the sixties, they have staged fewer and less often. Perhaps tastes in entertainment have changed, but the real difference is in women's lives. Women balancing families, career and volunteer commitments no longer have time to spend weeks rehearsing.

Thousands of young women, and sometimes their husbands, sang and danced to raise money for League projects in the last century. Nancy C. Connolly, an Augusta League Sustainer whose mother and daughter also performed in League Follies, shared her nostalgia for the League tradition when her League celebrated its 60th anniversary.

Admitted to the Association in February 1929, Augusta produced its first Follies in 1934–1935. Mrs. Connolly's essay first appeared in the Augusta League's *League Links* in 1989.

The Junior League of Chicago enjoying rehearsal almost as much as the performance.

The Junior League of Chicago

Dancers from the Junior League of Monroe Follies fundraiser.

The Junior League of Monroe, Louisiana

My earliest recollection of the Junior League Follies is of my mother taking me down the street to the Bon Air Hotel to watch her rehearse. There were all these ladies and mamas with bright red fingernails dancing around this big room, and when they weren't dancing around they were giggling and talking and smoking cigarettes all the time. It was great! At age five I knew I loved the Follies.

Thirty years later in 1962, I found myself dancing around the same big room at the Bon Air in rehearsal for "Rockets and Rockettes" and talking and giggling and smoking. And come to think of it, I took the youngest of my four children down the street to the Bon Air to watch us. She got stars in her eyes, too, because a few years ago she danced in her first Follies with the Atlanta Junior League. Bill Letters of Cargill was the director of "Rockets and Rockettes" and he was really dynamic and we had a ball. The show played at the Miller Theatre that year and of course was a big hit.

In 1967 we went into rehearsal for "Hearts-A-Go-Go" with a director who looked like a bulldog, acted like a bulldozer and our hearts were not all a-go-go over him. I was talent chairman for that production. It was a job I'd rather forget because it was rough going some of the time, but we all pulled together and had us another darn good show at the Bell Auditorium Music Hall. And did I ever have tales to tell afterwards.

Three years later I went Sustaining and the League went into rehearsal for "For Augusta With Love." . . . I chose to stay at home for a change and sit out this particular Follies. In fact, I didn't even attend a performance, which was my loss because naturally the show was another winner.

Time passed and for ten years the footlights were dark and the stage bare. The Junior League became involved in many good community projects. A major one was the Shelter for Abused Children which requires big financial support. By 1981 it was time again for Mr. Cargill and another Follies. "Sing For The Shelter" went into production and enthusiasm was riding high. While rehearsals were well underway, I received a telephone call from the talent chairman, Marie Perry. She was looking for "two old gals" who were dumb enough to get out there on the stage with all those young beauties and make fools of themselves. After I made lots of suggestions, namely every Sustainer I knew, who she really wanted was Lillian Cullum and me. Of course, we declined immediately because, after all, we were dignified Sustainers and much too old for such foolishness. But Marie convinced us to at least come on to rehearsal again at the Bon Air and see what we were not going to do. Well, my dear, we went, we saw,

they conquered. Lillian and I went armed with a million excuses why we couldn't or shouldn't "do" the Follies. But after we saw that we were to be cast as scrub women with buckets and mops (a la Carol Burnette) in a comic entr'acte skit, the ham in both of us rose up and took hold. Our rehearsals were minimal and we really were not caught up in the over-packed rehearsal schedule of the rest of the cast. The only "nights out" were the few and final dress rehearsals, so we never had to tell our husbands of our involvement other than that we were needed to "help out backstage." The hardest part was getting them to opening night, promising that we would join them in the audience after we had attended to our "backstage duties." To soften the blow of our surprise appearance on stage, we sent our two grown daughters, Nancy and Natalie, who knew all, to accompany their fathers to the show. Well, talk about a surprise, a shock, a mouth-opener!! WOW!! Lillian and I never had so much fun in our lives. We loved it, and naturally the show was magnificent.

Soon to follow was the last Follies in 1986, "Cause for Applause." Once again I'm sure husbands, homes and children were neglected for weeks but they all survived, they always do. Lillian was well into her Granny phase and I was approaching mine so, my only involvement was relaxing in the audience and enjoying my son, Tommy and his wife, Etta, doing the dancing and singing. This was the most fun of all.

For those of you who have yet to "do" a Follies, I shall just say that it is hard work, exhausting, time consuming, stressful and sometimes marriage threatening. There are many misunderstandings, hot tempers,

flare-ups, riffs, occasionally a few broken bones, hoarse voices, sore feet, aching backs, etc. But! Talent appears that you would never believed was there; you

The Follies have long been a source of fun and entertainment in the Junior Leagues, as well as a highly profitable fundraiser.

The Junior League of Chattanooga

discover best new friends and dance with a few old ones; you also dance off a couple of pounds which is rewarding; and you have the time of your life. There are times you swear you'll never, ever do this thing again . . . until the next time, and you might just end up being the chairman.

To use all those wonderful "F" words in describing the Augusta Junior League Follies: It's fabulous, it's fun, it's fantastic and believe me, it is unforgettable on either side of the curtain . . . and has been for sixty years.

—Nancy C. Connolly, Sustainer
Junior League of Augusta, Georgia

1952: How Average Are You?

The *Junior League Magazine* in October 1952 reported on a questionnaire that suggested a far different Junior League member than those who had replied to a survey in the 1920s. The "portrait" showed that the League had spent more money than ever on community services, the number of professional members was growing, one-sixth of the membership served on community boards, one-half of the Leagues had permanent headquarters and thrift shops were the most popular money-raising activities. The smallest Leagues were Waco, Texas, and Kingston, New York, with 110 members each. Boston was the largest with 1,548. And who was the "average" League member? Without immediately revealing the author or the League where the survey was taken, the magazine published an essay that reads like *American Demographics.* "How Average Are You?" asked the headline. Here is the article that followed:

She is thirty years old with light brown hair and blue eyes. She is 5 feet, 5-1/3 inches tall and weighs 127 1/2 pounds, wears a size 7 shoe and a size 12 dress. She is 89% married, has 1 3/4 children, boys prevailing. Her children attend public school.

Our average young matron has no help but a cleaning woman once a week (Only 11% boast of a maid). She does her own laundry, washes her own hair and manicures her own nails. About 50% sport red nail polish. Her pet housework-hates are ironing and washing dishes—but her husband does help with the crockery. Two per cent admit they dislike everything concerned with domestic chores, 4% don't like to cook, and 7% object to the dull repetition of it all. One gal's pet peeve is dusting the bottom rung on chairs. Another could do without making beds. Couldn't we all!

Our average member has two telephones, 3 1/2 radios and a television set for diversion. About 50% have a private telephone line (the rest of us just suffer!). Three per cent boast two television sets.

Our gal is a graduate of a four-year College, and had a paid job before she was married. She has had her tonsils out but not her appendix, drives a car and has never had an accident—not one that she admits.

She and her husband live in the city, own their own house, and have 1 2/5 cars. Nineteen per cent live in apartments and only 2% hang their hats in a rented house. Our heroine knew her spouse 3 2/3 years before they were married in a church wedding (Only 1% dispensed with the satin and lace, and eloped). She met the guy at college or on a blind date. Eleven per cent say they've always known him. And 2% met him on the golf course. One gal doesn't know how she met her mate (blinded by love, no doubt). Another met her better half at a party at which they were snowed in all night. (How cozy!) Our gal's husband was an officer in World War II and is a handy man around the house. Their abode is furnished with antiques, a dog, and a double bed in the master bedroom.

When she is not bogged down with diapers or dishes the average League girl finds plenty to do. She listens to semi-classical music, although 30% prefer Bach, Beethoven and Brahms. Thirty-five per cent play the piano and 27% enjoy painting or sketching. Thirty members find time to read a book a week, and 27% make some or all of their clothes. Nine per cent are Budding Authors, having had an article or poem published, while another 10% have braved the footlights—other than Ye Junior League Follies. Over 60% are pretty regular churchgoers—good Christians we!

Thirty per cent of us are outdoor girls who ski (witness the plaster casts all winter!). But the favorite sport is swimming. About 15% prefer golf and another 10% tennis. One brave soul likes to water-ski. Another prefers fishing—worms and all. Three per cent confess they like sports only as spectators. All but 11% play bridge.

Our gal's favorite color is blue, with green a close second. There are 22% who don't smoke and 7% who don't imbibe (*W.C.T.U.* take notice!). Six per cent have been divorced, and 4% have been married twice. Sixteen per cent have had a miscarriage. The care of League offsprings' sneezles and wheezles is pretty evenly divided between three local pediatricians.

What is her secret ambition? To travel (maybe we'll all get abroad yet). But there were 16% who had no secret ambitions (Come, come, girls, it doesn't cost anything to hope!). Five gals long for a bit of leisure; one would like to be a doctor; another wants to put aside domestic chores and run a big business. Nine per cent wish they could write and 3% would give their eye-teeth to be able to sing. One transient member longs to own a house and stay put. Three per cent would just like to get organized. Another gal longs for a million dollars (who doesn't!). Two per cent would like to be interior decorators. One gal wistfully wished for a family. Another secretly longs for a big bosom. Still another would like a well run house always spotless, her children always clean and never cross, her husband attentive and affluent, and herself serene and beautiful in Hattie Carnegie gowns. Oh, well, it was a nice dream.

Readers following the editor's instructions to turn to page 47, found that Martha Schue had written the essay originally for the *Buffalo Newssheet*.

Leagues Founded 1950–1959

Westchester on the Sound, New York
Springfield, Illinois
Westchester-on-Hudson, New York
Spartanburg, South Carolina
Birmingham, Michigan
High Point, North Carolina
Wilmington, North Carolina

Bangor, Maine
Northern Westchester, New York
Ogden, Utah
Lubbock, Texas
Abilene, Texas
Baton Rouge, Louisiana
Calgary, Alberta
Hampton Roads, Virginia

San Angelo, Texas
Kingsport, Tennessee
Greater New Britain, Connecticut
Greater Fort Lauderdale, Florida
Greenwich, Connecticut
Edmonton, Alberta
Fresno, California

Time to Take Stock

*Volunteer-supervised game time frees
a busy teacher for other duties.*

The School Volunteers for Worcester, Massachusetts

*T*he 1960s are remembered as a time of turmoil and dramatic social change, war protest, civil rights demonstrations, hallucinatory drugs, youthful rebellion and riots in the cities. The decade opened with the election of the first Catholic president in the United States, the Bay of Pigs rout and the Cuban Missile Crisis. A war the French had lost in Vietnam soon made the nightly news, the distant conflict ripping apart America.

At a Woolworth's lunch counter in Greensboro, North Carolina, four young black men, college freshmen, were refused service. "We don't serve Negroes," the waitress told them. The following day, 23 young black people returned to stage a peaceful "sit-in" to protest segregation. Not long after, black and white civil rights protesters faced angry mobs in the first of a series of Freedom Rides on public transportation.

John F. Kennedy, Robert Kennedy, Martin Luther King and Malcolm X were assassinated. Watts, Newark and Detroit burst into flames. Chicago police clubbed protesters at the 1968 Democratic convention in Chicago.

> It seems clear that the Junior Leagues do not have to change their basic ideas or ideals, but it may be that we shall have to change some of our areas of emphasis to fit a changing world.
>
> —Marjorie McCullough Lunken (Hiatt), 1961
> Association President

After a decade of silence in post-war domesticity, the feminist movement resurfaced, fueled by federal studies and legislation, new women's organizations, best-selling books and the civil rights and antiwar movements. In 1960, pressured by Eleanor Roosevelt and Esther Peterson of the Women's Bureau, President Kennedy created the Commission on the Status of Women and named Mrs. Roosevelt as chair. The Commission's report, issued three years later, detailed the discrimination women continued to face in society. In the same year, the Equal Pay Act was passed, and Betty Friedan published *The Feminine Mystique*, which encouraged women to find fulfillment in employment outside the home. The Equal Rights Amendment, first discussed by Congress in 1923, once again was an issue.

As in the late 19th century, women organized to make their voices heard in the public arena. In 1961, nearly 50,000 women were mobilized by the new Women's Strike for Peace. Growing out of state commissions on the status of women, NOW (National Organization for Women) organized to pressure the government for yet more changes. Other new women's organizations emerged, such as the Women's Equity Action League and the Women's Political Caucus. The new woman of the 1960s was embodied in women like Friedan, Gloria Steinem, Kate Millett and Bella Abzug.

The Junior League, 60 years after Mary Harriman founded the movement, entered the decade as a voice to be heard on local and national levels. Leagues in 199 North American cities involved nearly 80,000 women in community service. The Junior Leagues were actively engaged in the social issues of the decades at both the

Marjorie Lunken (Hiatt), President of the Association of Junior Leagues, 1960–62.

Photo: Harry Carlson

local and national levels, though they also understood that the social changes around them would very likely change Junior Leagues dramatically.

The Junior League was recognized as an important voice on many issues. Marjorie McCullough Lunken (Ittman Hiatt), 1960–1962 Association president, found herself in perpetual motion. She traveled regularly from Cincinnati to New York to preside over meetings at headquarters in the Waldorf-Astoria. She represented the League on national boards and committees, including the Council of National Organizations, the Women's Conference of the National Safety Council, the National Women's Advisory

Committee of the Office of Civil and Defense Mobilization and the American Educational Theatre Association.

She was in Atlantic City for the National Social Welfare Assembly at which Mrs. Victor Shaw, a former League regional director, was elected the organization's first lay leader. At the American Symphony Orchestra's convention, she accepted the Gold Baton Award for the Leagues' service to music and the arts. At the Children's Theatre Conference, she received a citation and plaque commending the Leagues for their contributions. She chaired a panel on volunteer recruitment at the National Conference on Social Welfare. And she visited the Omilos Ethelonton, the League's counterpart in Greece, as part of the Association's new goal to "enlarge the scope of the Junior League to encourage women throughout the free world to establish volunteer organizations encompassing the principles of the Junior League."

A Changing World

Attending meetings of other organizations that shared League interests was "a must" to keep up to date on services, trends and developments arriving with the new Space Age, she explained, reminding League members how fast the world was being transformed. The 1961 Annual Conference in Dallas delayed its opening to allow delegates to watch Alan Shepard become the first American in space. Within the year,

It is one thing to build a strong vibrant organization; it is something else again to maintain its effectiveness in today's atmosphere of expansion and diversification.

—Rita McGaughey, 1966
AJLA Public Relations Director

American astronauts had followed the Russians in orbiting the earth. Before the end of the decade, man would walk on the moon. Soaring birth rates in many of the new nations were sending the planet's population soaring even as scientists explored ways to extend the human life span. More and more people were living in cities and suburbs, fewer and fewer in small towns and on farms.

"You may ask what does all this mean to the Junior League," Marjorie Lunken said to delegates at the 1962 Conference. "I think it means a good deal.... Developments such as these mean that the Junior Leagues are working in a world changing more rapidly than ever before. But there is nothing wrong with change—for it involves growth and learning. It seems clear that the Junior Leagues do not have to change their basic ideas or ideals, but it may be that we shall have to change some of our areas of emphasis to fit a changing world."

She threw out a series of some rather disturbing questions. Would League services be adequate for the 1960s world? Were the Leagues helping members to develop their potential and do a "really significant" job? Should admissions policies be softened or tightened? Could the League find creative and new ways to fulfill its basic purpose as government agencies and other organizations began meeting society's needs?

Two "basic and glorious facts" gave her faith that the Junior League would surmount the challenges.

What's On a Woman's Mind?

Before Betty Friedan identified and shared her malaise in *The Feminine Mystique*, Betty Ruth Clark (Elizabeth Cless), president of the St. Paul League in 1951–1953, found a way to help wives and mothers fulfill their potential. In 1960, she and Virginia L. Senders, faculty members at the University of Minnesota, established the Minnesota Plan for the Continuing Education of Women, a pioneering program for "rusty ladies" that would become a model for hundreds of schools in the U.S. and around the world.

In the late 1950s, many married educated women not long out of college began to doubt that full-time domesticity could replace the intellectual stimulation and discipline they had enjoyed in the academy. The traditional role of wife and mother—often reinforced by advertising—was not enough, although they couldn't understand exactly why not.

The advertising executives eager to reach women didn't understand either. Women "baffled all understanding," an agency vice president confessed in a *Junior League Magazine* article in 1963. "The biggest unfathomable factor in manufacturing and marketing brand merchandise is the little housewife with the Mona Lisa smile—and heaven knows what's going on behind it."

A study by the Young and Rubicam advertising agency suggested that women in the early 1960s were introspective and worried "even when there's not much cause." Half the women surveyed felt something was wrong with them although they weren't sure just what.

Mrs. Cless, assistant to the dean of extension studies, approached the problem by engaging outstanding faculty members in the liberal arts college and professional schools to lecture in an experimental seminar taken by 16 women in the fall of 1959. The women with "better-than-average" educations brushed up on conceptual thinking and found an intellectual outlet in seminars on "New Worlds of Knowledge" and, later, "Arts of Reading," "Frontiers of Twentieth-Century Science" and "Ideas in America."

"Things have changed so fast that an older woman's B.A. practically isn't worth the paper it's written on," Mrs. Cless told a *Minneapolis Tribune* reporter in 1960. By the spring of 1960, she and Virginia Senders had a three-year grant proposal ready for the Carnegie Corporation. The objectives of the Minnesota Plan, were twofold:

- the full utilization of our resources of able and educated womanpower

- an increase in the personal happiness and satisfaction of many individual women, which will occur as they find ways to making full and productive use of their capacities and their time.

Carnegie awarded the program $110,000 and results were immediate. In the first year, more than 300 women enrolled. By 1965, over 2,500 women were participants. One of the students in the mid-1960s was Emily Seesel, who enrolled after completing her term as president of the St. Paul League. "The program got me so intrigued that I went back to law school," she said.

Prof. Senders introduced a course called "The Educated Woman in the United States," long before women's studies became part of the curriculum. "We were in orbit . . . It was very groundbreaking . . . It was absolutely a cultural shift," recalled Earl Notling Jr., a Minnesota Plan counselor. The Minnesota Women's Center at the university is an outgrowth of the program.

Mrs. Cless established a similar program at the Claremont Colleges and the Plato Society at UCLA. The Plato Society allowed retirees to organize their own courses and teach each other and was a forerunner of the Elder Learning Institute.

In 1963, she contributed an essay on "New Patterns for the American Woman" to the *Junior League Magazine*. In it, she said:

Many people are puzzled by all the sudden attention being given to mature women. Certainly every newspaper, every magazine and many television programs inform us that we have a problem. Books like Betty Friedan's The Feminine Mystique *become seven-day wonders. It has reached the point where those of us who are content with our lot feel as though something must be wrong with us.*

However, content though we may be as women, most of us are not sure of ourselves as people. We mustn't let the mass media get us down—but we must be realistic enough to admit that we are much like travelers in the Sahara. . . .

The things we have used as landmarks suddenly look different. This is not to say that what we learned at mother's knee is necessarily no longer true, but it is to say that it is not enough. To take poor old mother off the hook, let me quickly remind us that the wisdom you and I are handing on to our children probably will not be enough to produce security or happiness in the unpredictable world they will inhabit. . . .

Our world is in the agony of creation where at every turn the mists lift to show us something that no man before us has ever seen. Upon our flexibility, upon our willingness to understand, upon our ability to make correct judgements rests the survival of man.

"Fact No. 1 is that our founders built a solid structure—or design for achievement, if you will—and it is interesting to note that the many problems which surround us, some of them strange and new, can almost all be solved within the present framework of our Policies and Bylaws. We do not have to grope for principles. The groping, if any, is in the area of application of these principles. The second glorious fact is that Junior Leagues in their great history have never lacked for the skills, talent and ability to cope with problems. They have always found new ways to serve—and new solutions to problems—and they have dared to try."

She urged them to advance "beyond the borders of the usual, the tidy, the known" and "to march off the map" in pioneering new projects and meeting new human needs with new volunteer services.

"Many people will not venture outside of the known and familiar, but Leagues have a unique history of pioneering and a willingness to dare and to try," she said. "There are two ways to go when you find you have marched off the map. One is to retreat to the past. The other is to reach out and explore. I am confident that Junior Leagues will continue to reach out and explore."

Meeting New Challenges

Nobody at that meeting could have imagined how different the world would be a decade later. Leagues would be forced to consider how they could remain viable in a society where the traditional values League members had espoused were being challenged by a younger generation.

The Junior League of Boston assists the elderly.

The Junior League of Boston

At first, it was business as usual with the Leagues. The *Junior League Magazine* in 1961 reported that 37 Leagues had programs serving senior citizens and 100 League members had attended a regional Children's Theatre Conference in Shreveport. Planetariums were in the news, with the Dayton League giving $56,000 to build a planetarium for its city, Erie donating $19,091 to convert a museum barn to a planetarium and maintain it for two years, and Hamilton-Burlington in Ontario contributing $6,000 for a university planetarium project.

As the decade progressed, nearly half the Leagues had health and welfare projects, including alcohol programs, adoption services, clinics, convalescent care and hospital services. Central Westchester helped provide homes for unwed mothers. Morgan County, Alabama, furnished the entire pediatric wing of the local hospital.

New Orleans established a Cottage School for the Deaf after a League member with a deaf two-year-old discovered that the program for deaf preschoolers in the area had to limit enrollment because of a teacher shortage. Seattle created a series of training tapes for the learning disabled. Wilkes-Barre, Pennsylvania, was one of many Leagues working to make sure children received the new Sabin polio vaccine.

The Junior Leagues of New Jersey researched and produced "Portfolio U.S.A.," a lecture and slide series billed as "a panoramic view" of the best in American cultural, social and intellectual history. A Sears-Roebuck Foundation grant made the series available to schools, libraries, women's groups, PTA groups, historical societies and museums throughout the state. The New York League won international distribution from UNICEF for its slide show about an imaginary trip to five UNICEF countries.

Providing quality children's entertainment remained a League priority, although a trend toward League sponsorship of professional productions had emerged. In the mid-'60s, Edmonton sponsored the Hogarth Puppets of London, and the Minneapolis League worked with other community groups to bring professional Children's Theatre to the city instead of staging its own show. Leagues like Vancouver and New Orleans began to explore the therapeutic value of puppetry as they took their shows to children's hospitals.

Increasingly, Leagues turned their attention to television. Dubbed the Idiot Box or the Big Gray Eye, it had exploded into a big business, with America producing nearly $900 billion worth of sets a year early in the decade. League members got behind the camera and on the set to deliver educational programming that offered the public "good value from the electronic mentor in the living room." As early as 1960, the Central Delaware Valley Junior League (now the Greater Princeton League) pioneered with a television drug education program. By the mid-'60s, 11 Leagues were engaged in television projects, and many Leagues placed volunteers with local educational television stations.

In Rockford, the League produced a 30-minute television show for children, "Call on Casey," which was more popular in the Illinois town than Mickey Mouse. The Peoria League provided Sunday afternoon programming called "Spectrum," which explained modern life to junior high viewers. Guests included a scientist demonstrating Galileo's experiment and a state senator praising the genius of the American Republic. Both public and parochial schools used the series as a teaching tool. In Albuquerque, League members wrote, acted and helped produce "Donkey Tales" for preschool viewers, with four League members alternating as storytellers.

St. Louis sponsored an ambitious series called "Outside In," which took viewers to the city art museum, a shoe factory, a turkey farm and a stained glass art studio. The series also explained how a telephone worked, what western heroes were really like, what children of other nations ate, how a policeman was trained. Originally a 13-week summer program, it ran for seven months and was shown on CBS affiliates in Los Angeles, Chicago, Detroit, New York and Philadelphia. Across the state, the St. Joseph Junior League used television to promote family health by sponsoring a series called "Operation Shape-Up," hosted by a League husband who was a YMCA physical director. A League family billed as "The Bonebrakes" demonstrated how to stay fit.

The Leagues also used the medium to focus attention on issues. After pledging in 1960 to help emotionally disturbed and mentally retarded children, the Boston League

A hearing-impaired boy learns about sound at the New Orleans' League—sponsored Cottage School for the Deaf.

joined with WGBH-TV to produce hour-long documentaries in which League volunteers worked in every aspect. "The Innocents," which looked at schools, hospitals and training centers for the retarded, was shown throughout the country and won the Ohio State University Award for "intelligent, imaginative presentation of a sensitive subject . . . often moving, often frightening but always enlightening." Philadelphia received a National Educational Television Award for "The View from the Center," which provided a close-up of the city's Skid Row in a four-part series exploring community needs. Seattle researched and produced an eight-part television series on the vanishing Western American Indians, recording much information for the first time.

Focus on Education

The Leagues' longtime commitment to education was expressed most often in the 1960s through supplementing school programs. League members volunteered in the classroom and in after-school tutorial and enrichment programs helping culturally deprived and underachieving students. In 1965, eight Leagues were assisting in classrooms, doing anything they could to ease the teachers' workload and to provide more individual attention to students. A year later, that number had jumped to 22.

The Worcester League reported, "Like most volunteer programs, our initial requests were to fill 'safe' positions in libraries, etc. Direct student contact in a teacher situation was 'taboo.' But creative requests began to appear as volunteers proved their capabilities. Now our volunteers not only fill routine assignments as teacher aides or clerical

*I*n the mid-1960s, the women's section of the *Miami Herald* ran a small notice inviting women interested in continuing their education to show up at a local movie theater. To everyone's surprise, nearly 9,000 women turned out—bored housewives, mothers whose children were grown and women in economic need.

Out of that meeting grew the Council for the Continuing Education of Women, which became the largest program of its kind in the United States. Pulling together community resources, CCEW held annual job fairs attracting up to 15,000 women, established an outreach program targeting the growing Cuban exile community and served as a clearinghouse to help women complete their education, whether they needed a high school certificate or a doctorate.

Behind the notice and the Council was Marie Willard Anderson, a nationally acclaimed newspaper editor and a former Junior League president.

"Marie was the dreamer for it," remembered Betty Kaynor, the Council's coordinator and a League member first in Waterbury, Connecticut, and later Miami. "It became one of the prestigious groups in the nation and we were consulted by people all around the U.S., but it never would have flown without Marie's stories in the Herald. And she certainly put her civic/community resource Junior League training to work!"

A fourth-generation Floridian, Marie moved to Miami in 1939 after graduating Phi Beta Kappa from Duke University and completing a secretarial course. She always had wanted to be a reporter, but she spent the war years volunteering with Civil Defense, the American Red Cross and the Miami Beach Serviceman's Pier. She joined the Junior League in 1941 and only three years later was elected president. Under her leadership, the Miami League established a Public Affairs Committee, a forerunner of SPAC, which after the war investigated education and consumer issues. At the end of the war, she began her journalism career.

As women's editor of the *Miami Herald* in the 1960s, she drew from her League training to produce a women's section that reported on issues affecting the lives of women and families even if the topics were unpopular. She assigned women's page reporters to write about child molesters, alcoholism among women, anti-poverty programs, divorce and sexuality. Her section didn't just cover community issues. It defined

Marie Anderson
Miami Junior League

them. In the process, she led the transition from traditional women's pages to modern lifestyle sections.

The prestigious JC Penney-Missouri Awards, established in 1960 to make women's sections more relevant, recognized her section as the best among all the large news-papers in the country five times during the 12 years she was editor. Another five times she was "retired" from competition to give other newspapers a chance to win. Keynoting a session on "Issues" at the 1968–1969 awards workshop, she sounded more like a Junior League president than an editor: "Be a moti-vating force in your community. If your town doesn't do something call attention to that."

Under her leadership, the *Miami Herald* encouraged women to be motivating forces by sponsoring an annual club conference and competition to recognize and encour-age the contributions of volunteers. The Miami League's "Drugs Are Like That," a drug awareness program introduced in the late 1960s, won the newspaper's Club of the Year Award as well as White House citation for children's causes.

Marie Anderson chaired the CCEW and Governor's Commission on the Status of Women and was a member of local and state task forces on equal educational opportunities. She edited *Julia's Daughters*, a history of South Florida women.

assistants, they are also serving as aides in such specialized teaching fields as language, child study, science and physical education. A carefully developed training program—for both volunteers and teachers—is the one factor that makes such diversity possible."

The Eugene League qualified its members to tutor arithmetic; English and journalism graduates in the Palm Beaches, which had become a League in 1962, graded high school students' themes. A school volunteer pilot project sponsored by the Detroit League to battle the dropout problem had more than 5,000 community volunteers working in and outside of classrooms by 1966. Twenty-three Junior League members were directly involved as tutors, teacher aides and field trip assistants. A League committee administered the program in cooperation with the board of education and the principal of a local school. Experts called the program one of the best in the nation.

Leagues in Indianapolis, Palo Alto, Philadelphia, Fort Wayne and Buffalo sponsored community meetings on issues from urban poverty to public education. Buffalo also sponsored a conference on the shortcomings in public education. During the Vietnam War, the Des Moines League worked with other Iowa Leagues, 30 other community organizations and the U.S. Department of State in presenting a regional conference on foreign policy for 1,000 community leaders from four states.

> *It's amazing that the Junior League has held together at all given the pressures on women today and the social changes for young women.*
>
> —Barbara Yalich, 1968
> Association President

Midlife Crisis

Yet the Leagues slowly realized that what they were doing—how they were doing it—was no longer enough. The media began discounting the League's relevancy. Stephen Birmingham assessed the League in *Holiday* magazine in 1962 under the title, "The Ladies of the League: Is the Junior League a collection of snobs or social workers, post-debutantes or do-gooders? Even the ladies bountiful themselves aren't sure."

"Junior Leagues were overnight thrown into a frenzy of doubt about all the things they had done so well in the past," recalled Barbara Yalich of Colorado Springs, Association President in 1968–1970. "There were real questions about the worth and direction of such an organization. The concerns were compounded by the social programs funded generously by the Great Society—how could and should we meet with and take advantage of these new directions?"

In 1965, the Association of Junior Leagues hired a consulting firm to assess the organization. The report made one thing clear: it had to change where it was going and how it got there. "Some of this impetus for change comes from the belief that the Association is not maintaining its position of leadership. Individual Leagues are progressing beyond the Association's most advanced horizons," the consultants found. "Other voluntary organizations and the professional and business worlds are

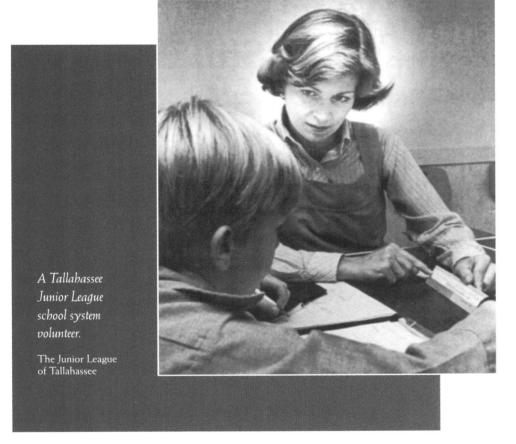

competing successfully for the time and energies of potential League members."

The most marked trend of the mid-1960s was a growing awareness of the need to intensify training for community leadership. The cover story of the July-August 1966 edition of the *Junior League Review* was on the trained volunteer. Under the headline, "To Make Their Service Efficient," Mary Louis Taylor, the publications editor, compared the Junior League volunteer to Alice in Looking Glass Land. "She found herself in a spot where she had to run as fast as she could to stay in the same place. She was assured that, to get anywhere, she would have run twice as fast as that."

She pointed out that League volunteers 50 years earlier had to make every effort to make their service efficient. "In 1966, specific problems may involve different groups and more refined techniques, but the need for training is ever present."

In the following issue, readers heard yet more. Rita McGaughey, director of public relations for the Association, wrote: "It is one thing to build a strong vibrant organization; it is something else again to maintain its effectiveness in today's atmosphere of expansion and diversification. More than ever before, the vitality of Junior League programs is dependent upon their flexibility to meet new needs. The past year was a particularly appropriate moment in our history to consider new directions for Junior League training and service."

An Association progress report that year noted growing awareness of the need for more intensive community leadership training and evidence that Leagues were banding together "to undertake collectively what they could not do alone."

"The Junior League of the 1960s was not an indivisible entity, but many separate groups, each indigenous to its community and with strong local traditions and values. Each League therefore was (and is) as much or more a part of its own community as it was a cog in an international organization," Janet Gordon and Diana Reische wrote in 1982 in *The Volunteer Powerhouse.*

Other organizations stepped up to lead the way in civil rights, feminism, urban decay, environmentalism and other issues of the times. The Junior League as a movement seemed hopelessly status quo, still laboring to meet community needs in education, housing, social services and employment, yet somehow no longer hearing community voices.

Although Mary Harriman and her friends had founded the Junior League to help heal the ills of the metropolis, the organization found it difficult to draw upon its experience in finding solutions for the urban decay and racial unrest in the 1960s. Eager to address the problems, some of the larger Leagues created advisory boards to help them understand the needs of a broader community. Advisors said Junior League must integrate if it wanted to be relevant. The African-American mayor of Washington, D.C., resigned from the League advisory board there to protest the all-white membership of the League. Lines were being drawn that separated the Leagues from the very work they had organized to do.

In 1968, one of the most explosive years of the decade, Barbara Yalich became president of an Association of Junior Leagues wracked by self-doubt.

"The questions were coming from the outside," she said. She remembered that reporters asked adversarial questions and made comments about white-gloved volunteers. "It was part of the whole climate of what was happening to organizations. The Y, the Red Cross, the National Conference on Social Welfare, every organization in those years was questioning their direction and questioning what their focus should be in a society in upheaval and obviously with so many unmet needs."

She remembers the painful questions Leagues had to ask themselves: Whom did the Leagues serve in the community? Should they try to meet all the new needs? Did they belong in the inner city? Could they continue to serve the arts and do traditional things? Where was the Junior League's place in the community?

"It's amazing that the Junior League has held together at all given the pressures on women today and the social changes for young women," she said. "Consider how many organizations have almost ceased to exist. Once we got over the shock of everything going on in the whole country, I think the League really did change direction and focus. The Leagues weren't just going to so-called safe project areas. I've always been proud that the Junior League learned to work in a different setup even though it was painful to go through this tremendous change."

Barbara Johnson Bonnell, Association President in 1962–1964, reflected a generation later, "In retrospect, it seems those years marked the ending of an age of relative innocence—for voluntary organizations like ours as well as for social, economic and political institutions throughout the world."

> *. . . it seems those years marked the ending of an age of relative innocence—for voluntary organizations like ours . . .*
>
> —Barbara Johnson Bonnell
> Association President, 1962–64

When Rachel Carson's *Silent Spring* appeared in the *New Yorker* in 1962, the environment suddenly became an issue. About the same time the Junior League of Toledo mobilized to save the Maumee River. Industrial wastes, agricultural chemicals and consumer demand threatened not only the river but an entire water system. The river begins in Fort Wayne in Indiana and travels more than 131 river miles, 105 of them in Ohio, before feeding into Lake Erie. Fort Miami was built on its banks, and generations had fished in its waters. Nearly 4,000 streams flow into the river, creating the largest drainage area of any Great Lake River. If the river died, so would the economic life of the region.

The League devised a comprehensive campaign to stir public concern, including a 1965 documentary called *Fate of a River*, which raised consciousness not only in Ohio but across the nation. When the U.S. House committee investigated pollution of the Great Lakes in 1966, Toledo League members testified as environmental specialists who had saved a river.

Other Leagues added the environment to their agendas, among them another Miami. In South Florida, the Miami River, whose Indian name had been "Mayamimi," meaning "sweet water," was also dying. The Miami League decided to clean up the Miami River, surveying the river, enrolling in pollution control courses and monitoring agencies. "If we pester enough . . . they'll realize the com-munity is interested," Mrs. Cynthia Whitney, the River Restoration Committee chair, told the *Miami Herald* in 1971. The paper headlined its report, "Women Plan to Be Meanies Until Miami River is Cleaned Up." The project not only cleaned up the sweet waters but also spearheaded the rebirth of the downtown waterfront.

The same year, the Chicago League and the Association co-sponsored a national environmental strategies conference attended by representatives of 203 Leagues. Nearly 40 percent of the Leagues had some environmental protection activities before the conference; 92 percent did after. League environmental projects included Stamford-Norwalk's program to train adults to teach river ecology to children.

Leagues Founded 1960–1969

Ft. Smith, Arkansas	Riverside, California	Bakersfield, California	Lake Charles, Louisiana
Tyler, Texas	Eugene, Oregon	Palo Alto & Mid-Penninsula,	San Jose, California
Tallahassee, Florida	Long Island, New York	California	Pensacola, Florida
Evansville, Indiana	Monterey County, California	Summit, New Jersey	Waterloo-Cedar Falls, Iowa
York, Pennsylvania	Albany, Georgia	Monmouth County, New Jersey	Wichita Falls, Texas
Palm Beaches, Florida	Midland, Texas	Fargo-Moorhead, North Dakota	

Defending and Reshaping Voluntarism

Community Answers, an information
resource for Greenwich residents.

The Junior League of Greenwich, Connecticut

A new feminist movement surfaced in the early 1970s as more and more women entered the workplace. By the end of the decade, slightly over half of all American women worked outside the home. More than 60 percent of those women had children of school age, and another 45 percent had children under age six. Women married later, and the divorce rate doubled between the early 1960s and the mid-1970s. In 1972 Congress approved the Equal Rights Amendment; the following year the Roe v. Wade decision by the Supreme Court legalized abortion. The decade saw women assuming increasingly prominent roles in society, with Shirley Temple Black of the Palo Alto League the U.S. Representative at the United Nations Conference on the Environment. In Great Britain in 1979, Margaret Thatcher became the first woman to serve as prime minister.

Women are more highly educated, more are working, many choose graduate work, career or Peace Corps . . . These changes in the role and expectations of women have profound significance for the Junior League and its place in the lives of these new women.

—Mary Poole
Association President, 1974–76

Junior League volunteers engage in training at an AJLI Multiculturalism Conference, 1990.

Working women found they had more career choices but less time, energy and incentive for volunteering in the community. "Women are more highly educated, more are working, many choose graduate work, career or Peace Corps when they might have chosen the League in the past. These changes in the role and expectations of women have profound significance for the Junior League and its place in the lives of these new women," Mary Poole of Albuquerque, then a League director, warned as the decade began.

Arva Parks McCabe, now a prominent Miami historian and League Sustainer, was a young wife and mother of two small children when she joined the League late in the '60s. "If an educated woman had things she wanted to do, she joined the League." In 1970 she was among League Actives, who took it upon themselves to organize a biracial summer camp at a Methodist Church to help prepare first graders to enter a court-ordered integration of school in the fall. "It was the most idealistic period in my life," she remembers. The camp operated for four summers, with a wait list after the first year. The women stayed involved in schools as their children grew up. "We were PTA presidents for years—the last gasp of a large group of educated women who were not working," she said of her fellow Actives.

For 70 years, the Junior League had provided leadership training and avenues for volunteer service to women, but the Junior League began to change with the times. In true League fashion, action was preceded by extensive research. In 1969, a committee of former and current Association board members, working with a consulting firm, examined the organization, purpose and membership of the Association of Junior Leagues of America in search of answers. A year later at the Annual Conference, the committee presented its 63-page "Proposal for Change," which recommended a major reorganization, a new name and a new purpose.

Proposal for Change

A stronger Association with more continuity of leadership would drop "of America" from its name. Instead of promoting Leagues' "individual purposes," the Junior League's united purpose would be "to promote voluntarism, to develop the potential of its members for voluntary participation in community affairs and to demonstrate the effectiveness of trained volunteers."

The new wording accurately described what the organization had been about from the beginning, but it came at a time when the very concept of trained volunteers dedicated to improving their communities had come under attack. The question many women had begun asking was not *how* or *where* to volunteer but *why* volunteer at all.

In the 1960s, government had assumed responsibilities for filling needs once met by volunteers. In the 1970s, inflation, recession and a gasoline crisis discouraged volunteer service. The economy had also diminished the amount of support the business community could contribute to League projects. Funding by the government and foundations dried up even as the cost of community programs escalated.

The National Organization for Women (NOW) went straight for the heart of the Junior League movement and voluntarism, contending that women who volunteered were depressing wages and taking jobs away from people who needed them. In September 1971, it passed a resolution calling volunteer work an "extension of unpaid household work." NOW argued that volunteerism forced "economic dependence of a woman by preventing her from earning money of her own." Skilled and educated women should be paid for their work in the new marketplace. The NOW National

Task Force on Women and Volunteerism lay down the challenge by declaring:

> The volunteer mystique is an ideology which hides the truth that volunteerism is yet another form of activity which serves to reinforce the second-class status of women; which is one more instance of ongoing exploitation of women; which takes jobs from the labor market, and therefore, divides middle class from poor and working women; which buttresses the structures which are keeping women in a subordinate role; which is antithetical to the goals of the feminist movement and thus detrimental to the liberation of women.

The League refused to back down. "There seems to be a pervading influence in most of the materials distributed by NOW that if you get paid for it, it's imminently worthwhile and if you don't get paid for it, it's not worth a darn," the *Junior League Review* reported. NOW's president, the article pointed out, didn't receive a salary. Prominent Junior League members rose to the defense of volunteerism, including Eudora Welty, the author and a Jackson, Mississippi, Sustainer, who won the Pulitzer Prize for *The Optimist's Daughter*.

Eudora Welty, member of the Jackson, Mississippi, Junior League, and Pulitzer Prize–winning author.

The joy is in the doing. I would hate to be prevented from volunteering.

—Eudora Welty

127

Conference on Voluntarism

About that time, the Minneapolis League was looking for a project to commemorate its 50th anniversary. Many Leagues use such occasions to give a special gift to their communities, such as a playground or a medical facility, but the League wanted to do something to celebrate voluntarism. The women considered staging a gala to raise money, but Marilyn Bryant, a member of the League, suggested something even more ambitious.

"The idea I sold was that after all we are community volunteers. We ought to have a conference on voluntarism," she remembered in 2000.

Out of her suggestion came a major national summit on voluntarism. Working with the Association, the University of Minnesota and several national voluntary centers, the Minneapolis League sponsored a three-day meeting in 1974. More than 700 delegates, mostly women, came from 30 states and Canada. More than 50 national volunteer organizations and hundreds of local and state groups were represented. Even women from NOW attended.

As conference chair, Marilyn was the ideal bridge. She was both a volunteer and a feminist and saw no contradictions in the roles. She had learned "how to speak in front of large groups, how not to be afraid to speak up for things you believe in and how to run a meeting" in what she calls "a very safe environment" of 9:30 a.m. League gatherings in a member's living room. But in the 1960s, as a wife and mother considering a law career, she became radicalized in a constitutional law course. Instead of applying to law school, she joined the Minnesota Women's Political Caucus. She was chairman six months later. In

2000, when the Minnesota Women's Consortium honored her with its Women Empowering Women Award, she was described as having earned "her credentials in the marches, rallies, political activities of the '70s and '80s." She often took her daughters along to introduce them to the issues. Her daughter, Anne Wight, later was president of the Minneapolis League.

The conference created more than a few ripples. Ralph Nader spoke on "Persistent Citizenship." George Romney, the former Michigan governor, told delegates, "America is great not primarily as a result of what government has done for the people. America is great primarily because of what the people have done for themselves." Delegates went back to their organizations with resolutions to be endorsed. The conference voted to ask the Junior League of Minneapolis "to act as a facilitator in forming a national coalition involving individuals and feminist and voluntary groups to work together to document and evaluate the role of the service volunteer."

Commitment to Advocacy

In line with its new commitment to advocacy, the Association of Junior Leagues issued a position paper on the importance of women as volunteers and then took action.

"Probably our most forward-moving achievement during my term was the Board's decision to issue a position paper in response to the National Organization for Women's attack on voluntarism," remembered Mary Poole, who served as Association President in 1974–1976. "This statement put the Junior Leagues on record validating voluntarism as a significant avenue for women to achieve leadership positions. We gained a platform from which to request, and sometimes demand, participation and involvement in decision-making roles at all levels of government."

During her presidency, the Association moved to train women not only for volunteer service in their communities but also for careers. Many Leagues had already introduced programs to help members assess their individual skills, set personal goals and realize their own potential. In 1975, the Association unveiled its Volunteer Career Development training program designed to improve members' skills, whether they wanted to be more professional in their volunteer service or translate volunteer experience into a paying job.

"All the issues of feminism have raised women's consciousness to the point where they want fulfillment in their lives and they want the full range of choices that are open to them, too," Mary Poole said at the time. "This program is an opportunity for ALL Leagues to offer their individual members a chance for the systematic acquisition of skills, through the Junior League, that they will need for a career."

Chair was Joan Ruffier, a former League president from Orlando, chosen an Outstanding Young Woman of America in 1975 because of her own voluntarism. "Volunteering is an elective occupation," she said as the program was launched. "Even when voluntarism is accepted as an essential and necessary activity, volunteering is a matter of individual choice and can be discontinued when it no longer fulfills a need of the volunteer. Voluntary organizations, if they are to survive, have no choice but to respond to the modern woman's search for self-fulfillment, meaningful work, personal identity, education, training, and even a career ladder. Junior Leagues surely are no exceptions."

Tuesdays for Women, part of the Volunteer Career Development Program, sponsored by the Junior League of Montclair/Newark, New Jersey, 1980.

Courtesy of Caroline Brady, photographer

The program was such a success that three years later, funded by the W. K. Kellogg Foundation, the Association developed a similar training program for youth and rewrote the adult model for use in the broader community. Soon Leagues were sponsoring seminars to adult and student groups across the continent to teach career-building skills and the value of voluntarism. By May 1981, even Betty Friedan, a NOW founder, was calling on women to demonstrate "impassioned volunteerism" in response to the pressing needs of the times.

Volunteer Career Development encouraged greater professionalism among League volunteers. The Association Management Process (AMP) taught Leagues to run their organizations like a business. The Association launched the program in 1973 under the direction of a former chief of staff at West Point, one of three men who would administer the Association between 1970 and 1977, AMP stressed management by objectives and a systemic approach to planning. "Only by setting objectives that are believable, achievable and measurable and the careful allocation of resources, which are increasingly scarce, can we, or voluntarism in general, survive a period of inflation/recession," Mary Poole wrote in 1975.

League members, from the Board down, received management training. The Chicago League first trained its own membership and then hosted a two-day training seminar for 63 community organizations to celebrate its 60th anniversary. A Chicago journalist wrote that Junior League members in his city could "match most corporations when you look at such management techniques as cost controls, long-range planning, defining objectives and executing projects."

ABOVE: *Volunteer visiting elderly person in nursing home through League's Project Reach Out.*

The Junior League of Tulsa

BELOW: *New York Junior League volunteers promote adoption opportunities.*

Photo: Stanley Seligson, The Junior League of the City of New York Archives

Community Issues

As it retooled itself for greater professionalism and efficiency, the Association also tackled major problems that were troubling all communities. Statistics made clear what was the number one issue. In 1972 more than one out of every five persons in the United States was a victim of crime, according to a Gallup Poll. In the major urban areas, the figures were worse. One out of every three persons had been victimized.

Crime was the number one social problem, yet few volunteer organizations had tried to fight it, and professionals in the field often looked with distrust and skepticism at any volunteers who tried. Undeterred, the Junior Leagues decided to mobilize all 223 Leagues in North America to decrease crime and delinquency and to increase the effectiveness of the criminal justice system.

In 1973, the Association in collaboration with the National Commission on Crime and Delinquency and the Justice Department launched IMPACT, a multifaceted effort focussing on delinquency prevention and rehabilitation, court reform, prisons' self-help programs, runaway shelter and return service, rape prevention and community services.

IMPACT grew out of the League work of Mary Whyte, who had been Mount Kisco president before it became the Junior League of Northern Westchester. She later served as an Association director and staff member. At her suggestion, the

Association took on crime and delinquency, sponsoring a five-day seminar in Houston in 1973, which attracted representatives from 205 Junior Leagues as well as others concerned about crime prevention. Within a month, 61 Leagues were involved in IMPACT-inspired projects. Two years later, that number had reached 114. In all, about 180 Leagues participated in the four-year program. One of the anticrime projects that resulted was Crime Stoppers, developed by the Albuquerque League and police department. Albuquerque sponsored the first national Crime Stoppers Conference in 1978.

The Junior League also mobilized to help all children receive their fair share and basic rights. Although the United States was the world's richest society, over 10.2 million children were living in official poverty and as many as one million a year were being abused or neglected. The welfare of children had always been a League priority, but in 1973 the League adopted child advocacy as an Association-wide program. Defining advocacy as action and class advocacy as interceding for the powerless, the Leagues officially declared themselves children's advocates. The Association and the Baltimore League co-sponsored a training conference on advocacy skills to help Leagues produce results.

The Leagues turned those skills to meeting needs in their individual communities. Boise discovered that 100 hard-to-place children identified as candidates for subsidized adoption were still in limbo and lobbied successfully for legislative funds. Alexandria, Louisiana, sponsored training programs for child abuse counseling volunteers. Detroit set up an emergency shelter for children at risk from abusive parents. Omaha cosponsored a runaway girls shelter. The Summit, New Jersey, League helped create a sex and health education program for elementary and junior high schools. Texarkana worked for drug education in the elementary schools. Oakland-East Bay opened a family stress center and established an auxiliary to support it. The Topeka League, whose members included Mrs. Roy Menninger, and the Menninger Foundation pioneered Children Have All Rights—Legal, Educational, Emotional or CHARLEE, Inc. to run homes for neglected, abandoned or abused children. The Atlanta League learned of CHARLEE in the late '70s and set to work to open a similar facility. By 1981, Atlanta had several homes in place and hosted a two-day conference for 17 Leagues on alternatives to institutionalization, which resulted in more League-sponsored residential programs for abused children.

The League in the 1970s also looked at the needs of senior citizens, not only in how to serve them but how to train them to serve. With a $790,000 grant from the Edna McConnell Clark Foundation, the Association designed Project VIE (Volunteers Intervening for Equity), a pilot project to develop retirees as a new reserve of community volunteers.

The first Baby Boomers were just hitting their stride in 1977 when the Junior League began planning for their retirement in the 21st century. The League looked ahead and saw an aging America not as a problem but as a solution. Community elders could be agents of constructive change in their communities.

Growing Up with the Girl Scouts

A decade after Marjorie Lunken (Ittman Hiatt) of Cincinnati served as Association president, she was heading up another national organization—the Girl Scouts of the U.S.A., whose board included about a half dozen League members. Long before the League adopted an official policy of collaboration, the two organizations had shared goals and outstanding volunteers. Marjorie Ittman was the third Junior League member to hold Scouting's highest office. At the local level, Leagues throughout the country had pioneered projects with the Girl Scouts for over 50 years.

"The Junior League and Girl Scouting grew up together, you know, and there are a number of interesting parallels in our histories," she wrote in the *Junior League Magazine* in 1973. "Even more reassuring was my discovery that Girl Scouting embraced the same philosophy of service that had made my Junior League years so personally fulfilling. In Girl Scouting, as in the Junior League, service opportunities are designed to give each volunteer sufficient challenge to draw on all her resources, and breadth and variety enough to develop her potential."

The parallels began to converge shortly after Juliette Gordon Low founded the Girl Scout movement in 1912 to "bring girls out of cloistered environments to serve their communities." Within five years the New York League had organized the first troop for disabled girls.

Anne Hyde Choate of New York followed Miss Low as president of the Girl Scouts, at the same time serving as a member of the first Association board. In the *Junior League Bulletin* in 1922, Mrs. Choate pointed out she had been "an enthusiastic Junior League member for the past 17 years and an equally enthusiastic Girl Scout for the past six years."

"It is my earnest conviction that there is no better way for a Junior League girl to serve her country than by taking the leadership of a group of younger girls, and giving them the benefit of the results of her own education, to the end that she may help these younger sisters to develop into the best kind of citizens," she contended.

She was delighted that "in constantly increasing numbers" League members were leading the Girl Scout movement at all levels. "In one town Junior League members formed the original Council; in another they are entirely responsible for the running of the local headquarters; in another they form the committee that arranges the examining of the Scouts for badges," she catalogued. "In many places they get up entertainments for the benefit of the Scout funds." Most of all, the number of League members serving as troop leaders was steadily growing.

Marjorie Lunken (Hiatt) (left) accepts an award from Mrs. Louis Gratz, a Girl Scout official, 1962.

Photo: Harry Carlson

One of those new troop leaders was Mrs. Alan H. Means of the Salt Lake City League. She served as national president of the Girl Scouts of the U.S.A. from 1941 to 1954 and later—by that time a Los Angeles Sustainer—chaired the World Association of Girl Guides and Girl Scouts.

Leagues as well as individuals worked in Scouting, providing funding and volunteers. "There really is no limit to the variety, the number, the tenure of Girl Scout service placements that need your kind of skills and concerns," Mrs. Ittman told fellow League members in the *Junior League Magazine* in 1973. She cited the DeKalb County (Georgia) League, then one of the newest, for sponsoring a troop for students with cerebral palsy and Fort Wayne for extending Scouting into the inner-city to ease urban tension. In Monterey County, California, the Junior League and the local Girl Scout Council were working together on a behavioral modification plan at Reality House, the League's rehabilitative project for delinquent girls. In Nashville, League members and Senior Girl Scouts were team-teaching ecology to seventh graders.

In urging Junior League members of the 1970s to continue the tradition of Girl Scout work, she wrote:

"It's no coincidence really that the Junior League and Girl Scouting were infant agencies during the same period, and that both became national movements at almost the same point in time. I think the historic parallels reflect a simultaneous recognition, by both sets of early leaders, that the Biblical injunction, 'To whom much is given, of him shall much be required,' also applied to women; and also had much broader meaning than the accepted female duty to home and family. The founders of Girl Scouting, like the Junior League's founders, believed that involvement in social problems, in youth work, in the welfare of their communities was the natural province of women with the time, capacity, and good will to be of service. Their vision went further. They knew that such service could be a fine and useful vehicle for developing women's potential. Whichever infant group they joined—the Junior League or Girl Scouting, or both—women were to discover that they could function successfully in a larger sphere, and could organize and lead others in useful enterprises."

After her term as national president, she chaired the Girl Scouts' National Advisory Council for nine years and served on the Juliette Gordon Low Birthplace Advisory Group and on the World Committee of the World Association of Girl Guides and Girl Scouts. A founding member of the Olave Baden Powell Society, the movement's fundraising arm, she was president from 1993 to 1996. She has also been a director and vice president of the World Foundation for Girl Guides and Girl Scouts. In 1997, World Association recognized her outstanding service to Girl Guiding and Girl Scouting

Marjorie Lunken Ittman (Hiatt), National President of the Girl Scouts of America, with First Lady Betty Ford, also a former Junior League member, surrounded by Girl Scouts on the Lawn of the White House, 1975.

Courtesy of Marjorie Hiatt

at a ceremony at the White House. In 2000, as Marjorie Hiatt, she received the Mary Harriman Award for her outstanding contributions to community service.

"Unlike most projects, VIE was not created in reaction to established problems. Rather, the project was designed to anticipate trends and address them before they became full-scale problems," Alice H. Weber of the Toledo League explained in 1979 when she was president of the Association. "The most significant of these trends is the shift in our society from a youth-dominated culture to a culture made up predominantly of older people. Rather than regard them as recipients of services, we must begin to see them as potential providers of services."

Alice Weber was also the first chair of Project VIE, a pilot project launched in nine cities by ten Junior Leagues. The Leagues matched seniors with challenging volunteer assignments in everything from working with young people in the criminal justice system to helping other older people obtain their rights and benefits. Cincinnati, Grand Rapids, Kansas City (Missouri and Kansas), Minneapolis, Providence, Omaha, Orlando-Winter Park, Rochester (New York) and Seattle set out to prove the model would work and to change the national agenda. More than 600 men and women between the ages of 55 to 89 were recruited and trained as volunteers meeting local needs.

In each city, Leagues had found different ways to tap the senior potential. Seattle, for example, organized volunteers into teams that specialized in senior needs.

We must have more programs like Volunteers Intervening for Equity: programs which reach out to older people, recognize their tremendous potential, and provide a way for them to become involved.

—First Lady Rosalynn Carter

Omaha established counseling services for seniors in 20 centers around the city. In Grand Rapids, VIE recruited older volunteers to design a comprehensive home health care plan, providing better and more humane care for people at substantially lower cost and offering an alternative to nursing homes. The pool of volunteers included retired college professors, local members of the American Association of Retired Persons—and Junior League Sustainers. In less than a year, VIE was producing results in all the cities.

In 1978, when representatives of private industry, government and the voluntary sector gathered in Washington to discuss Project VIE's performance in its first year, Rosalynn Carter saluted the program's success.

In Minneapolis in the late 1970s, Sustainer Elva Walker and Active Donna Anderson began building a partnership between the Junior League and businesses to recruit and train retirees. Mrs. Walker, a local businesswoman, had been involved with aging issues since the 1960s when she chaired the Minnesota Council on the Aging, serving under four different governors. Mrs. Anderson saw VIE as a way to change how society looked at older people. When Minneapolis-based Honeywell Inc. decided to develop a corporate retiree volunteer program, it turned to the Junior League for help. The St. Paul companies—Cargill Inc., Pillsbury, General Mills, 3M and First Bank—followed, and the program expanded throughout the Twin Cities. Soon out-of-state companies were also contacting the League. In 1985, a national conference on Corporate Retiree Volunteer Programs, held in Minneapolis, telegraphed the importance of such programs everywhere in the country.

Project VIE demonstrates what often has happened to League projects. The Association or an individual League identifies a need, establishes a successful program to meet that need and then turns the project over to other organizations on the local, state or national level. The Minneapolis VIE project grew into the National Retiree Volunteer Coalition, a nonprofit consulting organization with Donna Anderson as its director. NRVC helps employers in the United States and Canada channel the talents and expertise of their retirees into creative community programs under the banner of their former employers. In March 2000, NRVC joined Volunteers of America.

"We were too small and had too few resources to achieve our vision," said Donna Anderson. "By becoming part of Volunteers of America, we will be able to be more effective and reach more retired persons and provide opportunities for them to be of service to their communities."

Changing Membership

As the League was changing the face of voluntarism in the 1970s, it was also changing the face of its membership. "With the current battles, the demanding projects, and the need for young, intelligent and energetic women, the WASP image of the Junior League has not disap-

peared; but it seems to be fading away," Nan Birmingham wrote in a 1975 *Town & Country* article. Ms. Birmingham commended the League for dealing with "the nitty-gritty of contemporary life" and defending volunteer involvement in the community.

Some Leagues had simplified selection of members, encouraging women to join "without any reference to pedigree," Birmingham reported. Individual Leagues like Atlanta had already adopted policy statements that encouraged coalitions with groups of other races and creeds and membership for all young women regardless of race, color, religion or national original if they were dedicated to voluntarism. A few minority women had become members in Leagues, but the number was small.

In 1978 at the annual conference in Kansas City, the Junior Leagues of Saginaw and Birmingham, Michigan, introduced a proposal to change the Board's position on admissions in an attempt to introduce more diversity. Previously, how individual Leagues selected members was left to them. In the discussion that followed, Joan Ruffier, chair of the Ad Hoc committee developing the statement, explained that almost two years earlier Board members had begun preparing a policy statement that all Leagues could share. Conference delegates were asked to expand the Board's policy statement to read: "That member Junior Leagues reach out to all young women regardless or race, color, religion or national origin who demonstrate an interest in and a commitment to voluntarism."

When a straw vote was called, a majority agreed, signaling a League commitment to diversity and the first of many Association steps to achieve it.

The Canadian Connection

*I*n 1912, Montreal became the first League to organize in Canada, founded by young women addressing the same kinds of urban conditions and social concerns Mary Harriman recognized in New York. Working with the University Settlement in Montreal, they organized a Debutante League to raise funds for charities. No representative attended the first Junior League Conference held that year, but the editor of the *Junior League Bulletin* added this footnote: "The youngest League—Montreal—was not represented at the Conference nor did anyone appear from the Junior League of Holland, despite cited claims that a group existed there."

Although no League developed in Holland, the Montreal League thrived, organizing a free dental clinic and plunging into patriotic work during World War I. It wasn't until 1926, however, when Toronto became a League that the movement began to spread slowly across the country as urban centers grew. By 1934, Canadian Leagues numbered six, from Halifax on the Atlantic to Vancouver on the Pacific. From the beginning, Canadian Leagues have been full and equal partners in the Association of Junior Leagues, sharing programs and inspiration across the border.

Mary Ferguson of Winnipeg was president of the Association in 1940–1942.

By 1939, Canada was already at war. Winnipeg, as has been noted in Chapter Five, was the crucible for volunteer bureaus that the Leagues in both countries established in World War II. Building on a volunteer office Montreal had established, Winnipeg drew up the volunteer traditions of the Junior League to assess needs and serve as a clearinghouse for volunteers in both the war effort and ongoing community needs. The Roosevelt Administration drew heavily on the Junior League Central Volunteer Bureau concept to meet national needs. As Association President, Mrs. Ferguson urged Leagues everywhere in 1940 to establish such agencies. "The Leagues should be able, if necessary, to lead and not to follow."

After the War, with the addition of Calgary and Edmonton in the 1950s, Leagues often exchanged ideas. In the 1970s, Hamilton (later Hamilton-Burlington) adapted Buffalo's successful Haunted House fund-raiser.

In the late 1960s and early 1970s, however, the eight Canadian Leagues began to realize that they needed their own unified voice and a national image if they were to serve their communities effectively.

Delegates at the 1972 Conference voted to establish the Canadian Federation of Junior Leagues or the Federation Canadienne des Jeunes Ligues to help Canadian Leagues from Halifax to Vancouver communicate with each other, act in concert on national issues affecting voluntarism and address purely Canadian issues. It would be another four years before the Federation was fully launched.

"In Canada, it is difficult for voluntary organizations to escape the influence of government," Dyanne Gibson, a former Toronto League president explained in the *Junior League Review* in 1981. "Canadian Leagues, to be truly effective, have to work with government at all levels."

The Federation would research Canadian public issues, monitor government legislation and work with other organizations on subjects of common interest but not always in the same way as their sisters in the United States. Canada's parliamentary system created a different relationship between voluntary organizations and the government and allowed less opportunity for lobbying when a vote was at hand. Attempts to influence legislation had to begin much earlier—as the bill was being formulated, not after it was introduced.

From the start, the Federation broadened the League's exposure in Canada. In 1977, it was one of six national organizations convened to improve liaison and cooperation between the voluntary sector and the Federal government. The following year, the Secretary of State's Department included it in a meeting to discuss government policy among women's groups in the country.

One of the Federation's first acts was to establish a Canadian Public Issues Committee to research and represent the League's position on issues. In June 1979, the Federation made its first national statement, responding to a "People in Action" report by the National Advisory Council on Voluntary Action. It began looking into the freedom of voluntary organizations to function, pensions for women and the need for the government to coordinate its activities for children.

Individually, Canadian Leagues have pioneered many diverse projects over the years. Montreal was among the earliest Leagues to encourage and to make provisions for professional members, many with careers growing out of League placements. Halifax, a port city where fathers were often long absent at sea, early on recognized the problems of single mothers and established an "extra support" program. Hamilton-Burlington helped the Royal Botanical Gardens build a greenhouse that allowed hands-on experience for disabled adults and children. Toronto, with a focus on child development, life skills and safety, launched Growing Together, a prevention and early intervention program for preschoolers, in a downtown neighborhood in collaboration with a treatment center and the city health department.

Vancouver built the Children's Arts and Science Center and established the first arts council on the continent.

As early as 1987, Canadian Leagues began to attack the problem of domestic violence. Working with the local YWCA and the Albert Law Foundation, the Junior League of Calgary produced a 32-page pamphlet, "Law and the Abused Woman," which provided information on safety planning, legal options and negotiating the legal system. The pamphlet was distributed throughout the country. In 1984, the Federation held the first League-sponsored national conference to focus on violence against women. In 1998, it adopted domestic violence as a national public awareness campaign, using its collective voice to launch a local, provincial and national public awareness campaign.

Leagues Founded 1970–1979

Billings, Montana	DeKalb County, Georgia	Huntsville, Alabama	Pueblo, Colorado
Orange County, California	Lafayette, Louisiana	Cobb-Marietta, Georgia	Greater Alton, Illinois
Las Vegas, Nevada	Greater Lakeland, Florida	Sarasota, Florida	Fayetteville, North Carolina
Pine Bluff, Arkansas	Owensboro, Kentucky	Tuscaloosa, Alabama	North Little Rock, Arkansas
Clearwater-Dunedin, Florida	Alexandria, Louisiana	Springfield, Missouri	Gaston County, North Carolina
Champaign-Urbana, Illinois	Gainesville, Florida	Odessa, Texas	Reno, Nevada

A Powerful Voice for Social Change

Meredith Hallowell (right), from AJL Board,
testifying before a congressional subcommittee
on child welfare legislation.

Photo: Iris Rothman.

*T*he Junior League was back to business as usual in many ways during the 1980s. Mary Harriman would have felt at home at the 1980 Annual Conference in Toronto as delegates gathered to consider the urban future and the challenge for volunteers. The issues being discussed echoed the conversations of the earliest days of the League, but this time over 700 delegates from nearly 250 Leagues shared ideas and ideals and pondered the role the Leagues should play in improving their communities.

What could the Leagues do to stop the decay of residential neighborhoods and ensure a better education for all children? How could Leagues engage local governments to work with volunteers to make the most of diminishing tax dollars? And what voice could the Junior League have in the decisions to be made about the cities?

> . . . we are now a prime mover within the voluntary sector, leading the way into new areas of concern and raising new issues . . . a more dynamic and daring organization, willing to risk more and share more, to work with more partners.
>
> —Carole P. Hart
> Association President, 1984–86

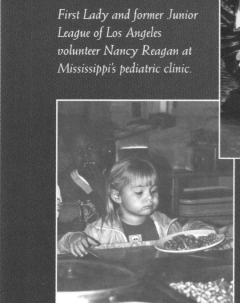

First Lady and former Junior League of Los Angeles volunteer Nancy Reagan at Mississippi's pediatric clinic.

The Junior League of Oklahoma City collected 275,000 pounds of food in the nation's most successful first-effort food drive.

The Junior League of Oklahoma City

The questions for the 1980s were posed within a framework established in the settlement houses of New York, Boston, Baltimore, Chicago and other cities where League volunteers had labored in the early days of the century.

The cityscape had changed, however, with urban issues of the '80s affecting even the smallest community. "What city today is not affected by the ebb and flow of populations? Dozens of new metropolitan centers have sprung up in areas formerly considered rural, while a disturbing number of older cities are shrinking with the exodus of their residents to other communities," the *Junior League Review* told its readers. "Indeed, Junior Leagues have felt the impact

of this population shift within their own memberships. In this increasingly urban world, whether in cities whose population is on the wax or on the wane, many issues emerge which demand attention and concerted effort from every sector of the community."

The Junior League was everywhere . . . pushing for welfare reform, working to end family violence and playing a major role in winning passage of the Family Violence Act of 1984 and later for reauthorization of the funding. To battle the growing problem of homelessness, the League pushed for adult literacy, joining with other national organizations in PLUS (Project Literacy U.S.). More than 25 Leagues cooperated in local efforts and another 15 had literacy projects of their own.

"These are exciting days for the Association of Junior Leagues, for we are now a prime mover within the voluntary sector, leading the way into new areas of concern and raising new issues. We have become in recent years, a more dynamic and daring organization, willing to risk more and share more, to work with more partners," Carole P. Hart, Association president, reported in the winter issue of the *Junior League Review* in 1986.

The decade saw women moving forward in many areas even though the Equal Rights Amendment failed to be ratified. In 1981, President Reagan appointed Sandra Day O'Connor, a former president of the Phoenix Junior League, as the first woman to sit on the U.S. Supreme Court. Sally K. Ride became the first female astronaut, and women served in the Gulf War. More women were being elected to public office and more were working, including members of the Junior League, who balanced careers with volunteer work.

Cutting Edge Projects

The Junior League moved into new, more controversial areas of service. In the spring of 1985, it launched Woman to Woman, a three-year international public awareness program to educate the public to the gender-specific impact of alcohol abuse cutting across socioeconomic boundaries. Alcoholism among women—wives and mothers—was a problem nobody wanted to talk about.

In the first phase of the campaign, Leagues undertook community-based surveys to identify the specific needs of at-risk women. Even taking the survey was considered a bold, risk-taking initiative. Leagues like New Orleans went head-on against the myth that ladies don't have drinking problems.

"By talking honestly and aggressively about alcohol abuse among local women, the Junior League took a very complex and life-threatening issue out of the closet," Brooks Emory, M.D., president of the Orleans Parish Medical Society, told the *Junior*

Woman to Woman

ALCOHOL AND YOU

More teen-age girls drink today than ever before.

Two out of three adult women drink.

Heavy drinking for women is defined as more than two drinks every day.

Women experience more serious health effects from alcohol after a shorter history of drinking than men.

Alcohol education and awareness for women becomes an important focus of the Junior Leagues in the 1980s through the Association's Woman to Woman project.

By talking honestly and aggressively about alcohol abuse among local women, the Junior League took a very complex and life-threatening issue out of the closet.

—Brooks Emory, M.D.,
Junior League Magazine, 1990

League Magazine in 1990. "They've forced a lot of women in this community to examine how they live." The League's drive prompted the medical society to devote an entire issue of its bulletin to women and alcoholism, leading to better diagnosis and treatment and a better prognosis for recovery.

The community studies everywhere showed that two things keep women from receiving treatment for alcoholism: a cult of silence and denial and the lack of available childcare during treatment times.

Within three years, Woman to Woman had more than met its objectives with more than 100 Leagues in the United States, Mexico and Canada participating. The Leagues had distributed almost a million copies of a brochure called, "Woman to Woman: Alcoholism and You." Each League devised an action plan according to local needs. Charlotte worked with the local PBS station to produce "Women Coming Out of the Shadows," a moving documentary shown around the country.

141

Former First Lady Betty Ford spoke at a media briefing sponsored by the Junior Leagues of Long Beach, Los Angeles and Pasadena. Charlottesville sponsored a pilot project at the University of Virginia. Buffalo established CoCare, a drop-in childcare center in collaboration with a local hospital's outpatient alcoholism clinic, increasing clinic attendance by eligible women by 50 percent.

"As an organization of women, it's critical for us to be involved in the issue of alcohol and women. What made us effective was the diverse perspectives of the women who worked on the project—a single parent, a child of an alcoholic, an artist. By putting it all together, we had a success," remembered Wendy Sanders, Junior League of Buffalo, Chair of the Woman to Woman Committee.

The Association partnered with others in the project. With funding from Allstate Insurance and the Blue Cross and Blue Shield Group, the League cosponsored a national conference in 1988 called "Alcohol Is a Women's Issue," the first major conference on women and alcohol. The following spring, the National Foundation for Alcoholism Communication gave its Markie Award for excellence in public information brochures to AJLI for conference brochures and information.

AIDS was another daring new addition to the agenda. The Los Angeles League became the first League to start an AIDS-related project in 1986, setting up a hotline and speakers' bureau to dispel fear and misinformation. It operated

> *LEAD has a triple focus where everyone benefits— youth, adults, the entire community.*
>
> —Anne Hoover
> Association President 1982–84

with six other Leagues to set up similar projects. The Mexico City League introduced AIDS education in the country, bringing together leading public and private health and education officials and following up by adding AIDS education at health clinics for low-income families. The Montclair-Newark, New Jersey, Provisional Class heard of plans to open Babyland, one of the first centers in the nation to provide education and care to AIDS children three months to three years and adopted the center as a project. "Federal grants simply do not cover everything, and this is where the Junior League women step in. And they do these things with fabulous spirit," said Mary Lou Madden, Babyland center's supervisor. By 1988, when AIDS was the major issue discussed at the Conference, more than 60 Leagues were involved in AIDS education projects. In San Francisco, the Junior League created Hope House, in face of community opposition to opening a halfway house for women recently released from the county jail, some of whom were HIV positive. In 1988, the Honolulu League began working with the Life Foundation and the Department of Health to produce "Bloodstream Follies," a comic book distributed in all Hawaiian schools to educate children about AIDS.

Needs of Children and Youth

Leagues had always focused their energies on meeting the needs of children, but by the 1980s, those needs—and many of the children—had changed. To illustrate just how

The Junior League of Boston provides transitional housing and support for homeless teenagers through their "Act Together" program.

The Junior League of Boston

Teens celebrate the completion of their initial training at the 1983 Project LEAD youth leadership conference in Philadelphia.

much, the *Junior League Review* published lists comparing the toughest discipline problems faced by public schools in the 1940s and 1980s. Talking and chewing gum topped the 1940s' list. Alcohol abuse was listed as number one 40 years later. The rest of the list looked more like a police blotter than a detention hall slip. Youth—and not just in troubled inner city neighborhoods—needed help. The League partnered with other concerned organizations to find ways to alleviate many of the educational, social and emotional problems being experienced by a growing number of teens.

With a grant from the W. K. Kellogg Foundation, the Junior League and The Quest National Center initiated a national leadership training program for youth called Project LEAD (Leadership Experience and Development), which began in early 1983.

"Leagues have worked extensively with such problems of youth as substance abuse, juvenile justice and teenage pregnancy. There is an opportunity to work *with* the youths *for* others in the community," Anne Hoover, then Association president, explained. "LEAD has a triple focus where everyone benefits—youth, adults, the entire community."

Using a mentor concept, adult volunteers—initially trained Junior League members, and, later, volunteers from other organizations—helped youth develop self-esteem as they worked together to identify community needs and then plan and execute specific programs. Students came from a broad mix of urban and rural schools and included young women, the handicapped and minorities who often were bypassed by traditional leadership opportunities.

Barbara Bush: First Lady of Literacy

First Lady and former Junior League of Houston member Barbara Bush reads to children in the White House.

Barbara Bush and her daughter-in-law Laura share more than the honor of being First Lady of the United States. Their Junior League roots (Barbara in Houston and Laura in Midland and Austin) led them to lifelong commitments to voluntarism, particularly in campaigning for literacy. Established in the late 1980s, The Barbara Bush Foundation for Family Literacy awarded more than $6 million to over 200 Family Literacy Programs in 44 states in its first decade. In 1998 when her husband was governor of Texas, Laura Bush launched an early childhood development initiative to prepare infants and young children for reading and learning before they enter school.

In 1989, Barbara Bush shared her thoughts on the Junior League, voluntarism and literacy in the *Junior League Review*:

Q. How was your Junior League training helpful to you in your activities concerning literacy?

A. I was a member of the Midland Service League before it became a Junior League, and most of my volunteer work at that time was in hospitals, the Next-to-New Shop, and at the children's school or church. Later, I became a member of the Houston Junior League. My League work certainly helped teach me the importance of volunteerism, the power of teamwork for a cause you care about and giving back some of what you have received. I also was lucky to have parents and a husband who taught me the same values.

Q. How and why did you become interested in the literacy issue?

A. I have been a lover of books my whole life, starting with the stories my mother used to read to me, and I still don't leave home without packing at least one or two good novels. But my formal involvement with literacy began about a decade ago, when George began his first campaign for the presidency. I realized I might have a chance to call attention to an important national cause. When I thought about all of the social problems that troubled me—crime, drug abuse, teenage pregnancy, homelessness—I realized many of our problems would be lessened if more people could read and write. I had found my cause.

Q. What role do you see the Junior League and other nonprofit organizations playing in the literacy cause?

A. So many Junior Leagues are getting involved in literacy programs, and it makes me very proud. One thing I can do is encourage that work, and be an active admirer and champion of your causes. Junior Leagues are doing some of the most serious and effective volunteer work in America today, and I use every opportunity to say so.

But as usual, we need more help. I would hope that Junior Leagues and other similar nonprofit groups would continue to support local literacy projects with funding and other material support, as well as provide volunteer assistance—not just in tutoring, but in administration, public awareness, fundraising, answering phones—you name it! In addition, Junior Leagues are in a good position to promote involvement of business and civic leadership, and help coordinate cooperation between the public and private sectors.

The League also launched several initiatives aimed at helping young women to avoid unwanted pregnancies. By the mid-1980s, some estimates put teen pregnancy at one in every ten young women. In collaborating with the March of Dimes, the League sponsored parent seminars on adolescent sexuality to help parents understand, clarify and share their values with their children. With the Children's Defense Fund, the National Coalition of 100 Black Women, the National Council of Negro Women and the March of Dimes, the League encouraged citizen monitoring and action through Adolescent Pregnancy Child Watch.

The broadest involvement in addressing teen pregnancy came through the Teen Outreach Program (TOP). Brenda Hostetler, director of pregnancy prevention programs in the St. Louis public schools, in 1978 began a program to develop self-esteem among teenage girls after some high school students asked if they had to get pregnant to participate in teen pregnancy programs. Brenda, who later became a member of the St. Louis League, and Jane Paine, a St. Louis Sustainer who had been involved in a pioneering Head Start project, took the project to the League where, with funding from the Danforth Foundation, the program was developed. In 1981, the St. Louis League began sponsoring the program with the goal of reducing teen pregnancy and increasing the rate of high school graduation.

The results were so encouraging that in 1984 the St. Louis League laid the groundwork for an even broader involvement by hosting the Teenage Pregnancy Prevention Conference, attended by over 100 Leagues

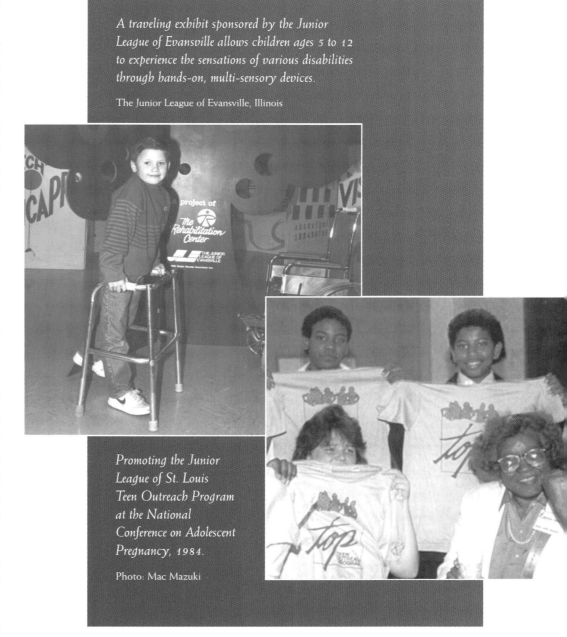

A traveling exhibit sponsored by the Junior League of Evansville allows children ages 5 to 12 to experience the sensations of various disabilities through hands-on, multi-sensory devices.

The Junior League of Evansville, Illinois

Promoting the Junior League of St. Louis Teen Outreach Program at the National Conference on Adolescent Pregnancy, 1984.

Photo: Mac Mazuki

and several outside organizations including the Urban League. Out of the conference grew seven pilot projects in other Leagues.

"Teen pregnancy has been emerging as a significant issue over the past year," Juliet Rowland, an Association Vice President, said at the time. "AJL first addressed the issue three years ago when it published an occasional

Juliet Rowland, AJL Board member, 1980–84.

paper on the topic and recently it has been active at the national level through advocacy programs. It is fortunate that a League prepared a model program, now ready for replication, that fits into that emerging need."

In 1987 the Association accepted sponsorship of TOP as a national program and continued to sponsor it until 1995 when it was turned over to the Cornerstone Consulting Group, a Houston firm that specializes in health and human services projects. The Leagues responded by taking the St. Louis model and creating cutting-edge programs tailored to local need.

Other Leagues established award-winning local programs targeting teens that continued into the 1990s. The Junior League of Springfield, Missouri, sponsored a teen parent program, which provided free day care for children of teenage mothers, enabling them to finish high school. Los Angeles established an adolescent pregnancy prevention education program. The Monmouth County, New Jersey, League included grandparents and teen fathers in its comprehensive Hand-In-Hand Toddler Center, which encouraged teen mothers to graduate from high school. Discovering that areas of Riverside, California, had higher adolescent pregnant rates than the national average, the League created a community collaborative program, which included Mother-Daughter Choices. Only one of 234 participants became pregnant during 1997–1998.

Civic Involvement

In tackling all the tough issues of the 1980s, the League also worked to influence public policy. Individual Leagues had public affairs committees, but the question of the League's role in public affairs was raised formally at the 1974 Conference in Boca Raton. Four years later, the Leagues adopted a policy directing the Association board to advocate on behalf of Association program interests.

The real landmark for the League in public affairs came in 1980 with the first Public Affairs Training Seminars (PATS), held in Washington. In the early 1990s, the name was changed to Policy Institute, held at the same time as the Presidents-Elect training session. The seminars reflected the growing importance Leagues place on taking active roles in monitoring and shaping public policy affecting their ongoing programs and the voluntary sector as a whole. That first national training seminar was entitled "By the People: A Route to Public Action," with 450 delegates representing 221 Leagues, 18 State Public Affairs Committees and 6 Area Councils. They spent three days in carefully organized sessions learning how the Federal legislative and regulatory process worked and how private citizens could affect government decisions.

"Increasingly, Leagues have found that their efforts on behalf of causes to which they are committed are frustrated because of public policy decisions and government regulations. This frustration has brought about the recognition among many League members that to be a responsible leadership organization the League must have access to government and its agencies, and make its voice heard," Carol Nutt, seminar chairman and past president of the Wichita Falls League, explained at the time. "The real challenge lies, not in receiving the information and training offered, but in accepting the responsibility to give of our knowledge and experience . . . to make a positive impact on the vital decisions being made at every level which affects our lives."

Marking its 60th anniversary in 1981, the Association of Junior Leagues embarked on a series of national

The Junior League of Washington, D.C., gets involved in public schools through its Public Education Legal Services, improving educational opportunities and facilities.

The Junior League of Washington, D.C.

symposiums and partnerships to focus greater attention on social issues, particularly those related to women and children. At a "Women, Work and the Family" symposium with Hunter College School of Social Work, over 150 representatives from women's organizations, corporations, universities, social agencies and local Junior Leagues met to explore family stress, older women returning to work, child care and balancing volunteer activities with work and family.

"In the dawn of the decade of the '80s, it is now time to shift the focus from an examination of the impact of 'women on work' to a study of the impact of 'work on women' as the pressures of double work roles—breadwinner and homemaker—take their toll on women and families," Juliet Rowland, symposium chairman, said at the time.

Saving a palace is no done-in-a-day project as the Honolulu League discovered when it stepped in to restore Iolani Palace, the only royal residence on U.S. soil. Completed in 1882, the last home of Hawaiian monarchs replaced an earlier palace, which had been destroyed by termites. By the 1960s, after service as capitol of the republic, the territory and the state, Iolani faced the same fate as its predecessor.

Founded in 1923, when Hawaii was still a territory, the Honolulu League came to the rescue as a new capitol was being constructed behind the palace. Collaborating with Princess Liliuokalani Kawananakoa Morris and members of her Civic Center Fine Arts Committee, the League established The Friends of Iolani. Nearly 100 League members spent 5,000 hours over three years cataloging the palace's history, establishing a database of details that would guide the restoration project over the next decades.

Whether saving a palace or a pioneer home, Leagues have been at the forefront of historic preservation since 1925 when San Antonio became the first League to use a historic building as its headquarters. The League restored Bright Shawl, an 1856

property, turning its stable into studios for artists and the house into a tearoom and library. League members in the U.S. and Canada have participated in both quiet and brave ways, from patiently surveying historic sites to standing in front of bulldozers.

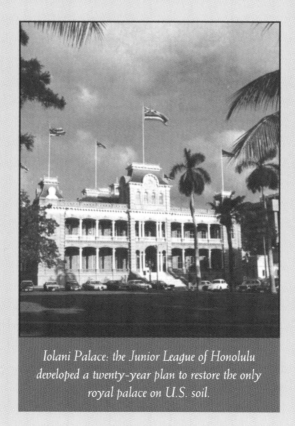

Iolani Palace: the Junior League of Honolulu developed a twenty-year plan to restore the only royal palace on U.S. soil.

Saluting League efforts in 1986, *Historic Preservation Magazine* noted that in 1985 alone the League had been involved in more than 60 preservation efforts, including a number that were "massive in scope and complexity." The sum of the efforts in 1989 brought the League the Thomas Jefferson Award from the American Society of Interior Designers for contributions to the preservation of American culture, intellectual development and national heritage. The same year the National Trust for Historic Preservation of the United States presented the Junior League with its Crowninshield Award, recognizing years of dedication at local, state and national levels to the preservation of historic sites and structures across America.

The Historic Preservation Act of 1966 spurred historic preservation, but Leagues pioneered in surveying and documenting historic sites. Savannah might not be the historic showcase it is today if it were not for a small band of women, including the first president of the Savannah League. The seven women formed Historic Savannah in the mid-1950s to save an early 19th century building. The next year the League formally adopted historic preservation as an ongoing project. League members surveyed buildings

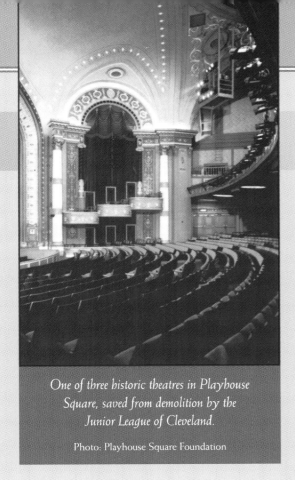

One of three historic theatres in Playhouse Square, saved from demolition by the Junior League of Cleveland.

Photo: Playhouse Square Foundation

and raised funds, led tours, held top posts in Historic Savannah. The effort saved over 1,000 buildings in what would become a two-and-a-half-mile historic district.

In 1962, the Junior League of San Francisco acted to save fine old buildings in the city and surrounding counties by launching an ambitious architectural survey. Dozens of League members went out in three counties to record historic buildings block by block. League members in Denver became historical detectives in 1966 when they prepared a building inventory that became a basic tool for the Denver Landmarks Commission and helped save the home of Molly Brown, nicknamed "Unsinkable" because of her heroism as the *Titanic* sank.

When the Charlotte, North Carolina, League discovered the schools needed audio-visual materials on local history, it initiated a five-year project in 1978 to produce and distribute videotape programs, which won a national award from the Corporation for Public Broadcasting in local history programming for grades 7–12.

Leagues published books celebrating the architectural heritage of their cities. Tulsa celebrated the city's Art Deco buildings; Greenwich, Connecticut, documented its great estates between 1880 and 1930; Evanston-North Shores, Illinois, and Lincoln, Nebraska, compiled architectural albums. St. Louis chronicled the creation and development of Forest Park, which was the site of the Louisiana Purchase Exposition (World's Fair) in 1904. Over the years, other Leagues such as Dayton, Duluth, Lancaster, Williamsport, Kingsport, Mobile, Evansville, San Jose and Wilmington, North Carolina, also chronicled the architectural treasures of their communities. When the Junior League of Washington, D.C., discovered no popular history of the capital was in print, 100 Active and Sustaining members gathered documents and personal recollections to produce one.

Everywhere Leagues were identifying and saving buildings of historic significance in their communities. Minneapolis League restored the John H. Stevens House, a five-room frame structure dating from 1850 and considered the birthplace of the city. The Edmonton League saved a forlorn little railroad station in 1979 only to find out a few years later that the underpinnings of the building, a hub of activity during the Klondike Gold Rush, were so rotten the building couldn't be restored at an affordable price. "It was a hard decision for us," Gwen Harris, chairman of the station committee, reported in the *Junior League Review* in 1983. "We had raised money on the basis that the station was being restored." The League decided if restoration was impossible, they would build a replica and their contributors happily agreed.

In Columbus, Ohio, in 1976 the League saved the Kelton House, an 1852 classical revival mansion, once a stop on the Underground Railroad, from destruction, turning it into a museum. The Cleveland League took on the largest theater restoration project in the United States in 1972, renovating three historic theaters and rejuvenating a decaying downtown. "The Junior League of Cleveland was able, literally at the midnight hour, to save them by coming up with $25,000," recalled Diann Scaravilli in 1986. "No one with any clout in the community was willing to come aboard. Everyone was convinced it would be nice to save the theaters, but there were not a lot of believers."

➤

Today Playhouse Square is a symbol of Cleveland's cultural renaissance—and the second-largest performance and concert hall complex in the United States.

In 1979, the Junior League of Las Vegas saved a 1912 California-style bungalow from destruction, renovating it and moving it to the city's Heritage Museum. In 1997, it rescued a 1929 Mission-Revival mansion, planning to use it as League headquarters as well as a working museum, but in August 2000, while the structure was still up on blocks awaiting its new foundation, a fire ravaged the building.

"I feel both for the loss of history and the loss of the Junior League," Mark Ryzdynski, a local museum administrator told a Las Vegas newspaper. "Back at a time before any other organization thought about saving Las Vegas history, back in the late '70s and early '80s, the Junior League was already doing that." The League returned the money raised, but another home with historical significance was donated to serve as League headquarters.

Wayside Cottage: the 18th-century house is maintained by the Junior League of Central Westchester, New York, as its headquarters.

Leagues like those in Indianapolis and Worcester, Massachusetts, have rescued historic mansions. Great Falls, Montana, created a cultural and community center in a massive three-story school building. Galveston, Texas, came to the rescue of a decaying commercial building with a unique facade of multicolored brick and ended up spurring economic development of an entire business district. While most League restoration projects have been in cities, the Junior League of Monterey County enlisted husbands, local tradesmen and the Soledad Correctional Training Facility in restoring a 19th century whaling station after the State of California asked for help.

Architectural preservation remains a League commitment, with more than 40 Leagues supporting projects at the beginning of the 21st Century. New York; Albuquerque; Scranton, Pennsylvania; San Angelo, Texas; and Miami are among Leagues housed in buildings of historical significance, preserved through League efforts.

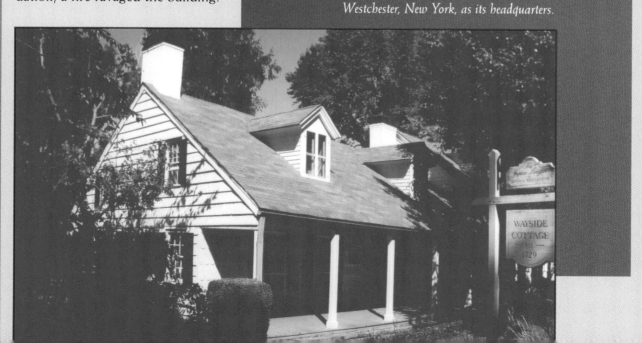

A few weeks later, the Association convened a second symposium, "Child Care: Options for the 80's," a conference held in cooperation with The Johnson Foundation at Wingspread in Racine, Wisconsin. After discussion sessions, attended by 45 representatives from universities, business, government, private agencies and 16 Junior Leagues that had been particularly involved in child care issues, the conference identified five major issues and developed nearly 40 strategies for improving day care at all levels.

"Every time I work with the Junior Leagues, I feel like the Marines have landed," Gwen Morgan, lecturer on policy and day care at Wheelock College, told the conference.

Wasting no time, the Leagues moved ahead on the child care issue. In March, the Association announced it had joined forces with the Children's Defense Fund on a nine-month citizen monitoring project designed to determine the effects of Federal cutbacks on programs for children and their families. Six Leagues—Baltimore, Hartford, Pittsburgh, Wichita, Albuquerque and Birmingham, Alabama,—would participate in Child Watch. Through interviews, volunteers would monitor how cutbacks would affect child health, child welfare, child care and Aid to Families with Dependent Children.

More national conferences at Wingspread followed: "Parental Leave: Options for Working Parents" in March 1985, "The New Homeless: Women, Children and Families" in 1987. In Canada in 1987, the Association and the Federation of Junior Leagues of Canada sponsored "Focus on the Family," a conference exploring issues surrounding the increase in single-parent families and families with two parents employed for pay.

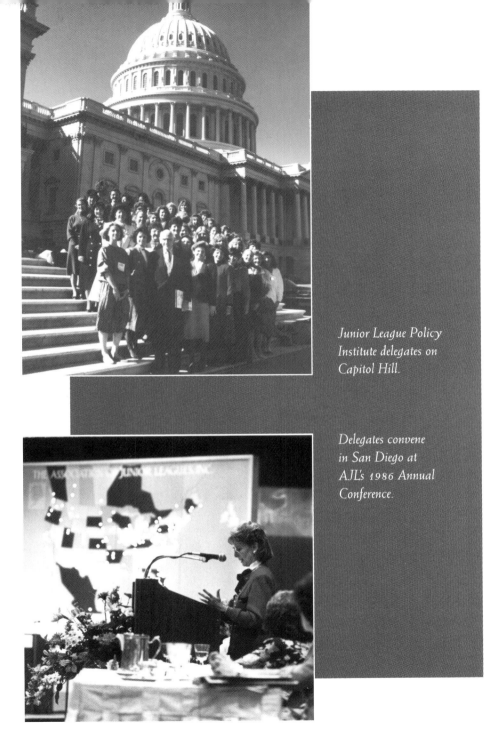

Junior League Policy Institute delegates on Capitol Hill.

Delegates convene in San Diego at AJL's 1986 Annual Conference.

151

President George Bush presenting the President's Volunteer Action Award to AJLI President Maridel Moulton, 1989.

addressing. In the spring of 1989, the Association of Junior Leagues received the U.S. President's Volunteer Action Award from President George Bush, assisted by his wife Barbara, a League Sustainer. "The Award took on an enhanced meaning. It came to symbolize the accumulation of 88 years of dedicated and caring service by wonderful women in every conceivable arena where the volunteer spirit can be fostered," said Maridel Moulton, Association president at the time. "I saw clearly how the Junior League experience is just the beginning— not the end—of a road of long and fruitful civic involvement."

More and more women began seeing the Junior League that way, too. Individual membership grew steadily in the 1980s: 154,000 in 1983, 160,000 in 1984, 162,452 in 1985, 168,358 in 1986. New Leagues joined the Association, too—from 253 in 1983 to 267 in 1986, with London joining in 1985. The membership profile was changing radically with nearly half of all Actives and almost 65 percent of the Provisionals in the workforce. Both Actives and Provisionals were older: the average age of Actives was 34.5 and Provisionals 31.2.

When nearly 1,000 representatives from 273 Leagues from the U.S., Canada, Mexico and Great Britain met for the 67th Annual Conference in Anaheim in 1989, the theme was "Advancing a Children's Agenda," the first time the League had devoted an entire conference to children.

Volunteers were making a difference and finding ways to solve social problems no one else was

Forging ahead in its own diversity efforts, the League started the 1980s committed to continue diversifying membership until "our Leagues represent a true mosaic of their communities." To help Leagues work together to achieve the goal, the League established the first Membership Diversity Network in

Every time I work with the Junior Leagues, I feel like the Marines have landed.

—Gwen Morgan, Wheelock College

1981. By 1987–1988, the Association had hired a coordinator of membership diversity to work with individual Leagues. In October 1988, the Junior League cosponsored a conference on "Minority Volunteers: Pluralism in the Volunteer Arena," at Hunter College in New York. The face of the League was changing, with more members of different religious, ethnic and racial backgrounds not only joining but also becoming League leaders.

The media began writing about the impact the Junior League was making on social issues. "In recent years the League has acquired impressive political strength," *Newsweek* reported in 1986. "On a national level the League proposes legislation to Congress, publishes its own literature and employs a full-time lobbyist in Washington."

Two years later *Time*, in warning that it was "High Noon for Women's Clubs," wrote, "The search for a fresh vision is most evident in the Junior League, that onetime bastion of society ladies that has gradually emerged as a powerful force for social change."

New York Junior League booth at the
Third Avenue Fair, *1984.*

Courtesy of Caroline Brady, photographer

Helping other volunteers to make the most of cable television opportunities, the Junior Leagues of Summit and the Oranges and Short Hills provide training sessions, c. 1983.

Photo: Brad Hess

Across the Atlantic

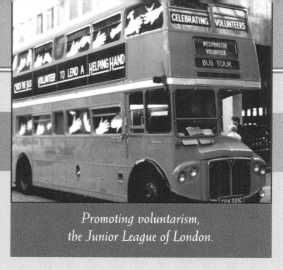

*Promoting voluntarism,
the Junior League of London.*

Eleven American women living in London in 1978 were homesick, but it wasn't for baseball games or fried chicken. What they missed was their Junior League volunteer work.

Wives of executives posted in Britain, they wanted to become involved in the community, but they quickly found that the British concept of voluntarism differed from what they had espoused in the Junior League at home. Women in Great Britain volunteered, but not in the same hands-on way as their American sisters. With the government providing many social services, voluntarism was primarily in fund-raising and single-faceted with one cause adopted for a lifetime.

They decided to organize a Junior Service League with the goal of becoming the first Junior League outside North America. After seven years as a Junior Service League, its mostly-American membership numbered over 250 and had included members of 61 Junior Leagues in North America, although previous League membership was not required. Most Junior League members planned to resume their League activities when they returned to North America. Anne Green, for example, became a League member in Evanston, Illinois, and in the 1990s affiliated with the New York League.

The London Junior Service League, using techniques and sometimes materials its members had acquired in the Junior League, initiated a full range of volunteer projects. They worked with learning-disabled children, volunteered with a substance abuse education project, staged special events at the zoo, undertook historic restorations (including Benjamin Franklin's London home) and compiled a comprehensive reference guide for living in London, now in its ninth edition. Its volunteer proposal for The Disabled Living Foundation so impressed the directors that the League project chairman was immediately asked to coordinate the whole volunteer program.

In every way, the London group reflected the best of Junior League traditions, yet controversy surfaced when it applied for Association membership. The issue was age, not geography. To meet Association requirements, each League first had to comply with regulations in its home community. The British saw the Junior League's age requirements as ageism, however, and refused to recognize any organization in which participation was limited by age.

"Every Conference has its issue. We were the issue that year," recalled Anne Green, who became London League president after it was admitted to the Association in 1985. "I know we opened the Pandora's box, but not many people recognize that." The concern wasn't over how old London League members were. Wives of middle and upper managers, they tended to be older than most Junior League members, but what would happen when London League members wanted to transfer to a U.S. League? In a compromise, the London League was admitted with no age limitations, but if any members wanted to affiliate later with North American Leagues, the local Leagues' membership requirements would apply.

By the next year the Canadian and Mexican Leagues also received permission to determine their own age requirements, and other Leagues began to discuss what was appropriate in their communities.

The London League made a similar impact at home. Susan Carr, president in 1990 when the League celebrated its fifth birthday, told readers of the *Junior League Review* that the League had come of age.

"In the beginning, our multi-focused approach to community needs (rather than a single focus on, say, cancer or heart disease) and our desire to be initiators of original projects to meet those needs, were met with incomprehension and mistrust," she admitted. "We took risks. We started projects without the certainty that we would be able to complete them, or, in established Junior League tradition, turn them over to the community, which perceived such an unheard-of procedure as abandonment."

True, some projects did fizzle out, but the League compiled and distributed Dyslexia Resource File throughout the country and then handed over the project to the British Dyslexia Association "as a natural conclusion to the project." The League soon was training community volunteers to take on other League projects such as "Kids on the Block." They established a popular Christmas boutique and introduced gingerbread houses, which the British called "Gingerbread cakes."

Most of all, they introduced the concept of the trained community volunteer when a training committee was established in 1982. "Our training committee worked not only with the Junior League of London but also involved other women from London. We taught group dynamics and leadership and human resource skills," said Anne Green, who later became a consultant in London and New York where she co-chaired the New York League's Nonprofit Boards Clearing House, a program training volunteers to serve on community boards.

In nearly 25 years of service, the London League often found itself bridging cultural and language divides. "Kids on the Block" scripts had to be rewritten to make sense to British children, spellings had to be changed in by-laws, the immunization campaign of the 1990s had to be adapted to a country where the government provided an almost universal program.

"We often put our foot in our mouth without realizing it," Anne Green laughed years later, but as she had said in 1985, "caring for one's fellow men and women transcends cultures and history."

Leagues Founded 1980–1989

Bristol, Tennessee-Virginia	Monroe, Louisiana	Kankakee County, Illinois	The Emerald Coast, Florida
South Brevard, Florida	Annapolis, Maryland	Northern Virginia, Virginia	Garland, Texas
Kalamazoo, Michigan	Central & North Brevard,	London, England	Ann Arbor, Michigan
Richardson, Texas	Florida	Sioux Falls, South Dakota	Morgan County, Alabama
Athens, Georgia	Norman, Oklahoma	McAllen, Texas	Bryan-College Station, Texas
Longview, Texas	Victoria, Texas	Harlingen, Texas	Bell County, Texas
Quad Cities, Iowa-Illinois	Boca Raton, Florida	Manatee County, Florida	Ocala, Florida
Yakima, Washington	Plano, Texas	Fort Myers, Florida	Florence, South Carolina
Charlottesville, Virginia	Daytona Beach, Florida	Fort Collins, Colorado	
Arlington, Texas	Johnson City, Tennessee	Lawton, Oklahoma	

Boldly Toward 2000

*A blue ribbon dialogue on maternal and
child health sponsored by the White House.
Representatives of 18 Junior Leagues, the
AJLI Board and staff exchange ideas with
Clinton Administration policymakers, 1994.*

Photo: Richard Greenhouse.

1990–1999

*T*he road women traveled in the 20th century *was not without bumps and detours, but by the end of the century they could be found heading major corporations, winning international athletic events, commanding space shuttles and serving at the highest levels of government. In the 1990s, a decade of prosperity, women were the primary wage earners in nearly half of all American families, earned half of nearly all law degrees and made up nearly 40 percent of the students in graduate schools of business. Women owned 8.5 million businesses, generating $3.1 trillion in revenues and employing nearly 24 million people. Faith Popcorn, a futurist, declared an EVEolution with women assuming new positions of power in the economy and the marketplace. Popcorn, who coined the term "cocooning" to describe a society turning inward, saw the 1990s as "the '80s with a conscience." "People do volunteer work with a 'this-is-who-I-am attitude,'" she observed.*

> *[The League's role is] leadership that emphasizes not only how to get things done . . . but understands and knows how to navigate the often turbulent waters of race, power, and class and is not afraid to talk about them.*
>
> —Mary Babson
> Association President, 1992–94

Suzanne Plihcik of Greensboro, North Carolina, Association President 1990–1992, often borrowed a fable from child advocates to explain how the Junior League changed its approach to voluntarism over a century of commitment. The story went like this:

Village women were doing their laundry in the river when one woman shouted out, "There's a baby in the water!" They quickly pulled it out and revived it. But soon more babies came downstream, more than the women could save no matter how fast they worked or how they organized the rescue.

Suzanne Plihcik testifying on child care before the Senate Finance Committee cites League experiences to substantiate the Association's position, 1989.

One woman hurried away from the bank and the rest called after her to stop. They needed all the hands they could get. "Why are you deserting us? Help us save these babies!" they shouted. Looking over her shoulder, she replied, "I'm going upstream to find out who is throwing these babies in."

From its inception, the Leagues have been saving "babies," often literally—alleviating the symptoms of social woes. Like the women at the river, Leagues—individually and as an Association—began to realize that wasn't enough. By the 1990s, devastating community issues like domestic violence, teen pregnancy, alcoholism among women, child abuse,

homelessness, AIDS babies and drug addiction required going upstream to eliminate the source of the problems.

"We have looked at more comprehensive and effective approaches to doing the same things. It is imperative that we change with the world," Suzanne Plihcik told the Associated Press in 1990. "But our basic values and goals remain the same. Everything is aimed at community improvements."

A decade before the countdown to the millennium began, the Junior League realized that a new kind of leadership would be required in the League's second century of service. "Boldly Toward the Year 2000" came the call in the 1989–1990 annual report, with Maridel M. Moulton of Oakland-East Bay, the Association president, exhorting nearly 200,000 professionally trained volunteers to ready themselves for the challenges ahead.

"For nearly a century, the Junior League has been empowering women to respond with courage, compassion and commitment to the needs of their communities. Today, thousands of professionally trained volunteers on two continents blend their talents, expertise and leadership into a mosaic of effective action. The growing diversity within our membership promises us a richness of perspective to meet the challenges ahead . . . We are in systemic pursuit of what we will become. Now we must match our vision with decisive action," she said.

New Strategies

The 1990s would be rich with decisive action from individual Leagues and from the Leagues as an association. Writing in the *Junior League Review* in 1993, Jennifer Leonard, a consultant for nonprofits, described the League in military terms. "League women work their wonders by deploying themselves as volunteer battalions for good—developing trained womanpower and investing it along with fund-raising profits in innovative programs, based on planning that would put most businesses to shame. In fact, Junior League women are more skilled, more capable, more *strategic* than many a paid professional—one reason the business and charity worlds scout local Leagues for talent."

With the motto "Meeting Community Needs, Fostering Societal Changes," the Leagues throughout the 1990s intensified their efforts in child health, education, family violence and multiculturalism, seeking out collaborations with other groups and advocating changes in public policy. The League's public policy office, established in 1986 in Washington, D.C., hired a lobbyist to work for such reforms as mandated job leaves for new parents. By 1990, the Associated Press was writing about how the League tackled "tough issues." The League set out to break what Peter Goldmark, president of the Rockefeller Foundation, writing in *Junior League Review,* called the "social gridlock."

"You start to wonder how you can change the system," Sally Orr, a New York League member for nearly 35 years and former Director of AJLI's Department of Public Policy, told the Associated Press in 1990. "The Junior Leagues

realized they had to influence the regulatory and legislative process to get changes in their community."

Mary Babson of Chicago, Association President 1992–1994, described the League's role as "leadership that emphasizes not only how to get things done, but also how to bring conflicting interests together to ensure that things do get done . . . leadership that understands and knows how to navigate the often turbulent waters of race, power, and class and is not afraid to talk about them."

More Leagues involved themselves in lobbying and more League members shaped policy through their own political careers, getting their start through League training courses such as public speaking and leadership development. Between 1985 and 1993, the number of League members in elected or appointed office had more than tripled, from 80 to 252. The Phoenix League prides itself in being a crucible for training women in public service careers.

"We have influenced the city of Phoenix by way of the many trained leaders and public figures that have emerged from our League," the League reported. In addition to U.S. Supreme Court Justice Sandra Day O'Connor, League members in public office include Betsy Bayless, Arizona Secretary of State, and Jacque Steiner, U.S. Senator. In Canada, the Honorable Rosemary Bodry, a League member, became Manitoba's Minister of Justice and Attorney General. "I have the

> *We have looked at more comprehensive and effective approaches to doing the same things. It is imperative that we change with the world...But our basic values and goals remain the same.*
>
> —Suzanne Plihcik, 1990
> Association President

responsibility and power to help people. I see women becoming really important in shaping government policy," she said. "Take your dream seriously. If you want to be a policy maker, you must take a risk."

Political office, elected and appointed, has been a natural extension of Junior League volunteer work. "When I was growing up, the Junior League was involved in some of the most interesting projects in my community. The Junior League is an ideal training ground for anyone who is interested in public service," said Carolyn B. Maloney, a congresswoman from New York. "It provides valuable lessons in identifying problems. More importantly, you learn what it takes to move a project from an idea into a reality. Through my experience in the Junior League in New York, I learned that it's not enough to know that something should change. I learned that I have to take responsibility for ensuring that it changes."

> *Take your dream seriously. If you want to be a policy maker, you must take a risk.*
>
> —Honorable Rosemary Bodry, Minister of Justice and Attorney General, Manitoba

Health Care Initiatives

Like the founding members, League members in the 1990s didn't hesitate to take risks, often venturing where nobody else would go. Together, the Leagues launched two major initiatives—an international immunization campaign and an ambitious association-wide domestic violence awareness and prevention effort.

The Cleveland League challenged all the Leagues to work in concert to fight the very childhood diseases early Leagues had helped eradicate early in the century. Simple diseases like measles had returned on a rampage. In the United States, childhood diseases, many of them preventable, were killing almost 40,000 infants a year.

In 1991, the Junior League, veteran of 90 years in maternal and child health activities, set forth to guarantee that all children, youth and pregnant women would have access to preventive and primary health care. During National Volunteer Week that year, Don't Wait to Vaccinate, the first Association-wide public awareness campaign, was launched. Empowered by their collective strength, all 276 Leagues began a massive effort to improve child health. Billboards, posters, handouts, multilingual radio announcements and legislative advocacy were among the weapons the Leagues employed.

They wanted more children vaccinated—pulling babies out of the river. They also wanted to tear down barriers to immunization—going upstream to the source of the problem. The Leagues identified the barriers as lack of insurance, language or literacy problems, unavailability of clinics, cuts in public health care budgets, lack of funding for vaccines and parental unawareness of how childhood diseases kill, and they went to work to eliminate them.

Results were immediate. A media blitz brought headlines like "A Shot in the Arm" and "Junior Leagues push campaign for vaccinations." Each League researched

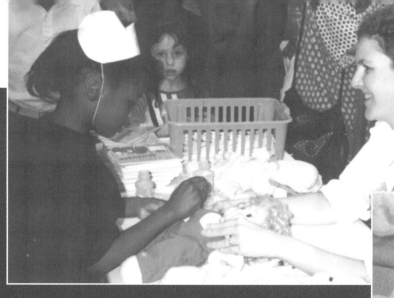

Kids learn about immunization at the Junior League of New Orleans Doll Clinic.

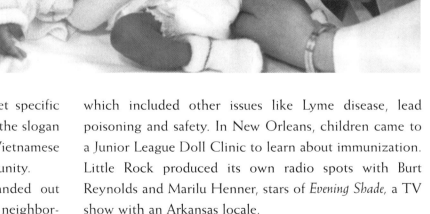

Baby being vaccinated as part of the Association-wide "Don't Wait to Vaccinate" campaign, 1991.

Courtesy of Ascherman Photographers

the issues in its community and then forged coalitions between other Leagues and local, county or state health agencies, tapping materials prepared by the Association or creating their own to meet specific populations. The Vancouver League translated the slogan not only into French but also into Punjabi, Vietnamese and Cantonese to reach everyone in the community.

In Jacksonville, Florida, the League handed out promotional balloons at a mall in a low-income neighborhood. More than 1,300 vaccinations resulted in a six-day period, over twice the number the previous month. In Orange County, New York, the League tallied "a 200 percent success: in creating a new children's Health Fair,

which included other issues like Lyme disease, lead poisoning and safety. In New Orleans, children came to a Junior League Doll Clinic to learn about immunization. Little Rock produced its own radio spots with Burt Reynolds and Marilu Henner, stars of *Evening Shade*, a TV show with an Arkansas locale.

St. Louis partnered in a five-year plan with the Missouri State Department of Health in which League volunteers would handle the department's health education program in the city. Before the first year was out, League

161

Many Marys

*L*ike Mary Harriman, many Junior League members have been leaders, visionaries and pioneers, making an impact on their communities and beyond through their volunteer contributions. Since 1991, the Association of Junior Leagues International has awarded the Mary Harriman Community Leadership Award to outstanding women who—like the Junior League founder—have made a lasting difference in their communities through their lifelong commitment to voluntarism. The Mary Harriman Community Leadership Award winners are:

Jane Krause Paine, 1991
Junior League of St. Louis

Roseann Knauer Bentley, 1992
Junior League of Springfield

Dorothy Weaver, 1993
Junior League of Miami

Jane E. Burdette, 1994
Junior League of Parkersburg

Helen Lowenfeld "Tilly" Chandler, 1995
Junior League of San Angelo

Jane Krause Paine (1991) of St. Louis was the force behind more than ten award-winning local and national programs improving the lives of children, particularly children at risk. In the early 1960s, she had initiated a Junior League–staffed preschool program at an all-black Y, a first for St. Louis and a model for Head Start. Her interest in parent/child education led to the development of the National Parents as Teachers Program. In the 1980s, as a Sustainer, she pulled together the St. Louis League's Teen Outreach Program (TOP), which became a national model for building self-esteem in at-risk adolescents.

I would have been a volunteer without the League. But frankly, I wouldn't have had the access I did or met wonderful volunteers all around the country.

Roseann Knauer Bentley (1992) of Springfield, Missouri, became an agent of change as a League volunteer when she chaired the committee that brought public television to her city only 16 months after contacting the Public Broadcasting System. She has served as president of the Missouri State Board of Education and the National Association of State Boards of Education and chaired the Children's Services Commission

as a state senator. *I believe in the Junior League tenet that joining forces makes a bigger difference. The League has helped me in the legislature with parliamentary procedure and bridging differences to be able to work with groups of divergent interests.*

Dorothy Weaver (1993) of Miami knew what to do after Hurricane Andrew leveled much of Dade County, Florida, in 1992. Daughter of Dee Dann Collins, a past president of the Dallas League, Dorothy was federal liaison for We Will Rebuild, a group of civic leaders organizing recovery. Overseeing $8 billion in federal hurricane aid and coordinating all federal, state, local, for-profit, and nonprofit government flood relief activities, she drew upon the Junior League model of *the organized, disciplined, trained volunteer . . . who will help lead the way, establish the model, set the standard, articulate the vision. When a community is stripped back to the basics, we find out who and how things get done . . . It was the volunteers who came thundering over the hill to the rescue.*

Jane E. Burdette (1994) of Parkersburg, West Virginia, the only League Active honored in the decade, is an advocate and model for the disabled. Confined by muscular dystrophy

to a wheelchair since age 13, she has been an outstanding volunteer since childhood, but she joined the Junior League when she was the 33-year-old executive director of the Parkersburg YWCA because of League commitment to community projects.

It was always involved in major projects— pages and pages of major projects. The League was known for taking on responsibility and following through. I wanted to tap into the League's training program. When the name "Junior League" is mentioned, people see strength.

Helen Lowenfeld "Tilly" Chandler (1995) of San Angelo, Texas, received her first Junior League award in 1958 as an El Paso Provisional. A League placement in an understaffed Child Welfare Office led her to write her first grant proposal for a special adoptions department, which placed over 30 children in the first 18 months of operation.

A fourth-generation Texan, she moved to San Angelo in the late 1970s and soon was known as "a one-woman gang" for her work in education, diversity, civic pride, art museums and historical celebrations. She co-chaired the town's centennial celebration in 1989 and developed tourism programs including a cowboy breakfast.

➤

Adele Hall (1996) of Kansas City was twice a Provisional—once in Lincoln, Nebraska, where her mother was a member and again after she moved to Kansas City.

Her hand can be seen in the Women's Public Service Network, a group of women in the Kansas City area who meet to exchange ideas, learn more about community issues and respond to needs. A longtime child advocate, she was instrumental in establishing Youth Friends, a pilot effort in six Kansas City school districts to connect caring adults with students K–12. Today 52 Kansas City school districts participate, and the

Adele Hall, 1996
Junior League of Kansas City

Pamela Yardley Paul, 1997
Junior League of Jacksonville

Sandra Day O'Connor, 1998
Junior League of Phoenix

Martha Rivers Ingram, 1999
Junior League of Nashville

Marjorie Hiatt, 2000
Junior League of Cincinnati

program has been introduced to six Michigan school districts.

The Junior League opened a great many doors. In the 1950s and 1960s, if you were a Junior League member, you knew you had a place at the table because League members had the reputation for being well trained and their word was good. If they said they'd be there, you could count on them to be there—and to stay.

Pamela Yardley Paul (1997) of Jacksonville found her volunteer future at a telephone answering service. *We established a hotline here, patterned after the one in New York. What crystallized was that all the calls involved children in some way.*

The hotline led her into a volunteer career, which mixed hands-on service and advocacy. In the early 1980s, as president of the Florida Center for Children & Youth, she transformed the "Tallahassee-focused" think tank into a statewide, membership-supported advocacy organization.

She also became the first woman to chair the United Way of Northeast Florida, overseeing a campaign in which 12,000 volunteers raised more than $14 million, setting a record as the highest increase in total contributions of any United Way in the nation.

Pamela Paul, who had Provisional Training in both New York and Jacksonville, said, *I give all the credit in the world to the Junior League for teaching me organizational skills.*

The Honorable Sandra Day O'Connor (1998) of Phoenix became the first woman to be appointed to the U.S. Supreme Court. Earlier as a state senator, she was the first woman in any state to serve as majority leader and the first woman appointed to the Arizona Court of Appeals.

As a state senator, she supported bilingual education and organized the repeal of "women's-work" law that prohibited women from being on the job more than eight hours a day. She worked to reform Arizona's marital property law, under which husbands managed and controlled assets.

Justice O'Connor, who served as president of the Phoenix League while assistant attorney general of her state, said, *One of America's most valued assets is its spirit of voluntarism, the spirit which is the heart of the Junior League.*

Martha Rivers Ingram (1999) of Nashville decided in the 1970s that her adopted city should become a regional cultural center and set out to lead the campaign, which began with federal bicentennial funds. By 2000, the Tennessee Performing Arts Center had an endowment of over $20 million, more than a million Tennessee children had experienced symphony music, drama and dance, and the Tennessee Symphony was playing at Carnegie Hall.

Her love of the performing arts began at Vassar College when she became a classical music DJ, assuming the pseudonym of Elizabeth Crawford and lowering her voice to conceal her youth. As a Provisional in Charleston, South Carolina, New Orleans and Nashville and as a Nashville Active, she learned the skills to share her love of music with an even greater audience.

League training also prepared her to head Ingram Industries, an $11 billion distribution conglomerate, when her husband died suddenly in 1995. Not long after, *Fortune* magazine called her one of the most powerful businesswomen in the country.

I never expected to find myself serving as Chairman and CEO of a major American corporation. You may never expect to run a business, to be head of a household, or to lead a non-profit board. Yet, effective Junior League training can prepare you for these experiences and many others.

Marjorie McCullough (Lunken Ittman) Hiatt (2000) of Cincinnati, saw beyond racial boundaries in the early 1950s, when the nation was still segregated, by serving on the board of her city's Urban League and cofounding the Urban League Guild. In more than half a century as a volunteer, she served as national president of the Junior League and the Girl Scouts, founding Cincinnati's children's theater and a preschool program for the deaf.

When Association president in 1961, she said, *We did not invent the voluntary approach to work that needs to be done, but the record shows that Junior League members have carried it forward.*

members had created a year-round traveling show, brochure and immunization card. "You got us started and now we can't stop," said Patrice Allen, who chaired the St. Louis initiative.

And in the Rose Garden, President George Bush, a Junior League husband and father-in-law, called the "Don't Wait to Vaccinate" campaign "a point of light."

Two years later, the Association shared what Leagues had learned in the campaign at a roundtable in Washington on "Improving Child Health: Enhancing the Effectiveness of Citizen Action and Collaborative Campaigns." From 30 to 40 participants had been anticipated; 64 came. No experts lectured, but representatives of 49 organizations sat at the table, sharing ideas and strategies in meeting the

A Junior League of Montclair-Newark volunteer consoles a victim of domestic violence, 1983.

Photo: Leslie Ellis Craw

international crisis in child health. Following the roundtable, the Association published a how-to manual, detailing how Leagues in collaboration with other agencies could create effective maternal and child health programs in their communities.

Throughout its history, the Junior League has marshaled its forces to fight epidemics, but in 1997 the Leagues voted to express a collective voice against domestic violence, an epidemic that claims the lives, livelihoods and welfare of women and children across borders. The following year, the Leagues approved a plan of action and set out to raise public awareness about the leading cause of injury to women in the United States and a major problem around the globe.

Domestic Violence Initiatives

Long before domestic violence became a national and international issue, the Junior League recognized that something had to be done to protect women and children. In the 1970s, individual Leagues began offering their services to help battered women. The Junior League of Bronxville was one of the first to initiate a project, working with the local probation department to develop a court assistance program for abused spouses. League volunteers provided information and support, including guidance through the family court system. When the League transferred the administration of the program to the social services department of a local medical center in 1981, mental health services were added to the program.

About that time, neighboring Northern Westchester League, after assessing the community needs, helped found a shelter for battered women and their children, which demonstrated that domestic violence could happen in the "best" of families. "I came here on my knees with my daughter and was watched over until I could get on my feet," wrote an executive's wife. By 1987, when the shelter became fully independent, the small League with only 97 members had helped nearly 1,500 people find safer, more productive lives. League volunteers continue to provide service and serve on the board.

The 1980s showed growing government awareness of just how big the problem was. Leagues, as individuals and as an Association, were called upon to testify before local, state and federal panels seeking solutions in the United States. In 1983, Maureen Hughes was among the Association directors who testified before U.S. Congressional Committees and the U.S. Attorney General's Task Force on Family Violence. She pointed up the role volunteers play in identifying the problem. "While the relationship between family violence and child abuse is not always clear within policies and programs, we believe the connection is visible to volunteers and paid employees who work on either problem in their communities," she said. Four years later, a League member from Columbia, South Carolina, testified before the Senate Committee on Labor and Human Services, urging—successfully—the reauthorization of the Family Violence Prevention and Services Act.

I came here on my knees with my daughter and was watched over until I could get on my feet.

—Victim of abuse

Canadian Leagues, too, identified the importance of the problem in their country. In 1987, the Calgary League, working with the YWCA and the Alberta Law Foundation, published "Law and the Abused Woman," a 32-page pamphlet League volunteers distributed throughout Alberta and other Canadian provinces.

During the 1990s, many Leagues joined the Silent Witness National Initiative, whose cochair was Jane Zeller of the St. Paul League. The Silent Witnesses, life-size silhouettes of 27 Minnesota women who died in 1990 as a result of domestic violence, were created by a grassroots group called Arts Action Against Domestic Violence in Minneapolis. Jane, advocacy chair of the St. Paul League, saw the figures and became an instant advocate, "mesmerized by the 'sound' of their silence." As codirector of the Silent Witness National Initiative, she organized marches, disseminated information, made presentations, enlisted corporate leaders to become involved. Leagues in the U.S., Canada and Great Britain spearheaded local campaigns. In Los Angeles, for example, the Junior League sponsored an extensive public awareness campaign, including an exhibit of 20 silhouettes near City Hall. On the steps of state capitols and the U.S. Capitol, the faceless cutouts made a silent plea for policy changes in a system that looked the other way at brutality in the home.

A 1993 Silent Witness exhibit on Capitol Hill raised awareness of domestic violence among senators and members of Congress and led to the addition of the Violence Against Women Act provisions to the 1994 Crime Bill. "What makes this so powerful around the country is that we're bringing the spirits of these women back to life," Jane Zeller said in 1997 as she organized a national march in Washington, D.C.

In many communities, Leagues spearheaded outstanding projects to help victims of domestic violence. Miami established Inn Transition, providing shelter up to two years and long-term support to help women reestablish their lives. In DeKalb County, Georgia, the League designed a program from crisis hotline to shelter to case management for battered refugee and immigrant women. In El Paso, the Junior League developed a bilingual multimedia campaign around the slogan "Break the Cycle That Breaks the Family." Cleveland, Phoenix, Kalamazoo and Lehigh Valley, Pennsylvania, also found ways to attack the cycle. In California, sixteen Leagues joined the California State Public Affairs Committee to introduce three domestic violence bills to the state legislature. A public awareness campaign sponsored by eight Alabama Leagues earned editorial praise in the *Montgomery Advertiser*: "That kind of cooperative attitude is critical in curbing domestic abuse, a societal problem of disturbingly great scale . . . The Junior Leagues deserve a salute—and support—for this project."

Silent Witness vigil led by Jane Zeller at the Minnesota State House, St. Paul.

Photo: Stormi Greener/*Minneapolis Star-Tribune*

By the end of the century, more than 100 Leagues were fighting the epidemic. Projects included direct support of safe houses and counseling services for women and children, sustained advocacy of progressive legislation on the statewide, national and international levels, and effective coalition-building across class, ethnic and institutional lines. At the 1999 Conference in St. Louis, Jan Langbein of the Dallas League and executive director of the Genesis Women's Shelter, called on the nearly 200,000 League members to make their voices heard on the domestic violence issue, not just for that year but for as long as it took in the century to come.

"Intimate partner abuse is at national epidemic proportions. It touches our lives, it touches the lives of every single one of us," she said. "It fills our emergency rooms, it fills our morgues, it keeps employees from going to work, it makes once happy children fearful and angry, it destroys homes and it destroys families. Truly we will not be able to prevent or eliminate this public epidemic, this public health problem, until three things happen. One is that public perception is changed, two is that community coordination is the norm and not the exception, and three is that individuals like you and me will do whatever we can wherever and whenever we can."

Civic Concerns

In the 1990s, even as the Junior League as an Association attacked broad issues like immunization and domestic violence, individual Leagues addressed a multitude of civic concerns. Parkersburg, West Virginia, established a halfway house for women with chemical dependency, but also worked towards establishing a discovery museum for children. The Memphis League established Hope House for juvenile victims of HIV/AIDS. The Junior League of Montclair/Newark began Orphans of AIDS, which

became a statewide project and a focus of the New Jersey State Public Affairs Committee (SPAC).

In Baton Rouge, the League launched a Juvenile Court project, the first major metro area with a high rate of urban crime to implement such a court. It also celebrated its 65th anniversary with a $100,000 gift to the local zoo to help create a Living Science Education Center.

In 1927, the Junior League of Houston made history by opening the first charity clinic for Houston's indigent children in the basement of a bank building. In March 2000, the League made history again when it gave the city a full-service mobile pediatric clinic as part of its 75th anniversary celebration. "The League wanted to do something that was forward-thinking and that would have as much impact on this community as the well-baby clinic did back in 1927," Dorothy Mathias Ables, 1998–1999 Houston League president, explained.

The Toledo League sponsored Toledo After Dark, a fund-raising lecture series which the *Toledo Blade* commended as "a nationally recognized powerhouse in attracting big-name speakers . . . that success has both tangible and intangible benefits to the Toledo area." Speakers have included former President George Bush, Gen. Norman Schwarzkopf and Queen Noor of Jordan. The Reading, Pennsylvania, League sponsored Town Hall Lectures. The Junior League of York, Pennsylvania, booked Gen. Colin

> *That kind of cooperative attitude is critical in curbing domestic abuse, a societal problem of disturbingly great scale . . . The Junior Leagues deserve a salute—and support—for this project.*
>
> —*Montgomery Advertiser*

169

Powell, Lady Margaret Thatcher, Walter Cronkite, former President George Bush and Katie Couric. The Pensacola League raised funds with lectures by nationally known figures in a "Lunch With The League" series.

Northwest Arkansas, one of the newest Leagues, went one-on-one with at-risk elementary school students with Fun Friends. The Peoria League, which had established the first maternity center in Illinois in 1938, worked with a sewing guild in the 1990s to create Keepsacks for Kids, sleeping bags that a local agency distributed to homeless children. The Junior League of Cedar Rapids teamed with the local YWCA to open the Madge Phillips Center, a comprehensive service center for homeless and near-homeless women and children. It was named for an outstanding community volunteer. When the Calgary League discovered that many female graduates of the local job training program couldn't afford clothing appropriate for job interviews, it established a "Suited for Success" program, providing outfits to more than 1,000 women, over 800 of whom found jobs.

In Austin, the League developed the Hispanic Mother-Daughter Program to encourage Hispanic girls to stay in school and seek higher education. Community Voice Mail, organized by the Junior League of Schenectady, New York, provided telephone voice mail to help

Mother and daughter gain practical experience and educational support in the Junior League of Austin's Hispanic Mother-Daughter model program, 1997.

Sue Stone Byrne, member of the Junior League of Seattle.

over to others after they were established makes it easy to forget that a community's hospital, women's shelter, museum, children's theatre, AIDS education program or a mobile health center exists because a League identified a need and initiated ways to meet it. No one has ever chronicled what League-trained women have accomplished as volunteers, professionals or public servants after they were no longer Active members. Memory is short but the reach is long, as Sue Stone Byrne, a Seattle Active, discovered when she attempted to tally just one League's community involvement by 1997. Her speech at the annual Dorothy Stimson Bullitt Community Service Award Luncheon that year is a case study of the legacy of Leagues everywhere.

The Junior League has a legacy of combining compassion with purpose and training to achieve profound results in our community. It is incredible what a difference trained volunteers—effectively mobilized into the community—can make. The League has been developing women who care into effective leaders—through excellent leadership training and hands-on volunteer experience in the community.

Since its inception in 1923, the Junior League of Seattle has recruited, developed and mobilized 5,000 women in Puget Sound. This League in its first year of existence opened the Eastlake Branch of the Seattle day nursery. That organization still exists and is thriving—known to us today as Childhaven.

The practice of initiating projects and turning them over to the community after their successful implementation and providing a resource of trained volunteers are among the League's many legacies.

homeless people find housing and employment. The London League established a playroom for homeless children. The Junior League of Winston-Salem dedicated all its resources to improving reading skills of area children and launched Read to Me, a program in which parents and caregivers were educated on the value of reading to children.

The Legacy of the Junior League

It's impossible to measure how much the Junior League Movement contributed in its first century. The League policy of turning projects

We are a training bed for volunteers and like the undercurrent in a river, this may be our least visible yet most powerful point.

—Sue Stone Byrne, 1997

Our League has 500 active members and today is run like a business by five management teams. We are in the business of developing and training women to successfully meet the challenge of pressing community needs. In the past five years, Junior League volunteers (in Seattle) have touched the lives of over 500,000 people through our direct service projects. In the last decade, the Seattle League contributed more than one million volunteer hours and provided over $1.5 million in funding for community projects.

League membership has changed with 70 percent of our members working outside the home. Age constraints have been removed and we encourage a diverse membership welcoming all women who are willing to work hard as a volunteer—willing to work hard to develop their leadership potential.

There is another legacy that is less visible in the community but perhaps even more important than the rest. Our members enter into a lifetime of service that extends well beyond their active time in the League. We are a training bed for volunteers and like the undercurrent in a river, this may be our least visible yet most powerful point.

While in the League, as Provisional, and then as Active members—these women are developed through formal classes and through hands-on experience with our JLS projects to become excellent fund raisers, project managers, promoters and organizers. In short, they are trained to become leaders. Long after their active time in the League has passed, these women will still be making impressive contributions in our community.

The League strives to build a strong foundation of expertise and a passion for lifelong voluntarism through its training. Our members typically continue to build on that foundation for the rest of their lives—making a huge impact on the organizations they touch and touching many organizations.

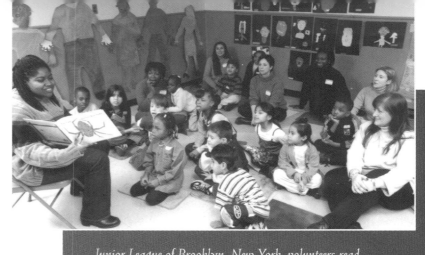

Junior League of Brooklyn, New York, volunteers read to children at Waverly Day Care Center.

Photo: Frank Moscati

I wanted to be able to stand up here and say how many non-profit groups in our area have a past or present League member on their board or working for them as a volunteer. Our committee started plowing through this year's Sustainer interest surveys. After looking at the paperwork for only the first 50 percent of that population, we had already identified nearly 500 organizations. We realized we were going about this wrong—we needed to start with all the organizations and make the list of the ones that DID NOT have one of ours involved.

Our members are out there in the community and will stay out there helping good, beautiful things to happen. This quiet powerful undercurrent of lifelong voluntarism is the true legacy—the one that makes a difference in the long run. The shelf life of the League effort is long. Many members come into their own fully mature and making their most dramatic contributions many, many years after their active time in the League.

The League is the best "school" for women who are serious about making a difference that I have ever seen. The League develops women to their top potential and those women in turn develop our community to be the best, kindest place that it can be.

172

The Junior League of Seattle developed CASA, the national court-appointed special advocate program for children who need caring adults to speak for them within the court system. Its members play prominent roles in local, state and national organizations. Pamela Eakes founded Mothers Against Violence in America (MAVIA). Colleen Willoughby, a former Seattle League President and Association board member, is cofounder of the Washington Women's Foundation, which helps women develop the confidence in financial giving by allowing them to be part of a major donor group. "For forty some years I have been a member of the Seattle Junior League. Each stage of experience has added to the next," she said.

> *This quiet powerful undercurrent of lifelong voluntarism is the true legacy....*
>
> —Sue Stone Byrne

"The founding of the Washington Women's Foundation is just a natural extension of previous experiences that maximize the potential of women to demonstrate effective leadership in our communities." The late Dorothy Stimson Bullitt founded King Broadcasting in 1946, pioneering children's, cultural and community affairs programming. Not long after giving the banquet speech, Sue Stone Byrne moved to Tennessee where she became a Knoxville Sustainer.

The Junior League had made its transition, achieving new strengths in leveraging "boldly, positively and productively" for social change. "Where a Woman Can Change the World" was adopted as the organization slogan in 1987–1988. As the 21st century opened, the slogan needed editing. In the course of a decade, the Junior League had demonstrated how many women working together could change the world even more.

As the 21st century begins, 296 Junior Leagues throughout the United States, Canada, Mexico and Great Britain had a collective membership of nearly 200,000 women of diverse national origins, religions and races. What held them together has been more than the training and support services provided by the Association of Junior Leagues International Inc., a not-for-profit organization headquartered in New York. The Junior League movement established by Mary Harriman remains true to its century-old vision of voluntarism: developing the potential of women and serving the communities in which they live.

Colleen Willoughby, Junior League of Seattle and founder of the Washington Women's Foundation.

Making an Impact on Communities

The AJLI/BMW Community Impact Award, established in 1987, honors Leagues and their community partners for creating innovative programs to address community needs. The award underscores the importance of collaboration in successful community programming. Those needs have included domestic violence, homelessness, teen pregnancy, substance abuse, literacy, juvenile crime, child care and family health. For a complete list of winners, see page 190.

Recipients have included some of the smallest Leagues like Northern Westchester, New York, which received the first BMW Award for its shelter for domestic violence victims, to the largest Leagues like Atlanta. Atlanta received a merit award for its Family Literacy Collaborative project in 1993 and another in 2000 for its Prejudice Awareness Summit. Several Leagues have been honored more than once:

■ Norfolk-Virginia Beach received the 1988 award for its Coalition for Adolescent Pregnancy (CAPP) program, which included a forum on teen pregnancy with Oprah Winfrey as guest speaker, a teen telephone information hotline and ongoing workshops to help parents learn how to communicate with 10- to 15-year-olds. In 1994, an ambitious public awareness campaign, Growing Up Great, which focused on child health from prenatal through early childhood, received a merit award.

■ Greensboro, North Carolina, received two merit awards, the first in 1989 for initiatives for day care for poor children, which they funded through a citywide recycling program, and the second in 1993 for its Greensboro Pharmacy project.

■ Oakland-East Bay in 1991 was the grand award recipient for its Chemical Addiction Recovery Effort (C.A.R.E.), a three-year program serving drug-exposed infants and also legislating for the rehabilitation of addicted mothers. Seven years later, the League received a merit award for its partnership with Battered Women's Alternatives, which led to relationship education curriculum for seventh graders and other programs helping youth to find non-violent ways to solve conflict.

■ Buffalo in 1992 received its first merit award for working with a local hospital to help encourage alcoholic mothers to seek and complete treatment. Its second came in 1995 for Learning, Empowerment and Families (LEAF), an initiative to help meet some of the critical needs of the educationally at risk. The project has become a model for international development (see Postscripts and Prologues).

■ Nashville received a merit award in 1992 for Recovery Residences of Nashville, Inc., a residential aftercare program for adolescent boys with chemical dependencies. The program began in 1983 after a League task force researched the needs and then joined with a group of treatment professionals who were developing an aftercare program. Two years later came the grand award for "Kare for Kids: A model for Systematic Change," which provided child care for homeless families while parents looked for jobs and raised public awareness. In 1998, it received another grand award for Renewal House, the longest running residential program in Tennessee where mothers receiving treatment for substance abuse can remain with their children.

■ Mexico City, which received a merit award in 1996 for the first substantive recycling and environmental project, was honored with the grand award in 2000 for an even more ambitious recycling program aiming to reduce the growth of garbage dumps that had begun to suffocate the city.

Inauguration of the Junior League of Mexico City's recycling program, 1993.

The Junior League of Mexico City

From the start, the Junior League of Mexico City was unlike any other. The language of the League was English, but the language of its city was Spanish and the volunteer tradition— apart from the church—was as foreign as the 14 American women who decided in 1927 to form a League. Wives of international businessmen, they began by sewing for the British and American Hospital but soon expanded their commitments to include a lending library to help support charity work at the Granja School for Newsboys and the Cuna Foundling Home. In 1930, their League won membership in the Association of Junior Leagues.

In 2000, with Mexican women making up nearly 70 percent of the Active membership, the Mexico City League proved that voluntarism knows no geographic or language borders when it received the BMW Community Impact Award. Partnering with supermarkets and the municipal government, the League organized a recycling campaign, collecting more than two tons of milk and juice cartons a month. The "Recyclable by Nature" project included an educational program targeting teachers and communities.

Throughout its 70-year history, the Junior League of Mexico has created community service projects impacting not only the Mexican capital but beyond the borders of the country. In those years, the League has grown into a predominantly Mexican organization with members from many nations.

"What do these cultural differences mean to our volunteer organization?" asked Reha Braniff in 1987 when she was president. "They mean adapting, learning and enjoying different customs . . . we broaden not only our own horizons but those of the community and the Junior League as well."

Like Mary Harriman and her contemporaries, the League decided in 1939 to survey the community to identify the greatest needs. Blind people, the women discovered, were all but ignored, and few Braille materials in Spanish existed anywhere in the world. Not a single book in Braille could be found for sale anywhere in Mexico.

They contacted the Asociation Ignacio Trigueros, a small group of blind men "whose desire for obtaining some adequate educational facilities for blind people in Mexico had been a struggle carried on over a period of years but with poor results," Dorothy Ellis, the League president reported in the early '40s. The volunteers went to work, first learning Braille themselves and then laboriously transcribing Spanish books into Braille. Eighteen League members learned to use Braille typewriters, freeing up an antiquated press to print textbooks for children in the country's one school for the blind.

"Over a two-year period our work with this private Mexican organization was so satisfactory that we became convinced that we must do something more for the underprivileged blind of Mexico," Mrs. Ellis wrote.

The women approached the Department of Public Welfare early in 1941, shortly after a new administration had closed the government's school for the blind because of terrible conditions. Nobody even knew how

➤

175

many blind people lived in Mexico. Most were illiterate and the few literate blind had "pitifully few advantages." The challenge was enormous.

The League decided to establish a library with talking books as well as books in Braille. The following year, on a budget of $420, the League's library opened in the reorganized National School for the Blind. On the shelves were a few books purchased from Argentina, 50 books from the Asociation Ignacio Trigueros and the few books League members had transcribed. At first, only children at the school could use the books, but soon the word spread and others started coming. The library, staffed by League volunteers, became a sort of community center for the blind, with not only books but games like chess and dominos.

League volunteers introduced English and French classes and read textbooks to blind high school students in public schools. One boy who had been tutored in English won a scholarship to study at the Institute for the Blind in New York and returned with the first seeing-eye dog in Mexico. The League began hiring blind Mexicans to transcribe books as read aloud by a sighted person.

The Mexican government supplied more and more space for the activities, but the ancient press needed replacing. The

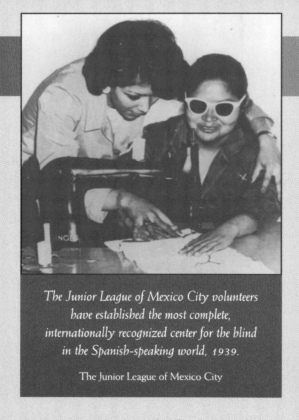

The Junior League of Mexico City volunteers have established the most complete, internationally recognized center for the blind in the Spanish-speaking world, 1939.

The Junior League of Mexico City

women went looking for funding, enlisting Mrs. Ellis' husband Allen to contact sources when on a business trip to the States. As an expression of the Good Neighbor Policy, the Office of the Coordinator of Inter-American Affairs contributed $1,000 in 1943 to equip a Braille Print Shop, the Centro Editorial Braille, the first of its kind in Latin America.

The new printing facilities allowed the League to supply books for general readership and also texts for Mexican schools for the blind, six more having opened after the press made books available. Soon schools and

individuals in Spain, Cuba, Argentina, Peru, Colombia, Puerto Rico, Honduras, Panama, Guatemala and the United States were asking to buy books. After receiving a list of books available, a little girl in Spain wrote back saying she had written every country where she thought she might find books in Braille, but only Mexico had replied. Could the Print Shop please send her all the books available so she could learn something about the world?

The project grew with a visit from Helen Keller and grants from the Kellogg Foundation and the American Foundation for Overseas Blind. Professionals took over the direction of the Print Shop while League volunteers concentrated on the library and workshops for the blind. The League expanded services to include job placement, swimming lessons and excursions. By the end of the 1950s, the League was laying plans to turn the program over to a community board, Comite International Pro-Ciegos, to consolidate all private welfare work for the blind. By 1962, the League had completed the turnover of the project—the most complete center in the Spanish-speaking world.

The League opened the world to the blind people of Mexico, but it also worked in child health, traffic safety, child abuse, nutrition, learning disabilities, women's health.

Hellen Keller visiting the Mexico City Junior League, 1954.

Among its most ambitious projects was the Centro de Recuperacion Para Ninos Convalescientes de Fiebre Reumatica, a model pilot project that grew into the first center in Latin America for preventing and treating rheumatic fever, which was attacking at least ten out of every 1,000 school-age children in Mexico City. By the early 1970s, the annual budget was nearly $50,000, with all funding coming from the League. In 1974, the League turned its energies to prevention, supplying volunteers to take throat cultures, and ended its involvement by producing a film on the disease, which was shown in movie theaters around the country.

In the late 1980s, the Mexican League created and implemented an alcohol and drug awareness project, funded by the Ford Motor Company in Mexico. It also offered Mexico City's first AIDS information forum, with a follow-up education program in health clinics for low-income families and in public middle and high schools.

In many of its projects, the Mexican League tapped the successes of other Leagues, translating materials into Spanish. "We've found we need to make few changes," Mrs. Braniff reported in the 1980s. "It's amazing how something that works in New York or Chattanooga will also work in Mexico."

Leagues Founded 1990–2001

Douglas County, Georgia
North Harris County, Texas
Gwinnett & North Fulton Counties, Georgia
Greater Winter Haven, Florida
Anniston-Calhoun, Alabama
Anderson County, South Carolina
Eau Claire, Wisconsin
Olympia, Washington
Madison, Wisconsin
Gainesville-Hall County, Georgia

Ottawa, Ontario*
Indian River, Florida
Greater DuKane, Illinois
Jackson County, Oregon
Las Cruces, New Mexico
Palm Springs Desert Communities, California
Napa-Sonoma, California
Murfreesboro, Tennessee
Lufkin, Texas

Flint Hills, Kansas
Lee County, Alabama
Moore County, North Carolina
Greater Covington, Louisiana
Northwest Arkansas, Arkansas
Martin County, Florida

(*League that disbanded in the 1990s)

Postscripts and Prologues

Clotilde Perez-Bode Dedecker, 1998–2000
AJLI President and Cochair of the
International Year of the Volunteer (IYV),
and Kofi Annan, UN Secretary-General,
at the opening reception in New York,
January 2001.

Swing open the door to your future as you celebrate, Clotilde Perez-Bode Dedecker as Association President told Junior League members preparing for their centennial anniversary. "Embrace all the opportunities that change brings. Remember the League is all about change—changing communities for the better and changing women for the better," said the Cuban immigrant who became the first Hispanic woman to lead the Association of Junior Leagues when she was elected in 1998. Clotilde's story tells just how much the League itself has changed.

Clotilde's family came to the United States in search of a better life in 1967. Clotilde was a third grader clutching a doll, the only toy she was allowed to bring from Havana. Although her father had been a dentist and her grandfather a prominent surgeon in Cuba, the family had volunteers to thank for clothing, public housing and emotional support in the two years her father studied to revalidate his degree. From those roots grew Clotilde's commitment to voluntarism. She joined the Buffalo Junior League in 1983 and by 1993, when that League celebrated its 75th anniversary, was president.

> We've made it to the ripe old age of one hundred by balancing tradition and change. . . . We will remain vital and relevant because we will always try to find new ways to serve and new solutions to the challenges facing our communities.
>
> —Deborah Brittain
> AJLI President, 2000–2002

*Deborah Brittain,
AJLI President,
2000–2002.*

Photo: Columbus
Lee

a 49-year-old single professional woman, was elected League president; Dr. Brenda Armstrong, a Duke Medical School faculty member, headed the local chapter of The Links. Before their terms were out, they were initiating ways their groups could work together to serve their community even more.

Today's League member can be a college student, a retiree, a professional woman or a stay-at-home mom— or even a debutante. Membership in the 21st century is a mix that cuts across demographics like age, job status, ethnicity and religion and reflects the profile of the women in the individual community. For example, the *Dallas Morning News* in 1999 headlined "A quiet revolution: Junior League, no longer a domain of Dallaselite (sic), welcomes working women" in a report on "the new face" of the Dallas League, which is one of the Association's largest Leagues with membership around 5,000.

Deborah C. Brittain, a Greater Princeton, New Jersey, Sustainer who followed Clotilde as Association president, illustrates yet another change. She holds a master's degree from the Simmons School of Social Work and has been a leader in the Junior League and The Links, Inc., an international African American women's service organization founded in 1946. The first African American elected Association President, Deborah laid the groundwork for historic collaborations between the Urban League and Junior League when she served as president of the Junior League of Northern Virginia in 1991–1993.

In Durham, in the year 2000, two African Americans, undergraduate roommates at Duke University nearly 30 years ago, made their own history. Alice Sharpe,

International Role

The Junior League has also swung open the door to the world. From its earliest days, the Junior League has been a model for women's service organizations in other countries. It became an international organization in fact, though not in name, when the Montreal League formed in 1912. The growth of the Canadian Leagues, the addition of Mexico in 1930 and London in 1985 demonstrated that the model could be exported. In 1989, at Annual Conference, the Junior Leagues voted to officially add "international" to the Association's name.

The League's international role grew steadily in the 1990s. The Buffalo League took its grassroots LEAF

(Learning, Empowerment and Families) initiative to Vienna in 1994 and to Beijing in 1995, becoming the first League to present at a United Nations conference on women. The project was set up to break the intergenerational cycle of illiteracy plaguing families in Buffalo but offered strategies other countries could modify, using their own resources.

"We wanted governments and countries worldwide to recognize women's voluntary organizations, specifically the Association of Junior Leagues International, as catalysts for change in the community," Beth Simons, then president-elect of the Buffalo League, explained.

Junior League representatives from Canada, England, Mexico and the United States shared their experiences in 1998 when the World Volunteer Conference of the International Association for Volunteer Efforts met in Edmonton. At the same conference, the Canadian Federation of Junior Leagues trained volunteers to be advocates for change. The League was already mobilizing to tackle issues of worldwide concern and extend the unifying force of voluntarism beyond national boundaries.

By coincidence, the Junior League centennial coincided with the UN's International Year of the Volunteer 2001, but it was no coincidence that the Junior League, represented by Clotilde Dedecker, was chosen to cochair the U.S. Committee. Under the leadership of the League and The Points of Light Foundation, the committee set out to celebrate and advocate volunteerism, engaging more volunteers in alleviating social problems and strengthening society.

Alice Sharpe and Brenda Armstrong, Junior League of Durham and Orange Counties, North Carolina.

Clotilde Perez-Bode Dedecker, AJLI President, 1998–2000.

The Junior League of Buffalo presents their literacy project at the NGO Forum on Women, Beijing, China, 1995.

Junior League of Houston volunteers work with Habitat for Humanity to provide housing for the poor.

Photo: King Wong

The Face of the League

Each of the 296 Leagues—like League cookbooks—continues to have a local flavor, but collectively they also have an image. Over the century, newspapers and magazines have regularly reported on the changing look of the Junior League, often using cliches involving white gloves and pearls. Anecdotal information charted a change from debutante to sorority girl to affluent young matron to women espousing a variety of lifestyles, but at the end of the 1990s, the Junior League commissioned a more scholarly examination. Roper Starch Worldwide conducted a survey of membership that resulted in a portrait much different in many ways from League members who had gone before.

The founding members had been little more than schoolgirls, often still in their teens. A hundred years later, 75 percent were 35 with an average age of 47. The average age of new members was 31. Some Leagues had done away with age requirements altogether and had a few Provisional members in their seventies and eighties. Rules mandating that women become Sustainers automatically at age 40 had all but disappeared. Now instead of a sea of bouffant hairdos on young matrons of the 1950s, gatherings of presidents and presidents-elect had become sprinkled with graying heads of women of 50. College degrees had become the norm, with 88 percent having at least a bachelor's. League members could be found in every sector of public life: doctors, lawyers, accountants, elected officials, nonprofit administrators, teachers, aerospace engineers, investment counselors, journalists and psychologists. The vast majority reported being employed, most of them full time. Fully

Three Junior League Presidents in the Equen family: Mom Anne Equen and her two daughters, Anne Equen Ballard and Carol Equen Miller.

The Junior League of Atlanta

Three generations of League volunteers: Diana Duncan Hepting (left), New York and Columbia, South Carolina, Leagues; Anne Hepting Flegenheimer (center), President of Saginaw Valley, Michigan, League; and Mildred Hooker Duncan (right), New York League, 1994.

two-thirds said the skills developed as League members had been useful to them outside the League.

Nearly half of the membership—46 percent—was identified as "Roper Influentials," a term Roper Starch has used since the early 1940s for people who influence the lives of others in their communities. The qualities that make Influentials stand out in their communities—their passion, knowledge, experience, self-confidence and hunger for information—typify Junior League members. The study also determined that women join the Junior League today for the same reasons they did a century ago: 1) they want to make a positive impact on their community; 2) they gain personal satisfaction from volunteering;

3) they value the friendships they develop with other women through their service.

Business Savvy

The Junior League remains vibrant and relevant even as other service organizations have withered and even died. In writing about the Dallas League in 1996, *The Dallas Morning News* observed that the Junior League had become

183

"a more business-savvy group," asking tough questions about projects and "strengthening a tradition of women who use their heads along with their hearts and hands."

Junior League training today prepares members to run the Leagues like small corporations as well as to serve in the community. Traditional Junior League fund-raisers like tearooms have matured into centers like the St. Louis League's dining room and banquet facilities, which the *St. Louis Business Journal* ranked as the third-largest luncheon club in the city. When it celebrated its 75th anniversary in 1999, the Junior League of Columbia, South Carolina, made the cover of the *Greater Columbia Business Monthly*, which cited the League for its good business practices. "A big part of making sure the organization is prepared for the future is building a strong financial foundation," the writer noted.

Many Leagues have established endowments to support projects no matter what the economic climate. In Baton Rouge, the League launched a campaign to create an endowment covering League operating expenses in order to continue "producing a good product" of women trained in community leadership and to keep dues from being a barrier to membership, according to Emily Distefano, League president in 1999–2000.

But the answer to why the Junior League has survived and thrived over the century goes beyond personal satisfaction and good business practices. "We provide and train

When we send volunteers out into the community, they are ready to hit the ground running. After several years with the Junior League, these women are well prepared to serve on the boards of charitable organizations.

—Ellen Rose, President
New York Junior League, 2001

women volunteers for the community. Period. End of story," says Emily Distefano. "The overriding thing over time is that we provide volunteer leaders for the community."

Training for Leadership

There's no better place to assess the future of the Junior League in the 21st century than in the Junior League of New York City, where the movement began more than a century ago. Mary Harriman's bold vision is stronger than ever in the League. Membership in the year 2000 had grown to more than 2,500, with 85 percent holding full-time jobs, but members still volunteered an average of two hours a week in the community. Collectively the women contribute over 100,000 hours of direct community service to the city each year, with volunteers staffing nearly 30 League-run projects in four areas of community need: Domestic Violence, Healthy Foundations, Family Life Skills and Cultural Enrichment for Youth.

The emphasis since the League's beginning has been on the well-being of women and children. For over 100 years, the League has called upon the skills of its members for planning, fund-raising, recruitment, training and collaboration with community-based organizations and government agencies to make life better for the city's children. From its earliest days, the League has always worked to expand playgrounds. A

Central Park playground honors Mary Harriman Rumsey's contribution early in the 20th century. In the 21st century, the League partners with New York City Parks and Recreation and the City Parks Foundation to renovate one school playground every year, with League members spending five spring weekends installing new equipment, painting murals on exterior walls, replanting gardens, creating surface games in play areas.

Continuing in the tradition of those first volunteers who worked with mothers and babies in the Settlements, League members provide support and education to homeless pregnant teenagers and to pioneering pregnancy prevention programs. A League "warmline" reaches out to new, at-risk parents to answer parenting questions and to identify concerns. Volunteers work with residents of transitional housing to educate them on alcohol awareness and nutrition.

RIGHT: *The positive development of adolescent girls is the focus of the Junior League of Boston's "Leader Within" program.*

The Junior League of Boston

The New York Junior League paints a mural in a city playground as part of their Playground Improvement Project, 1994–95.

The Junior League of the City of New York Archives

185

The Junior League of Fayetteville, North Carolina, promotes National Volunteer Week, with supermarket fund-raiser, Working Together.

The New York Junior League Health Education Center housed in a new Settlement Health Primary Care Clinic in East Harlem delivers health education programs on nutrition, AIDS prevention, asthma, diabetes, infant care, and smoking cessation. Volunteers staff the center, which includes the latest in on-line information that clients can access directly.

At the turn of the last century, the young women like Eleanor Roosevelt taught dance, music and art at the Settlement Houses. Today League volunteers teach in a variety of arts projects, including hands-on instruction for at-risk youth at contemporary "Settlement Houses" and work with hospitalized children.

When the League was founded, members worked to improve deplorable living conditions in the Lower East Side where more than nine million immigrants crowded into a neighborhood that was perhaps the most densely populated area in the world. In recent years, the New York Junior League has stepped in to provide housing for homeless families in the city. In 1985, the League partnered with the Children's Aid Society to buy and renovate three abandoned buildings in northern Manhattan to provide transitional housing and support for more than 30 homeless families at a time. League members supply training to help families gain control over their own lives and find permanent housing. Over 600 families were helped in the project's first decade.

Trained League volunteers can be found at every level of volunteer work throughout the city, getting their hands dirty, pushing for legislation, serving on nonprofit boards. "Training volunteers to be effective is one of the things we do best," said Ellen Rose, president of the New York League in 2000–2001. "When we send volunteers out into the community, they are ready to hit the ground running. After several years with the Junior League, these women are well prepared to serve on the boards of charitable organizations."

One of the most successful League projects of recent years is its Not-for-Profit Boards training course, which prepares both women and men for board service and has matched interested candidates with organizations seeking board members since 1994.

The New York League continues to reach out in many new directions, but it also honors the past, pointed

The Junior League of Raleigh's "Safe Child" program.

The Junior League of Raleigh, North Carolina

The Junior League of Philadelphia's "Learning Lunches" and "Dynamite Dinners" projects.

The Junior League of Philadelphia

out Ellen Rose, who happens to be the daughter and grand-daughter of League members elsewhere.

"The New York Junior League was founded by women with brave hearts and bold vision who cared enough to try to make a difference," she said. "Their spirit lives on in an exceptional organization which combines heartfelt compassion with the practical training to make a positive, meaningful impact on people's lives. The League volunteers carry on this legacy every day through our efforts to tackle the City's toughest problems."

That legacy guides Ellen Rose every day. "Whenever I have a problem to solve," she said, "I always ask myself, 'What would Mary Harriman do?'"

Mary Harriman, early 1900s.

187

Acknowledgements

*I*n the course of researching and writing this book, I have spoken with countless thoughtful, distinguished and dedicated people in hundreds of communities around the world. I cannot possibly thank by name everyone who deserves to be thanked and express my appreciation to all who took the time to talk with me and proudly share their stories, photos and memorabilia.

I am particularly indebted to all of the book's readers, especially Suzanne Plihcik, Association President 1990–1992, Anne Dalton, Director of Governance for the Association of Junior Leagues International and Julia Siebel, Ph.D. They read multiple drafts of the book and provided critical commentary while under tight deadlines of their own. Their insights and remarkable understanding of the organization's history and strategic issues were critical to the book before us now.

Finally, I must express my heartfelt thanks to everyone at the Association of Junior Leagues International, especially Jane Silverman, Executive Director, and Cheryl Bundy, Director of Centennial Planning, whose faith in the book and vision for the Centennial Celebration helped keep the book on track. The book would not have been possible without the impeccable archival resources, fact-checking and editing by Diane Moran, the energy and resourcefulness of Evelyn Twitchell, and the steadfastness of Melanie Monroe, Anabel Schnitzer and Rachel Kelstein.

Finally, my profound appreciation to the hundreds of thousands of Junior League volunteers who have given their hearts, hands and minds to help improve our communities over the past century. I admire your commitment and I am honored to write of your accomplishments.

Nancy Beth Jackson
New York City
August 2001

The best way to understand the Junior League is to talk to its members. This study includes interviews in person, by telephone and by e-mail with members of many Leagues. An even richer source is the *Junior League Magazine* (also published as the *Junior League Bulletin* and *Junior League Review*). In it, the voices of members over the century can still be heard. The magazine is archived at the Association of Junior Leagues International. The Association and individual Leagues also have preserved documents relating to specific League activities.

Consumer magazines, particularly *Town and Country*, and local newspapers also have reported on the Junior League. Specific articles are mentioned in the text. The Internet offers not only the Association's website <www.ajli.org> but also women's and general history sources. Here are some books that were especially useful in this centennial history of the Junior League.

Abramson, Rudy. *Spanning the Century: The Life of W. Averell Harriman*. New York: William Morrow and Company, 1992.

Banner, Lois W. *Women in Modern America: A Brief History*. New York: Harcourt Brace Jovanovich, Inc., 1974.

Beer, Thomas. *The Mauve Decade*. New York: Vintage Books, 1960 (originally published by Alfred A. Knopf, Inc. in 1926).

Cook, Blanche Wiesen. *Eleanor Roosevelt* (Vol. I: 1884–1933). New York: Penguin Books, 1992.

Evans, Sara M. *Born for Liberty*. New York: Free Press Paperbacks, 1997.

Fisher, Ellen Kingman. *Junior League of Denver, 1918-1993*. Denver: Colorado Historical Society, 1993.

Gordon, Janet and Diana Reische. *The Volunteer Powerhouse*. New York: The Rutledge Press, 1982.

Klein, Maury. *The Life & Legend of E. H. Harriman*. Chapel Hill: The University of North Carolina Press, 2000.

Lash, Joseph P. *Eleanor and Franklin*. New York: Konecky & Konecky, 1971.

Simbeck, Rob. *Daughter of the Air: The Brief Soaring Life of Cornelia Fort*. New York: Atlantic Monthly Press, 1999.

AJLI/BMW Community Impact Awards

Since 1987, the AJLI/BMW Community Impact Award has honored the best in collaborative, community programs created by Junior Leagues and their community partners. The programming has implemented changes and improved conditions in almost every sector of society, including the areas of child abuse and neglect, domestic violence, pregnancy prevention, senior care, substance abuse prevention, literacy, multicultural awareness, HIV/AIDS education and historic preservation. In the first two years only one program was recognized. Merit awards were added in 1989.

1987   Award to Northern Westchester, NY for Northern Westchester Shelter for Domestic Violence

1988   Award to Norfolk-Virginia Beach, VA for CAPP (Coalition for Adolescent Pregnancy), in partnership with church and agency representatives

1989   Grand Award to Binghamton, NY for Children's Shelter for Abused, Abandoned and Neglected Children, in partnership with Broome County's Department of Social Services and the Children's Home of the Wyoming Conference

Merit Awards to
    Greensboro, NC for Initiatives for Day Care for Poor Children
    Milwaukee, WI for Foster Care Citizen Review Board
    St. Louis, MO for Emergency Shelter for Homeless Families
    South Brevard, FL for the Haven for Children

1990   Grand Award to Oranges and Short Hills, NJ for Isaiah House for Homeless Families, in collaboration with the United Way of Essex and West Hudson

Merit Awards to
    Detroit, MI for Children and Youth Initiative
    Jackson, MS for Center for Family Education
    Lehigh Valley, PA for Turning Point II
    Miami, FL for Inn Transition
    Springfield, MO for Teen Parent Program

1991   Grand Award to Oakland East Bay, CA for Chemical Addiction Recovery Effort (CARE) for drug exposed infants.

Merit Awards to
    Orange County, CA for Child Abuse Service Team (CAST)
    Seattle, WA for Child Haven Crisis Nursery
    Baltimore, MD for Side by Side: A Day Care Coalition for Children
    Tuscaloosa, AL for First Gafford Neonatal Intervention Program
    Fort Collins, CO for The Children's Clinic

1992   Grand Award to San Francisco, CA for Hope House, a halfway house for women released from prison, in partnership with the Sheriff and San Mateo County Alcohol & Drug Dept. and Adult Probation Dept.

Merit Awards to
    Nashville, TN for Recovery Residences of Nashville, Inc.
    Omaha, NB for WELLSPRING Collaboration
    Daytona Beach, FL for Project WARM
    McAllen, TX for Palmer Drug Abuse Program
    Buffalo, NY for CoCare (child respite at alcoholism clinic)

1993 Grand Award to Greenville, SC for Partnership for Families, a family support program to empower families living in an at-risk neighborhood of Greenville to become self-sufficient

Merit Awards to
Albuquerque, NM for Family Focus Center at Zia Elementary School
Atlanta, GA for Family Literacy Collaborative
Birmingham, MI for Pontiac Area Transitional Housing
Greensboro, NC for the Junior League of Greensboro Pharmacy
Los Angeles, CA for Adolescent Pregnancy Prevention Education

1994 Grand Award to Nashville, TN for Kare for Kids: providing child care for homeless families as well as training and advocacy to achieve a model for systemic change, in partnership with the Salvation Army

Merit Awards to
Hartford, CT for Friends of the Family
Norfolk-Virginia Beach, VA for Growing Up Great
Phoenix, AZ for YWCA Transitional Housing Program
San Jose, CA for George Travis Center
Spokane, WA for Senior to Senior Peer Counseling Program

1995 Grand Award to Roanoke Valley, VA for Project H.O.P.E. (Hurt Park Organization for Prevention and Education), a program to provide support and self-sufficiency for the residents of Hurt Park, a city-owned housing community of at-risk families

Merit Awards to
Buffalo, NY for Learning Empowerment and Families (LEAF) Program
Parkersburg, WV for the Halfway House Project
Durham & Orange Cos., NC for Middle School After-School Initiative
Kalamazoo, MI for HealthConnect
Waco, TX for McLennan County Youth Collaboration

1996 Grand Award to Chattanooga, TN for the Westside Community Development Program, a multi-dimensional initiative that includes economic, educational, health and social development

Merit Awards to
Albuquerque, NM for Family Focus Center at Zia Elementary
El Paso, TX for Midnight Basketball
Mexico City for Recyclable by Nature
Portland, ME for the Beacon Teen Center
Richmond, VA for Family Resource Program

1997 Grand Award to Cedar Rapids, IA for Madge Phillips Community Center, a comprehensive 24-hour emergency shelter for women and children, in collaboration with the YWCA of Cedar Rapids

Merit Awards to
Austin, TX for Hispanic Mother-Daughter Program
Kalamazoo, MI for Family Violence/Abuse Project
Memphis, TN for Hope House Day Care Center
San Jose, CA for Legal Advocacy Program
Schenectady, NY for Community Voice Mail

1998 Grand Award to Nashville, TN for Renewal House, a residential treatment facility where mothers can remain with their children for treatment for substance addiction

Merit Awards to
Arlington, TX for Dental Health for Arlington
Boca Raton, FL for In the Pines, Inc. Migrant Farmworker Community
Columbia, SC for Smart Matters
Little Rock, AK for Potluck, Inc.
Monmouth County, NJ for Hand-In-Hand Infant Toddler Center

➤

AJLI Awards & Tributes

1999 Grand Award to Riverside, CA for Challenges of Youth: Adolescent Pregnancy Prevention and Parenting

Merit Awards to
    DeKalb County, GA for International Women's House
    Lancaster, PA for the Crisis Nursery Project
    New Orleans, LA for Teen Court
    Oakland-East Bay, CA for Battered Women's Alternatives
    Pasadena, CA for James Madison Center

2000 Grand Award to Mexico City for Recyclable by Nature, a milk and juice carton recycling program

Merit Awards to
    Atlanta, GA for the Atlanta Prejudice Awareness Summit
    Charlotte, NC for Connecting Links
    The Oranges and Short Hills, NJ for the Pink Ribbon Program
    Portland, ME for the Kids First Center
    Sacramento, CA for the Sacramento Crisis Nursery

Since the 1950s, the Association of Junior Leagues International has received honors on behalf of Junior Leagues, including:

U.S. President's Volunteer Action Award, presented at the White House in 1989 for outstanding volunteer achievement in mobilizing volunteers

The Association for Women in Communications: 2000 Clarion Award for excellence in communications for *Safe Homes Safe Communities, The AJLI Resource Guide for Ending Domestic Violence*

National Association of Hospital Hospitality Houses Inc.: for the continued endorsement, involvement, volunteerism and financial support of hospital hospitality houses

American Society of Association Executives (ASAE): for Excellence in Communications materials for the Association's Annual Conference

American Legion Auxiliary: for strengthening and reshaping our communities into safer, more positive places to live through the active promotion of voluntarism and community involvement

Christmas In April, Proclamation: for the Junior Leagues' role in launching home rehabilitation programs, providing outstanding, trained and dedicated leadership, financial support and a primary volunteer force in rehabilitating homes for low-income homeowners

Magazine Week: for publishing excellence in civic magazines

Society for National Association Publications (SNAP): for publishing excellence in newsletters

National Trust for Historic Preservation's Crowninshield Award: for years of dedication to the preservation of historic sites of local, state and national significance

American Society of Interior Designers, Thomas Jefferson Award: for outstanding Junior League contributions to the preservation of American culture, intellectual development and national heritage

Shelter Aid Award: in recognition of significant contributions to helping women and children affected by domestic violence

Association for Volunteer Administration (AVA),
National Service Award: for exceptional
leadership in the field of volunteer
administration

National Foundation for Alcoholism, Markie
awards: five awards for excellence in
communications about women and alcohol

*The National Council on the Aging Inc., VIAA
(Voluntarism in Action for the Aging)*
Certificate of Appreciation: for
significant contributions on behalf
of older Americans

*The National Committee for Prevention of Child
Abuse*, Mary Ellen Citation Award:
in appreciation for outstanding
contributions to the field of Child
Abuse Prevention

*Court Appointed Special Advocate Association
(CASA)*: Outstanding Service Award

Alexander Graham Bell Association For The Deaf:
for the exceptional efforts of thousands
of volunteers in Junior Leagues for
pioneering, funding and maintaining
outstanding speech and hearing centers

American Association of Career Education Coordinators,
Certificate of Appreciation: in recognition
for national leadership in and outstanding
contributions to the promotion and
advancement of career education

The Association for the Care of Children's Health:
for outstanding service to children in
health care settings

American Academy of Pediatrics, Distinguished
Public Information Service Award: for
the five-year national program promoting
community awareness, advocacy and
action on behalf of the special needs of
infants, children and adolescents

Tribute of Appreciation, U.S. Department of
State: for support of the first World
Conference for Women in 1975, and for
U.S. contribution in 1978 to the United
Nations Voluntary Fund for the Decade
for Women (1976–1985)

National Recreation and Park Association,
National Volunteer Service Award: in
recognition of dedicated volunteer service

*National Citizens Committee for Educational
Television*, Citation: for pioneering vision
and outstanding public service in helping
to bring to the American community the
advantage of educational television

National Foundation for Infantile Paralysis, March
of Dimes Service Award: for educational
interpretation of the polio program,
encouragement of the use of the vaccine
and humanitarianism concern for the
rehabilitation of the handicapped

National Legal Aid and Defender Association, Public
Service Citation: for volunteer contribution
of time and talent in the financing,
establishment and operation of Legal
Aid Societies in many communities

National School Volunteer Program Inc.,
Recognition Award: for significant
contributions to school volunteer program

Girls Scouts of the United States of America,
on its Golden Anniversary: gratefully
acknowledged the Junior Leagues for
their cooperation and support

American Educational Theater Association,
Children's Theater Conference, the
Monte Meacham Award: for continued
support of the best in children's theater

American Symphony Orchestra League: for many valued
services on behalf of music and the arts

The American National Red Cross, on the
occasion of its 75th Anniversary: in
appreciation for the Junior Leagues'
devoted support and participation in the
humanitarian work of The Red Cross

Boys' Clubs of America, Golden Anniversary
Award: in appreciation for the
outstanding support and cooperation
given to member Boys' Clubs of America

Abilene, TX	1956	Brooklyn, NY	1910	Durham and Orange		Greensboro, NC	1928

Abilene, TX	1956	Brooklyn, NY	1910	Durham and Orange	
Akron, OH	1926	Bryan-College Station, TX	1988	Counties, NC	1938
Albany, GA	1964	Buffalo, NY	1919	Eastern Fairfield	
Albany, NY	1917	Calgary, AB	1956	County, CT	1920
Albuquerque, NM	1948	Canton, OH	1937	Eau Claire, WI	1993
Alexandria, LA	1975	Cedar Rapids, IA	1934	Edmonton, AB	1959
Greater Alton, IL	1977	Central & North		El Paso, TX	1933
Amarillo, TX	1946	Brevard, FL	1983	Elizabeth-Plainfield, NJ	1923
Anderson County, SC	1992	Central Westchester, NY	1947	Greater Elmira Corning, NY	1931
Ann Arbor, MI	1987	Champaign-Urbana, IL	1972	The Emerald Coast, FL	1987
Annapolis, MD	1982	Charleston, SC	1923	Erie, PA	1925
Anniston-Calhoun, AL	1992	Charleston, WV	1923	Eugene, OR	1962
Arlington, TX	1982	Charlotte, NC	1926	Evanston-North Shore, IL	1924
Asheville, NC	1927	Charlottesville, VA	1981	Evansville, IN	1961
Athens, GA	1980	Chattanooga, TN	1917	Fairmont, WV	1927
Atlanta, GA	1916	Chicago, IL	1912	Fargo-Moorhead, ND	1966
Augusta, GA	1929	Cincinnati, OH	1920	Fayetteville, NC	1977
Austin, TX	1934	Clearwater-Dunedin, FL	1972	The Flint Hills, KS	1998
Bakersfield, CA	1965	Cleveland, OH	1912	Flint, MI	1928
Baltimore, MD	1912	Cobb-Marietta, GA	1976	Florence, SC	1989
Bangor, ME	1953	Colorado Springs, CO	1924	Fort Collins, CO	1986
Baton Rouge, LA	1956	Columbia, SC	1925	Greater Fort	
Battle Creek, MI	1948	Columbus, GA	1936	Lauderdale, FL	1959
Beaumont, TX	1946	Columbus, OH	1923	Fort Myers, FL	1986
Bell County, TX	1988	Corpus Christi, TX	1944	Fort Smith, AR	1960
Bergen County, NJ	1933	Greater Covington, LA	1999	Fort Wayne, IN	1941
Berkshire County, MA	1933	Dallas, TX	1922	Fort Worth, TX	1930
Billings, MT	1970	Dayton, OH	1920	Fresno, CA	1959
Binghamton, NY	1932	Daytona Beach, FL	1984	Gainesville, FL	1975
Birmingham, AL	1922	DeKalb County, GA	1973	Gainesville-Hall	
Birmingham, MI	1952	Denver, CO	1919	County, GA	1994
Boca Raton, FL	1984	Des Moines, IA	1931	Galveston County, TX	1949
Boise, ID	1928	Detroit, MI	1914	Garland, TX	1987
Boston, MA	1907	Douglas County, GA	1990	Gaston County, NC	1978
Bristol, VA	1980	Greater DuKane, IL	1995	Grand Rapids, MI	1925
Bronxville, NY	1948	Duluth, MN	1921	Great Falls, MT	1938

Greensboro, NC	1928
Greenville, SC	1947
Greenwich, CT	1959
Gwinnett and North Fulton	
Counties, GA	1991
Halifax, NS	1933
Hamilton-Burlington, ONT	1934
Hampton Roads, VA	1956
Harlingen, TX	1985
Harrisburg, PA	1929
Hartford, CT	1921
High Point, NC	1952
Honolulu, HI	1923
Houston, TX	1926
Huntington, WV	1933
Huntsville, AL	1975
Indian River, FL	1994
Indianapolis, IN	1922
Jackson County, OR	1995
Jackson, MS	1941
Jacksonville, FL	1924
Johnson City, TN	1984
Kalamazoo, MI	1980
Kankakee County, IL	1984
Kansas City, MO	1914
Kingsport, TN	1958
Kingston, NY	1922
Knoxville, TN	1921
Lafayette, LA	1974
Lake Charles, LA	1967
Greater Lakeland, FL	1974
Lancaster, PA	1924
Lansing, MI	1948
Las Cruces, NM	1995
Las Vegas, NV	1971
Lawton, OK	1986

Location	Year	Location	Year	Location	Year	Location	Year
Lee County, AL	1998	The City of New York, NY	1901	Quad Cities, IA	1981	Summit, NJ	1965
The Lehigh Valley, PA	1943	Norfolk-Virginia Beach, VA	1925	Racine, WI	1916	Syracuse, NY	1921
Lexington, KY	1924	Norman, OK	1983	Raleigh, NC	1930	Tacoma, WA	1921
Lincoln, NE	1921	North Harris County, TX	1990	Reading, PA	1924	Tallahassee, FL	1960
Little Rock, AR	1922	North Little Rock, AR	1978	Reno, NV	1978	Tampa, FL	1928
London, England	1985	Northern Virginia, VA	1985	Rhode Island	1921	Texarkana, AR	1947
Long Beach, CA	1948	Northern Westchester, NY	1953	Richardson, TX	1980	Toledo, OH	1933
Long Island, NY	1962	Northwest Arkansas, AR	1999	Richmond, VA	1927	Topeka, KS	1937
Longview, TX	1981	Oakland-East Bay, CA	1935	Riverside, CA	1962	Toronto, ONT	1926
Los Angeles, CA	1926	Ocala, FL	1989	Roanoke Valley, VA	1928	Troy, NY	1929
Louisville, KY	1921	Odessa, TX	1977	Rochester, NY	1933	Tucson, AZ	1933
Lubbock, TX	1954	Ogden, UT	1953	Rockford, IL	1930	Tulsa, OK	1923
Lufkin, TX	1996	Oklahoma City, OK	1928	Sacramento, CA	1942	Tuscaloosa, AL	1976
Lynchburg, VA	1929	Olympia, WA	1993	Saginaw Valley, MI	1934	Tyler, TX	1960
Macon, GA	1937	Omaha, NE	1919	St. Joseph, MO	1921	Greater Utica, NY	1918
Madison, WI	1993	Orange County, CA	1971	St. Louis, MO	1914	Greater Vancouver, BC	1931
Manatee County, FL	1986	Orange County, NY	1922	St. Paul, MN	1917	Victoria, TX	1983
Martin County, FL	2000	The Oranges and Short Hills, NJ	1913	St. Petersburg, FL	1931	Waco, TX	1946
McAllen, TX	1985	Greater Orlando, FL	1947	Salt Lake City, UT	1934	Washington, D.C.	1913
Memphis, TN	1922	Owensboro, KY	1974	San Angelo, TX	1957	Greater Waterbury, CT	1923
Mexico City, Mexico	1930	The Palm Beaches, FL	1962	San Antonio, TX	1924	Waterloo-Cedar Falls, IA	1968
Miami, FL	1927	Palm Springs Desert Communities, CA	1995	San Diego, CA	1929	Westchester on the Sound, NY	1950
Midland, TX	1964	Palo Alto * Mid Peninsula, CA	1965	San Francisco, CA	1912	Westchester on Hudson, NY	1950
Milwaukee, WI	1916	Parkersburg, WV	1925	San Jose, CA	1967	Wheeling, WV	1940
Minneapolis, MN	1924	Pasadena, CA	1926	Santa Barbara, CA	1925	Wichita Falls, TX	1968
Mobile, AL	1931	Pelham, NY	1941	Sarasota, FL	1976	Wichita, KS	1925
Monmouth County, NJ	1966	Pensacola, FL	1968	Savannah, GA	1926	Wilkes-Barre, PA	1934
Monroe, LA	1982	Peoria, IL	1936	Schenectady, NY	1932	Williamsport, PA	1929
Montclair-Newark, NJ	1921	Philadelphia, PA	1912	Scranton, PA	1940	Wilmington, DE	1918
Monterey County, CA	1963	Phoenix, AZ	1935	Seattle, WA	1924	Wilmington, NC	1952
Montgomery, AL	1926	Pine Bluff, AR	1972	Shreveport-Bossier, LA	1933	Winnipeg, MB	1928
Montreal, QUE	1912	Pittsburgh, PA	1922	Sioux City, IA	1921	Winston-Salem, NC	1923
Moore County, NC	1998	Plano, TX	1984	Sioux Falls, SD	1985	Greater Winter Haven, FL	1992
Morgan County, AL	1988	Portland, ME	1922	South Bend, IN	1944	Worcester, MA	1925
Morristown, NJ	1936	Portland, OR	1910	South Brevard, FL	1980	Wyandotte & Johnson Counties, KS	1949
Murfreesboro, TN	1995	Poughkeepsie, NY	1919	Spartanburg, SC	1951	Yakima, WA	1981
Napa-Sonoma, CA	1995	Greater Princeton, NJ	1921	Spokane, WA	1925	York, PA	1961
Nashville, TN	1922	Pueblo, CO	1977	Springfield, IL	1950	Youngstown, OH	1932
Greater New Britain, CT	1958			Springfield, MA	1922		
Greater New Haven, CT	1923			Springfield, MO	1976		
New Orleans, LA	1924			Stamford-Norwalk, CT	1923		

Famous Junior League Members

MEMBER	POSITION AND COMMUNITY SERVICE	JUNIOR LEAGUE
Mary Harriman Rumsey	Founder of the Junior League—1901; First defender of consumer rights as Chair of the Consumers' Advisory Board of the National Resource Administration in President Franklin Roosevelt's Administration, 1933	The City of New York
Eleanor Roosevelt	First Lady; social reformer; humanitarian; author. As U.S. Delegate to the United Nations, she chaired the Human Rights Commission during the drafting of the Universal Declaration of Human Rights—adopted 1948	The City of New York
Oveta Culp Hobby	First Commander of Women's Army Corps 1941; First U.S. Secretary of Health, Education & Welfare 1953	Houston, TX
Sandra Day O'Connor	First female U.S. Supreme Court Justice, appointed 1981	Phoenix, AZ
Barbara Bush	First Lady; literacy activist	Houston, TX
Laura Bush	First Lady; literacy activist	Austin, TX
Betty Ford	First Lady; substance abuse prevention activist	Grand Rapids, MI
Nancy Reagan	First Lady; substance abuse prevention activist	Los Angeles, CA
Eudora Welty	Author; Pulitzer prize for *The Optimist's Daughter*, 1972	Jackson, MS
Shirley Temple Black	Child actress; Delegate to the United Nations (1969); U.S. Ambassador to Ghana; Czech and Slovak Republics	Palo Alto, CA
Katherine Hepburn	Actress; women's issues activist	Hartford, CT
Sarah Palfrey Cook Danzig	Tennis champion and activist; two-time Wimbledon champion	The City of New York

Elected to Government — U.S. House of Representatives

Ruth Baker Sears Pratt	Served 1929–1933; first woman elected by NY	The City of New York
Isabella Selmes Greenway	Served 1934–1937	The City of New York
Frances Payne Bolton	Served 1940–1969	Cleveland, OH
Mary E. Pruett Farrington	Served 1954–1957	Honolulu, HI
Lynn Martin	Served 1981–1985; U.S. Secretary of Labor 1991–1993	Rockford, IL
Jennifer Dunn	1993–present	Seattle, WA
Anna Eshoo	1993–present	Palo Alto, CA
Tillie Fowler	1993–present	Jacksonville, FL
Carolyn Maloney	1993–present	The City of New York
Judy Biggert	1998–present	Chicago, IL

Elected to Government

Elected to Government	**U.S. Senate**	
Margaret Chase Smith	First woman elected to the Senate	Bangor, ME

Elected to Government	**Canadian Parliament**	
Margaret McTavish Konantz	Member, Canadian Parliament, 1963–1968	Winnipeg, MB
Florence Bird	Member, Canadian Parliament, 1978–1983	Winnipeg, MB
Bobbie Sparrow	Member, Canadian Parliament, 1984–1988	Calgary, AB

Association Presidents

1921–1922	Mrs. Willard Straight	New York City, NY
1922–1924	Mrs. Arthur Swann	New York City, NY
1924–1926	Mrs. Charles S. Brown, Jr.	New York City, NY
1926–1928	Mrs. Carleton H. Palmer	Brooklyn, NY
1928–1930	Mrs. Foskett Brown	Nashville, TN
1930–1932	Mrs. Roger S. Sperry	Waterbury, CT
1932–1934	Mrs. John G. Pratt	New Orleans, LA
1934–1936	Miss Elizabeth P. Taylor	Little Rock, AR
1936–1938	Mrs. Peter L. Harvie	Troy, NY
1938–1940	Miss Helen W. Leovy	Pittsburgh, PA
1940–1942	Mrs. George V. Ferguson	Winnipeg, MB
1942–1944	Mrs. Linville K. Martin	Winston-Salem, NC
1944–1946	Miss Cecil Lester Jones	Washington, D.C.
1946–1948	Mrs. Ralph Jones	Charleston, WV
1948–1950	Miss Dorothy Rackemann	Boston, MA
1950–1952	Mrs. James M. Skinner, Jr.	Philadelphia, PA
1952–1954	Mrs. DeLeslie Allen	Rochester, NY
1954–1956	Mrs. Robert L. Foote	Chicago, IL
1956–1958	Mrs. Frank S. Hanna	St. Joseph, MO
1958–1960	Mrs. George W. Vaughan	Los Angeles, CA
1960–1962	Mrs. H. Edmund Lunken	Cincinnati, OH
1962–1964	Miss Barbara G. Johnson	Baltimore, MD
1964–1966	Mrs. Warner Marsden	Pasadena, CA
1966–1968	Mrs. David A. Whitman	Boston, MA
1968–1970	Mrs. Milo Yalich	Colorado Springs, CO
1970–1972	Mrs. William H. Osler	Harrisburg, PA
1972–1974	Mrs. Rufus C. Barkley, Jr.	Charleston, SC
1974–1976	Mary D. Poole	Albuquerque, NM
1976–1978	Susan R. Greene	Buffalo, NY
1978–1980	Alice H. Weber	Toledo, OH
1980–1982	Margaret M. Graham	Washington, D.C.
1982–1984	Anne B. Hoover	Fort Wayne, IN
1984–1986	Carole P. Hart	Greater New Haven, CT
1986–1988	Virginia T. Austin	Oklahoma City, OK
1988–1990	Maridel M. Moulton	Oakland-East Bay, CA
1990–1992	Suzanne Bond Plihcik	Greensboro, NC
1992–1994	Mary Burrus Babson	Chicago, IL
1994–1996	Nancy H. Evans	Cedar Rapids, IA
1996–1998	Carol Kleiner	Colorado Springs, CO
1998–2000	Clotilde Perez-Bode Dedecker	Buffalo, NY
2000–2002	Deborah C. Brittain	Princeton, NJ

Junior League Cookbooks

Abilene, TX
  Landmark Entertaining 1996
Akron, OH
  Beginnings 2000
Albany, GA
  Quail Country
Albuquerque, NM
  Simply Simpatico 1981
Alexandria, VA
  Secret Ingredients 2000
Ann Arbor, MI
  The Bountiful Arbor 1994
Annapolis, MD
  Of Tyde and Thyme 1994
Asheville, NC
  Mountain Elegance 1991
Atlanta, GA
  Atlanta Cooknotes 1982
  *True Grits—Tall Tales and Recipes
    from the New South* 1995
Augusta, GA
  Tea-Time at the Masters
  2nd Round: Tea-Time at the Masters
Austin, TX
  Necessities and Temptations 1987
Baltimore, MD
  Hunt to Harbor 1996
Baton Rouge, LA
  River Road Recipes 1959
Binghamton, NY
  Family & Company 1992
Birmingham, AL
  Food for Thought 1995
  Magic 1982
Boca Raton, FL
  Savor the Moment 2000
Boise, ID
  *Beyond Burlap . . . Idaho's Famous
    Potato Recipes* 1997
Buffalo, NY
  *Great Lake Effects: Buffalo Beyond
    Winter and Wings* 1997

Charleston, SC
  Charleston Party Receipts 1993
  Charleston Receipts 1950
  Charleston Receipts Repeats 1986
  Joseph's Charleston Adventure 1998
Charleston, WV
  Mountain Measures 1984
  *Mountain Measures,
    A Second Serving* 1987
Charlotte, NC
  *Dining By Fireflies, Unexpected
    Pleasures of the New* 1994
Chattanooga, TN
  Dinner on the Diner 1983
Chicago, IL
  Celebrate Chicago 1996
Cincinnati, OH
  I'll Cook When Pigs Fly 1998
Cleveland, OH
  A Cleveland Collection 1992
Cobb-Marietta, GA
  Georgia on My Menu 1988
  Southern On Occasion 1998
Colorado Springs, CO
  Nuggets 1983
Columbia, SC
  Down By the Water 1997
Columbus, GA
  *A Southern Collection—
    Then & Now* 1994
Corpus Christi, TX
  Delicioso 1982
  Fiesta 1973
  VIVA Tradiciones 1996
Dayton, OH
  Causing a Stir 2000
DeKalb County, GA
  Peachtree Bouquet 1987
  Puttin' On The Peachtree 1979
Denver, CO
  Colorado Cache 1977
  Colorado Collage 1995

  Créme de Colorado 1987
Greater Elmira-Corning, NY
  Thru the Grapevine 1998
El Paso, TX
  Seasoned With Sun Co. 1989
The Emerald Coast, FL
  Sugar Beach 1995
Eugene, OR
  A Taste of Oregon 1980
  Savor the Flavor 1990
Fayetteville, NC
  Sweet Pickin's 2000
Greater Fort Lauderdale, FL
  Made in the Shade 1998
Fort Myers, FL
  Tropical Settings 2001
Gainesville, FL
  Gracious Gator Cooks 1997
Gainesville-Hall County, GA
  *Perennials,
    A Southern Celebration of
    Food and Flavor* 1984
Galveston County, TX
  Rare Collections
Gaston County, NC
  Southern Elegance 1987
  *Southern Elegance:
    A Second Course* 1998
Grand Rapids, MI
  Cookbook I 1976
Greensboro, NC
  Out of Our League 1998
Greenville, SC
  Uptown Down South 1986
Greenwich, CT
  The Greenwich Gourmet 1997
Hampton Roads, VA
  Children's Party Book 1996
  Very Virginia 1995
  Virginia Hospitality 1975
Harlingen, TX
  Rio Riches 1997

Harrisburg, PA
  A Capital Affair 1996
Honolulu, HI
  A Taste of Aloha 1983
  Another Taste of Aloha 1993
Houston, TX
  *Houston Junior League
    Cookbook* 1968
  *Stop and Smell the
    Rosemary* 1996
  The Star of TX Cookbook 1983
Huntington, WV
  Almost Heaven 1984
Huntsville, AL
  Huntsville Heritage 1967
  Sweet Home Alabama 1995
Indianapolis, IN
  Back Home Again 1993
  Winners 1985
Jackson County, OR
  Rogue River Rendezvous 1992
Jackson, MS
  Come On In! 1991
  Southern Sideboards 1978
Jacksonville, FL
  A River Runs Backwards
Johnson City, TN
  Smoky Mountain Magic 1995
  Treasures of the Smokies 1994
Kansas City, MO
  Above & Beyond Parsley 1992
  Beyond Parsley 1984
  Company's Coming 1975
Knoxville, TN
  *Dining in the Smoky Mountain
    Mist* 1995
Lafayette, LA
  Talk About Good 1967
  Talk About Good II 1979
  Tell Me More 1993
Lake Charles, LA
  Pirate's Pantry 1992

Las Vegas, NV
Glitter to Gourmet 2001
Lawton, OK
Family & Friends 1994
Little Rock, AR
Apron Strings 1997
Long Island, NY
It's Our Serve
Los Angeles, CA
Gourmet LA 1988
Louisville, KY
Splendor in the Bluegrass 2000
Lufkin, TX
According to Taste 1985
Lynchburg, VA
In Good Company 1999
McAllen, TX
La Pinata 1997
Some Like It Hot 1992
Memphis, TN
Heart & Soul 1992
Memphis Cook Book 1952
Party Potpourri 1971
Mexico City, Mexico
Buen Provecho 1994
Mobile, AL
Bay Tables 1998
One of a Kind 1981
Recipe Jubilee 1964
Monroe, LA
Celebrations on the Bayou 1989
The COTTON COUNTRY Collection 1972
Morgan County, AL
Beyond Cotton Country 1999
Cotton Country Cooking 1974
Morristown, NJ
A Matter of Taste 1998
New Orleans, LA
The Crescent City Collection 2000
Jambalaya 1980
Plantation 1972
The City of New York, NY
I'll Taste Manhattan 1994
Norfolk-Virginia Beach, VA
Tidewater on the Half Shell 1995
North Little Rock, AR
Rave Reviews 1993

Northern Virginia, VA
What Can I Bring 1999
Odessa, TX
Blue Denim Gourmet 1998
Wild Wild West 1991
Ogden, UT
The UT Dining Car 1996
Greater Orlando, FL
Sunsational Encore 1998
Palm Beaches, FL
A Slice of Paradise 1996
Pasadena, CA
California Sizzles 1992
Dining by Design 1998
Pensacola, FL
Some Like It South! 1984
Philadelphia, PA
Settings—From Our Past To Your Presentation 1990
Phoenix, AZ
Desert Treasures 1992
Pine Bluff, AR
Southern Accent 1994
Pittsburgh, PA
Without Reservations 1995
Portland, ME
Maine Ingredients 1995
RSVP 1982
Portland, OR
From Portland's Palate 1998
Pueblo, CO
From an Adobe Oven to a Microwave Range 1972
Racine, WI
Udderly Delicious 1989
Raleigh, NC
You're Invited 1998
Rhode Island
Windows 1995
Richardson, TX
Appetites & Victuals 1973
Plain and Fancy 1984
Texas Sampler 1999
Richmond, VA
Virginia Fare 1994
Virginia Seasons 1984
Roanoke Valley, VA
Oh My Stars! 2000

Rochester, NY
Applehood & Motherpie 1998
For Goodness Taste 1998
Rockford, IL
Brunch Basket 1994
Generations 1995
St. Louis, MO
In the Kitchen 2000
Saint Louis Days . . . Saint Louis Nights 1994
Salt Lake City, UT
Always in Season 1998
Heritage Cookbook 1975
Pinch of Salt Lake 1986
San Angelo, TX
Pearls of the Concho 1996
San Francisco, CA
Encore 1984
San Francisco á la Carte 1979
San Francisco Flavors 1999
Santa Barbara, CA
Slice of Santa Barbara 1991
Savannah, GA
Downtown Savannah Style 1996
Savannah Style 1994
Seattle, WA
Simply Classic Cookbook 1998
South Bend, IN
Great Beginnings, Grand Finales 1991
Nutbread & Nostalgia 1979
Spokane, WA
Gold'n Delicious 1995
Springfield, IL
Honest to Goodness 1990
Springfield, MO
Sassafras! The Ozarks Cookbook 1985
Women Who Can Dish It Out 1997
Tallahassee, FL
Thymes Remembered 1988
Tampa, FL
Gasparilla Cookbook 1961
Tampa Treasures 1991
Tucson, AZ
Purple Sage and Other Pleasures 1986
Tuscaloosa, AL
Winning Seasons 1994

Tyler, TX
And Roses for the Table 1997
Waco, TX
Hearts and Flour 1988
Washington, D.C.
Capital Celebrations 1997
Capital Classics 1990
Waterloo-Cedar Falls, IA
Buttercups and Brandy 1978
First Impressions 2001
Pig Out 1986
Westchester on the Sound, NY
Sound Seasonings 1990
Wheeling, WV
The Best of Wheeling 1994
Treat Yourself to the Best 1984
Wichita, KS
Women of Great Taste 1995
Wichita Falls, TX
Home Cookin' 1976
Williamsport, PA
Victorian Thymes & Pleasures 1998
Wilmington, DE
Savor the Brandywine Valley, A Collection of Recipes 1993
Wilmington, NC
Seaboard to Sideboard 1998
Worcester, MA
A Taste of New England 1990
Wyandotte & Johnson Counties, KS
Treasures of the Great Midwest 1995

Association of Junior Leagues International
Centennial Cookbook 1996
Celebration Cookbook 2000

Note: *This list was compiled from League responses to the 2000 Annual Directory questionnaire, and, therefore, is not a complete list of all League cookbooks.*

Index